OPEN
WINDOWS

Philip Yancey

OPEN WINDOWS

Thomas Nelson Publishers
Nashville • Camden • New York

Published in Nashville, Tennessee, by Thomas Nelson, Inc. and distributed in Canada by Lawson Falle, Ltd., Cambridge, Ontario.

Printed in the United States of America.

Some of the writing in this book has appeared, in different form, in *Christianity Today, Leadership*, and the *Christian Century*. The chapter "Pitfalls of Christian Writing" grew out of ideas that originally appeared in *Publishers Weekly*.

The publisher and author express appreciation for permission to quote from the following:

Four Quartets by T.S. Eliot, taken from *Collected Poems 1909-1962*, copyright © 1963; used by permission of Harcourt Brace Jovanovich, Inc.

Pilgrim at Tinker Creek (Pulitzer Prize winner, a Harper's Magazine Press book) and *Holy the Firm* by Annie Dillard, copyright © 1974 and 1977 respectively; used by permission of Harper & Row.

Open Windows was first published in 1982 by Crossway Books, a division of Good News Publishers, 9825 West Roosevelt Road, Westchester, Illinois 60153.

Library of Congress Cataloging-in-Publication Data

Yancey, Philip.
  Open windows.

  1. Religious literature—Authorship—Addresses,
essays, lectures. 2. Theology—Addresses, essays,
lectures. 3. Suffering—Religious aspects—Addresses,
essays, lecture. 4. Gandhi, Mahatma, 1869-1948—
Addresses, essays, lectures. I. Title.
BR44.Y36   1985   200   85-18727
ISBN 0-8407-5960-6

To Janet, my wife,
who fills the word
love
with meaning

Contents

Writing has its occupational hazards: a constant fear of rejection, the anxieties that come with free-lancing, and a peculiar, numbing sense of loneliness. But one great benefit makes up for all these: unlike some other jobs, it doesn't lock you in.

For example, I spent four years working on books with Dr. Paul Brand, a surgeon and leprosy specialist. Those projects took me to medical libraries, into operating rooms, even to a leprosarium in India. But once the books were finished I could go on, to other subjects, to other fields.

New interests had stirred along the way. India had kindled a curiosity about Mahatma Gandhi. My study of pain had led me to the survivors of Nazi death camps, then to Solzhenitsyn, and then to the great Russian novelists. That's the way a writer's life works. It makes the best sense when seen in reverse order.

Now I can look back and see that the chapters in this book, though written over several years, have much in common. Writing is a way of thinking, and *Open Windows* represents stages of my own discovery. It includes some introspection, thoughts about the process of writing itself.

Each spring when my wife and I open the windows of our Chicago apartment, fresh air rushes in. The streets outside are filled with happy sounds as people shed their coats and rediscover the outdoors. But open windows also let in city dust, the blaring horns of taxis, the throbbing music of a late-night bar. You'll find glimpses of both in this book: the lovely and the unlovely. I have tried to see both with a steady gaze.

PART ONE

The Arts

When asked what specifically brought them to a relationship with God, many Christians will cite a moving sermon, a praying family, an evangelistic meeting, or an acquaintance with the Bible. I would have to answer that nature and classical music were decisive factors in awakening my spiritual life. I grew up in an environment clotted with key phrases, memorized Bible verses, and prescribed spiritual activities. Before long, I could no longer distinguish a true prayer or an authentic act from a hypocritical one.

In a sense, I had been vaccinated against spiritual truth; I had heard it all before and learned to reject it. About that time, something began to stir in me: an appreciation for beauty. I would take long walks in the Carolina pine forests, follow butterflies across fields, stare at the Milky Way creasing the heavens. And late at night I would slip into the college chapel and play Chopin, Schubert, and Beethoven on the concert grand.

It is a terrible thing to be grateful and have no one to thank, to be awed and have no one to worship. Gradually, very gradually, I came back to the castoff faith of my childhood. Rather, I was drawn back by the Sehnsucht, *or sense of longing for, in C.S. Lewis' words, "a scent of a flower we have not found, the echo of a tune we have not heard, news from a country we have never yet visited."*

I am fully aware that music and nature are subjective experiences, that a Japanese Shintoist draws different conclusions from nature, that a moonstruck lover may listen to Bach's Wedding Cantata *thinking only of his beloved, not of Christ. And yet, nature and art are also manifestations of God's grace. I can let them fill out the objective content I derive from revelation. Without nature and art, I could hardly relate to awe and glory and joy. With them, I can better respond to such concepts as estrangement, redemption, and, finally, resurrection.*

1

The Music of God

I AM leaning back in a padded seat listening to a speaker recite well-worn words: "I believe in one God, the Father almighty, maker of heaven and earth and of all things visible and invisible. And in one Lord Jesus Christ, the only-begotten Son of God, begotten of his Father before all worlds, God of God, Light of Light, very God of very God, begotten, not made, being of one substance with the Father...." the words drone on, a repetition of the familiar Nicene Creed, words that once stirred heated debate and massive church councils but which, encrusted with the barnacles of time, today normally elicit ritualistic mumbling or a stifled yawn.

Yet when the speaker finishes, the audience erupts into vigorous cheering. Some stomp the floor, some shout "Bravo!" and a few even whistle through their fingers. I look around me. These are not charismatics at a prophecy rally; they are stockbrokers, lawyers, executives, and society figures, all of whom have forked over at least ten dollars to hear the Nicene Creed. For the most part, they fail to see the irony that looms large to me: half-empty churches stand throughout Chicago where scarcely a stray "Amen!" (let alone wild applause) is heard, while these nonreligious types pack Orchestra Hall to hear Beethoven's *Missa Solemnis*.

The "speaker" in this case, if I have misled you, is the Chicago Symphony Chorus and its featured soloists. But they are faithfully rendering the words handed down by the Council of Nicaea in A.D. 325. Those same words, as interpreted by Mozart and Haydn or linguistically adapted by Brahms or Berlioz, are often repeated by skilled professionals in every major city in the Western world.

I know a few musicians and would not intimate that they perform the clergy function in any willing sense. Fortunately for the unbelievers of the Chorus, these highly charged words of grace are neatly packaged in rhythmic Latin phrases that glissade safely off the tongue. Yet as I watch, something approaching a miracle seems to occur. A Jewish tenor on the third row, who stiffened up for this performance with three Manhattans and a pack of Camels, who gives not a rip for "the only begotten Son of God," whose chin is marked with styptic pencil, whose collar is flecked with blood from a hasty shave—that tenor's face is transformed. Harshness drains from it; he sucks a deep breath of hope and release from the anxious world offstage and belts out "Agnus dei, Agnus dei" ("Lamb of God, who takest away the sins of the world, have mercy upon us") as though it is the only true plea he has ever made. Perhaps, for a moment, he does mean it.

Perhaps crusty old Beethoven, who, it is said, angrily shook a fist at the thundering heavens before relaxing into death, meant the words as he rolled them over and over in his mind, searching out the most profound way of communicating them. The music, so powerful a carrier of thoughts too unearthly to be fully expressed, assumes its own power, possessing composer, conductor, performers, audience. For a few hours, performers' thoughts about the union wage scale and postperformance parties, as well as my own concerns about a day filled with deadlines and jangling telephones, yield to a sublime contemplation of the unfathomable.

I am not alone—even hardened music critics are vulnerable. Reviewing the Chicago Symphony's recent recording of Brahms' *German Requiem*, Heuwell Tircuit of the San Francisco *Chronicle* wrote, "The performance is divine (in several senses). It constitutes an overpowering experience, one which is not only technically and stylistically perfect, but moving in an uncanny, religious way. When the chorus sings of 'The Living Christ' even an atheist can believe in Him."

After reading scores of articles decrying Western civilization and the economic structure that fostered Beethoven and Mozart, and others lamenting the production of computer disks, plastics, and the internal combustion engine, I would offer a deeply felt vote of gratitude for music and the technology that makes it democratically available.

When we total the dollars per hour of gospel preached across the National Religious Broadcasters' airwaves or the attendance in Sunday morning services, do we somehow forget the stunning impact of these monuments to a living Christ voiced by history's musical geniuses?

While I have my doubts about the neutron bomb, the Concorde, and a hand-held television, I am daily blessed by an ability shared by no other generation in history: I can invite into my study the Munich Bach Choir or the Concertgebouw Orchestra. I can sit before my speakers and listen transfixed, as did the European gentry who commissioned these works for their great halls and private chapels. Or, I can turn down the volume and use it as background music, even as I write these words.

As music, no one questions the value of the enduring religious works of Mozart, Handel, or Bach. But what of their value as a reflection of the personal faith of the composers? Were they indeed intended as a testimony to deep religious sentiments?

The answer, of course, varies with each composer. A few lived disciplined lives of humble spirituality, best exemplified by pious César Franck and Anton Bruckner. The latter especially wrote his works to reflect his belief that God is good and that everything we do should honor him. While hard at work on his Tenth Symphony, he remarked to Gustav Mahler, "Now I have to work very hard. ...Otherwise I will not pass before God, before whom I shall soon stand. He will say 'Why else have I given you talent, than that you should sing my praise and glory? But you have accomplished much too little.'" Bruckner at first evoked the scorn of his university students for his humble faith. Clad in a rural jacket from his native Upper Austria, with an oversized head and wrinkled face, he would abruptly stop his lectures when bells sounded from a nearby church. There on the classroom floor he would kneel and pray before resuming his lecture. Few, however, failed to come away impressed with his devout sincerity and the cathedral-like music of belief he produced.

Two other famous composers, Handel and Mendelssohn, served almost as evangelists, memorializing great biblical stories and themes in colorfully staged epics. Handel created twenty such oratorios, including *Saul, Israel in Egypt, Jephtha*, and probably the most performed classical piece of all time, *The Messiah*. He treated Bible stories as operas, infusing them with tension and drama. Handel's audience wept openly when in *Samson* the lead character cried out, "Total eclipse—no sun! All dark amid the blaze of noon!"; the elderly Handel himself was standing on stage, totally blind.

Mendelssohn contributed two oratorios, *St. Paul* and *Elijah*, as well as two delightful but seldom heard religious symphonies: *Hymn of Praise*, centered on the hymn "Now Thank We All Our God," and *The Reformation Symphony* constructed on the great hymns of the Protestant Reformation. Because of a cruel twist of history, Mendelssohn is not performed often today, due in part to Hitler's program to rid the concert stage of Jewish influence (though Felix's grandfather Moses was a Jewish philosopher, Felix and his father converted to Christianity).

Two orthodox Catholics, Mozart and Haydn, produced volumes of church music, but admittedly they drifted toward religious themes mainly for economic reasons—commissions for special church events made it worthwhile. Neither could be described as mystical; yet Mozart was so moved by the *Requiem Mass* he was working on until his death that his doctor sought to take the manuscript from him lest he become too agitated.

Profound religious music has even flowed from the pens of men whose lives were decidedly irreligious. Consider Tchaikovsky, an unhappy, paranoid homosexual who drank too much and yet somehow gave us a remarkably rich setting of "The Lord's Prayer." Or Brahms, raised in brothels and exhibiting no personal piety, who came up with the brilliant *German Requiem*, which enfolds phrases from Luther's Bible with music so fitting it seems as if the words were created just for his melodic setting.

Beethoven wrote few religious works, but both he and his successor Mahler struggled with issues vocalized by Mahler: "Whence do we come? Whither does our road take us? Why am I made to feel that I am free while yet I am constrained within my character, as in a prison? What is the object of toil and sorrow? How am I to understand the cruelty and malice in the creations of a kind God? Will the meaning of life be finally revealed by death?" However, musically the two asked these questions in dramatically different ways: Beethoven shook a titanic fist at the heavens; Mahler wrung his hands in despairing *angst*.

Religious music has consistently called the great composers to their highest artistic achievements. Of his hundreds of works, Beethoven only wrote two masses; yet he asserted the *Missa Solemnis* was his greatest composition. The not-so-religious, such as

Brahms and Schubet, as well as composers on the church payroll, found unequalled inspiration in Christian themes.

Part of the reason lies in the implicit challenge of rendering themes that had been attempted by nearly every composer. Imagine the task of giving novel treatment to a text so devoid of literary images as the Nicene Creed. Palestrina churned out ninety-three such masses. Those who followed him agonized over how to express the familiar in startling, arresting ways. Like Olympians, each competed with the great composers who had preceded him.

I believe the real secret, though, must be found in the implicit depth of those Christian themes. In contrast, during its recent twenty-fifth anniversary, the United Nations commissioned a composer to write a piece entitled "To Posterity." Fresh music can come from small thoughts—occasionally a good piece surfaces from all the current drivel extolling teenage love, for example. But give a genius like Beethoven a concept such as "God of God, Light of Light, very God of very God" or assign Handel the surrealistic setting of "Worthy is the Lamb" in Revelation 5, and you can begin to understand what has ignited music through the centuries.

A case can be made for the theory that music would never have reached its glorious zenith in Western civilization without the combustive energy of Christian themes. I will leave that question to the theorists. I do know, however, that when I read Revelation 5 and then drop the needle on Handel's version, chills race up my spine. Music short-circuits the senses with a direct pathway into human emotion. My beliefs about God and grace and redemption are transfigured by the creative products of musical geniuses who plumbed those same wild, liberating concepts.

Above all others, one man symbolizes the perfect blending of musical religious ideals. I refer, of course, to Johann Sebastian Bach, father of most major developments in Western music. What other figure has earned a cover portrait on *Time* magazine 250 years after his birth? Essayist Lewis Thomas was asked what composer he would choose to represent earth in interplanetary communication. His reply: "I would vote for Bach, streamed out into space over and over again. We would be bragging, of course, but it is surely excusable for us to put the best possible face on at the beginning of such an acquaintance. We can tell the harder truths later."

Born in the shadow of the Wartburg castle where Luther translated the Bible into German, Bach became the single composer most identified with the church, in his case the Lutheran Church. Bach was no saint: he was always offending students and opposing any authority who restricted his musical freedoms. But he had a clear goal. The purpose of his music, he said, "should be none else but the glory of God and the recreation of the mind." Bach attacked his goal with an insatiable thirst for perfection and a formidable knowledge of the Bible (he possessed an impressively large ecclesiastical library). He wrote as though God himself, not a wealthy patron, was scrutinizing every note and phrase, beginning most manuscripts with the abbreviation *JJ* ("Jesus, help") and ending with *SDG—Soli Deo Gloria* ("To God alone the glory").

Bach's 295 church cantatas (two-thirds of which have survived) range from meditations on the relationship between Christ and his Bride the Church to exultant celebrations of the final resurrection. In his last days he could confidently dictate this message: "Come, sweetest death, come blessed rest and take my hand and gently lead me on." While literally at the edge of death he dictated one last cantata to which he gave the superscription "With This I Step Before Thy Throne."

Of Bach's most important works *The Passion According to St. Matthew* is generally acclaimed as the greatest choral work ever written in German. It received one performance in Bach's day, caused little stir, and lay unperformed for exactly 100 years. Then in 1829 Felix Mendelssohn obtained a copy of the magnificent manuscript from his teacher, who had allegedly bought the original from a cheese merchant using worthless manuscript pages to wrap cheese. Mendelssohn staged a revival of *The Passion*, unleashing a tidal wave of enthusiasm for Bach that has never ebbed. Before he had finished preparing the work for performance, the twenty-year-old Mendelssohn had been converted to faith in Christ.

I heard that great work in a summer concert by the Chicago Symphony Orchestra and Chorus at Ravinia Park near Chicago. Three thousand people gathered in the park for the four-hour performance. Once again I was struck by the irony of that crowd: upper-class patrons, bedecked in evening finery, dining by candlelight on Ravinia's spacious grounds, balanced by a strong contingent of the scruffy blue jean set. Chicago's North Shore Jewish population was liberally sprinkled throughout. All these listened enraptured to a forthright retelling of Jesus' crucifixion adapted from Matthew's gospel.

Five times in the performance the entire choir sang the haunting refrain from which the hymn "O Sacred Head Now Wounded" is taken.

The scene was as far removed from that dusty, bloody night on Calvary as any I can imagine. Yet somehow the master had woven his spell. Paid performers in evening gowns and tuxedos rendered the agony and horror of that dark day, as well as its profound significance for all mankind, far better than any heavy-breathing Southern evangelist macabrely describing nailprints and thorn marks.

Who knows what impact the performance had? I know of no church revivals sparked by classical music. But in me, a believer, the delicate care invested by music's greatest mind in expressing the one event that split history in two found reward. C.S. Lewis referred to great art as the "drippings of grace" which can awaken in us a thirst for the true Object. Under the right master, those drippings can become a flood of God's presence. *SDG.*

Every so often a writer comes along who creates a new creative category. In my opinion, Annie Dillard did just that with Pilgrim at Tinker Creek, *for which she was awarded the Pulitzer Prize.*

If you ask what the book is about, a loyal Dillard fan will stare at you vacantly. About? Well, a woman takes walks in the woods and sees tadpoles and water striders and things, and relates unusual facts about trees and creeks. Not much of a plot, really. Yet behind her observations lies a natural theology that has not been attempted with such ambition since perhaps Joseph Butler.

Annie Dillard is a Christian who lives in a post-Voltaire, post-Darwin age of naturalistic skepticism and yet somehow avoids the blinders of that age. She knows that nature contains, in Rudolf Otto's phrase, Mysterium tremendum. *Even in a broken and twisted world she sees enough to leave her breathless.*

When I read Pilgrim *and later* Holy the Firm, *I knew I had to meet Annie Dillard. Before long I was sitting in her office on Puget Sound conducting the interview which follows. For those unacquainted with Annie Dillard, I have interspersed appropriate selections from her work.*

2

A Face Aflame: Annie Dillard

Question: Annie, when I mention you to my friends, I get one of two reactions: either a sigh of appreciation from a fervent admirer or a puzzled "Who?" It seems most evangelicals are in the second category.

Answer: Well, I admit I am consciously addressing the unbeliever in my books, though I have great empathy for evangelicals. I was raised Presbyterian, in Pittsburgh, and during my development I had only one short fling of rebellion against God.

For four consecutive summers I had gone to a fundamentalist church camp in the country. We sang Baptist songs and had a great time—it gave me a taste for abstract thought. But I grew sick of people going to church just to show off their clothes, so I quit the church. Instead of quietly dropping away, I wanted to make a big statement. I marched into the assistant minister's office and gave him my spiel about how much hypocrisy there was in the church. This kind man replied, "You're right, honey, there is."

Before leaving, I said, "By the way, I have to write a senior paper for school—do you have any C.S. Lewis books?" He gave me an armful and I started a long paper on C.S. Lewis. By the time I finished I was right back in the arms of Christianity. My rebellion lasted a month.

Question: You gained stature in the publishing world so quickly. It's amusing to be with publishers who think they have the whole literary scene predicted and portrayed on graphs and charts. Then out of nowhere comes a young woman with her first book, which gets the Pulitzer Prize. Were you shocked?

Answer: Sure, but what excited me more was the acceptance of the first chapter from *Pilgrim* for *Harper's* magazine. That day I was happy. I was out playing softball when the phone call came. I ran in, ate an apple very quickly, and called everyone I knew. Twenty-four hours later I got happy all over again. The Pulitzer came much later—over a year later.

Question: You did, however, become a public person suddenly. How did that affect you?

Answer: It was confusing at first. Offers came in from everywhere: offers to write texts for photography books, to write for Hollywood, write ballets and words for songs. And I received hundreds of invitations to speak and teach.

That whole business is a dreadful temptation for an artist. I thought about it, and finally made my choice by turning down an appearance on the *Today* show. Now I give only one reading a year and virtually no other public appearances. I have chosen to be a writer—and I must stick to that; the craft demands my full energy.

Question: Did you get many personal letters from readers of *Pilgrim?*

Answer: Yes. One man, a professor of theology at a Catholic university, wrote that he resigned his job immediately after reading it. Another woman, a devout Catholic, was a book editor for *The National Observer.* She wrote a very sympathetic, intelligent review

---

There is one church here, so I go to it. On Sunday mornings I quit the house and wander down the hill to the white frame church in the firs. On a big Sunday there might be twenty of us there; often I am the only person under sixty, and feel as though I'm on an archaeological tour of Soviet Russia. The members are of mixed denominations; the minister is a Congregationalist, and wears a white shirt. The man knows God. Once in the middle of the long pastoral prayer of intercession for the whole world—for the gift of wisdom to its leaders, for hope and mercy to the grieving and pained, succor to the oppressed, and God's grace to all—in the middle of this he stopped, and burst out, 'Lord, we bring you these same petitions every week.' After a shocked pause, he continued reading the prayer. Because of this, I like him very much. 'Good morning!' he says after the first hymn and invocation, startling me witless every time, and we all shout back, 'Good Morning!' (Holy the Firm, *pp. 57-58*).

---

for her paper, discussing the religious angle thoroughly. On the same page with the review, the paper ran her obituary; she had died shortly after finishing the review.

Many people who responded with the most warmth were struggling with cancer or some similar burden.

Question: You seem easily moved by people. And yet you write about them only rarely; you prefer objects and nature. Why? Don't people fascinate you in the same way?

Answer: Oh yes—they do. I just don't think I'm good enough to write about people yet. I'd love to try some day.

Question: I have heard that you have come in contact with rigid fundamentalists. How do they affect you?

Answer: I have great respect for them. When I lived in Virginia, I did readings for the blind at a nearby Bible college. Fundamentalists have intense faith. Many educated people think them naive. But fundamentalists know they have chosen the narrow way; they know the social scorn they face.

You must remember, however, my prime audience is the skeptic, the agnostic, not the Christian. Just getting the agnostic to acknowledge the supernatural is a major task.

Question: Your latest book, *Holy the Firm*, differs greatly in structure from *Pilgrim at Tinker Creek*. It's a fraction of the length, more narrative in style, more abstract, more directly theological. Many people consider it less penetrable. What did you hope to accomplish?

Answer: I chose an artistic structure. I decided to write about whatever happened in the next three days. The literary possibilities of that structure intrigued me. On the second day an airplane crashed nearby, and I was back where I had been in *Pilgrim*—grappling with the problem of pain and dying. I had no intention of dealing with that issue at first, but it became unavoidable.

I kept getting stuck. Those forty-three manuscript pages took me fifteen months to write. In *Pilgrim* I would get stuck for three days at a time and I would just plow through. But in *Holy the Firm* the problems were enormous. The question I constantly faced was, "Can it be done?" After the second day's plane crash...how could I resolve anything on the third day?

I would have to crank myself up to approach the stack of manuscript pages. Then I'd read what I had written on the last pages and even I couldn't understand it. I don't live on that kind of level.

Question: People who know you through your writings probably assume you do live on that level, don't they?

Answer: Yes, that's an unfortunate error. As a writer, I am less a creator than an audience to the artistic vision. In *Holy the Firm* I even inserted a disclaimer. I said, "No one has ever lived well." I do not live well. I merely point to the vision.

People, holy people, ask me to speak at their monasteries and I write back and say no, keep your vision. In *The Wizard of Oz* there's a giant machine that announces "Dorothy!"; behind the curtain a little man is cranking it and pushing buttons. When the dog pulls back the curtain to expose the little man, the machine says, "Pay no attention to that man behind the curtain! Look at the light show."

So I ask the monks to keep their vision of power, holiness, and purity. We all have glimpses of the vision, but the truth is that no man has ever lived the vision.

Question: How does your own vision penetrate your life? You don't write much about ethics.

Answer: No, I don't write at all about ethics. I try to do right and rarely do. The kind of art I write is shockingly uncommitted—appallingly isolated from political, social, and economic affairs.

There are lots of us here. Everybody writes about politics and social concerns; I don't. I'm not doing any harm.

About five years ago I saw a mockingbird make a straight vertical descent from the roof gutter of a four-story building. It was an act as careless and spontaneous as the curl of a stem or the kindling of a star.

The mockingbird took a single step into the air and dropped. His wings were still folded against his sides as though he were singing from a limb and not falling, accelerating thirty-two feet per second through empty air. Just a breath before he would have been dashed to the ground, he unfurled his wings with exact, deliberate care, revealing the broad bars of white, spread his elegant, white-banded tail, and so floated onto the grass. I had just rounded a corner when his insouciant step caught my eye; there was no one else in sight. The fact of this free fall was like the old philosophical conundrum about the tree that falls in the forest. The answer must be, I think, that beauty and grace are performed whether or not we will or sense them. The least we can do is try to be there (Pilgrim at Tinker Creek, *pp. 7-8*).

Question: You write as an observer, perched on the edge of but also immersed in the world. You ask us to see it with new, enlightened eyes. But how are your powers of observation affected by what has happened to you in the last few years? Can you maintain an innocent gaze when you know you could make a pile of money on your walk through the woods, or on your trip to the Galápagos Islands, or even on your visit to the hospital to visit the plane crash victims?

Answer: That's not been a problem. I'd certainly not walk in the woods thinking I'd write a book about it. That would drive me nuts in no time.

Question: In *Holy the Firm*, you lived those three days knowing you'd write a book about them.

Answer: True. I started it as a poem. I merely waited to see what was going to happen and I wasn't looking at my reactions. I simply needed a certain amount of events—whatever might happen—to make a minor point: that days are lived in the mind *and* in the spirit.

Question: In other words, what we perceive happening in a day is really just the surface layer; something much greater and more profound is occurring behind the curtain?

Answer: Yes. How does the world look from within? And that brought in the concept of *Holy the Firm*.

Every day has its own particular brand of holiness for us to discover and worship appropriately. The only way to deal with that was to discover the relationship between time and eternity. That single question interests me artistically more than any other.

If you examine each day, with the events and objects it contains, as a god, you instantly have to conclude there are pagan gods. And if you believe in a holy God—how does he relate to these pagan gods that fill the world? That is exactly the same question as the relationship between time and eternity. Does the holy God bring forth these pagan gods out of his love?

Here I depart from the British rationalists like C.S. Lewis, G.K. Chesterton, and George MacDonald. I am grounded strongly in art and weakly in theology. There is a profound difference between the two fields. If I wanted to make a theological statement I would have hired a skywriter. Instead, I knock myself out trying to do art, and it's not so airtight. It isn't reducible to a sealed system. It doesn't translate so well.

Question: Then that's why in your books you give us both hope and despair, anger and love.

Answer: I guess. I must stay faithful to art. I get in my little canoe and paddle out to the edge of mystery. It is unfortunately true that words fail, reason fails; and all I can do is to create a world which by its internal coherence makes a degree of sense. I can either do that or hush. And then I learn to make statements about that world, to furrow deeper into the mystery.

Every single thing I follow takes me there, to the edge of a cliff. As soon as I start writing, I'm hanging over the cliff again. You can make a perfectly coherent world at the snap of a finger—but only if you don't bother being honest about it.

Question: You seem driven to that mystery. You describe the beauty of nature with such eloquence in *Pilgrim at Tinker Creek*— but just as I'm exulting, you strike me with its terror and injustice.

Answer: As I wrote *Pilgrim*, I kept before me the image of people who are suffering. They were right there in the room as I wrote the book. I could not write a cheerful nature book or a new version of the argument from design—not with a leukemia patient next to me. I

In the Koran, Allah asks, 'The heaven and the earth and all in between, thinkest thou I made them in jest?' It's a good question. What do we think of the created universe, spanning an unthinkable void with an unthinkable profusion of forms? Or what do we think of nothingness, those sickening reaches of time in either direction? If the giant water bug was not made in jest, was it then made in earnest? Pascal uses a nice term to describe the notion of the creator's, once having called forth the universe, turning his back to it: Deus Absconditus. *Is this what we think happened? Was the sense of it there, and God absconded with it, ate it, like a wolf who disappears round the edge of the house with the Thanksgiving turkey? 'God is subtle,' Einstein said, 'but not malicious.' Again, Einstein said that 'nature conceals her mystery by means of her essential grandeur, not by her cunning.' It could be that God has not absconded but spread, as our vision and understanding of the universe have spread, to a fabric of spirit and sense so grand and subtle, so powerful in a new way, that we can only feel blindly of its hem. In making the thick darkness, a swaddling band for the sea, God 'set bars and doors' and said, 'Hitherto shalt thou come, but no further.' But have we come even that far? Have we rowed out to the thick darkness, or are we all playing pinochle in the bottom of the boat?* (Pilgrim, p. 7).

---

had to write for people who are dying or grieving—and that's everybody. I can't write just from my safe position.

When I worked on *Holy the Firm* and the plane went down, I thought, *Oh no, God is making me write this damn problem of pain again.* I felt I was too young, I didn't know the answer and didn't want to—but again, I had to.

Question: C.S. Lewis said something like this about nature: you don't go to her to derive your theology. You go to her with your theology and let her fill those words (*glory, redemption, love*) with meaning.

Answer: I like that.

Question: Yet I get the idea, in *Pilgrim* especially, that you did go to nature to derive your theology.

Answer: In a way, that's true. I approached the whole chaos of nature as if it were God's book. From it I derived symbols and themes that gave me some structures for truth.

Question: But only God can tell you about God. Nature merely tells you about nature. What if something you learned from nature contradicted other revelation?

Answer: If I thought I had to make the choice between God and nature, I would choose God. But I don't think I have to make that choice.

Question: When you studied nature, you came away with a simultaneous sense of awe and horror?

Answer: It can't be reduced to those terms. In *Pilgrim* I wrote about the *via positiva* and the *via negativa.* The rich, full expression of God's love bursts out in all the particulars of nature. Everything burgeons and blossoms—and then comes a devastating flood. There is spring, but also winter. There is intricacy in detail, but also oppressive fecundity as nature runs wild. It all starts collapsing; I see sacrifice and then prayer and everything empties and empties until I'm at the shores of the unknown where I started—except much more informed now.

Question: Chesterton said about nature that it's wrong to refer to her as mother nature. She's really sister nature, a separate, parallel creation to man with all his flaws and inconsistencies. She's half good and half bad.

Answer: Well, I sure as heck deal with that. I don't have a summary sentence for my view. It's all in the books somewhere.

That something is everywhere and always amiss is part of the very stuff of creation. It is as though each clay form had baked into it, fired into it, a blue streak of nonbeing, a shaded emptiness like a bubble that

not only shapes its very structure but that also causes it to list and ulti-
mately explode. We could have planned things more mercifully, perhaps,
but our plan would never get off the drawing board until we agree to the
very compromising terms that are the only ones that being offers.

The world has signed a pact with the devil; it had to. It is a covenant to
which every thing, even every hydrogen atom, is bound. The terms are
clear; if you want to live, you have to die; you cannot have mountains
and creeks without space, and space is a beauty married to a blind man.
The blind man is Freedom, or Time, and he does not go anywhere with-
out his great dog Death. The world came into being with the signing of
the contract. A scientist calls it the Second Law of Thermodynamics. A
poet says, 'The force that through the green fuse drives the flower/Drives
my green age.' This is what we know. The rest is gravy (Pilgrim, *pp. 180-*
181).

Question: The group you referred to as the British rationalists, notably Lewis, would explain this planet as the condemned planet, an
outpost of the universe where evil runs rampant. Perhaps that's why
he makes the statement that you can't get your theology from nature.
You are on the carbuncle planet and you may come up with a carbuncle theology. Do you view the universe as filled with God's love
and the earth as a marred exception?

Answer: That's nuts. We live in the age when we have the photo-
graphs of earth from space. Here is one absolutely beautiful sphere
floating among the others. There's more beauty in the variety and
richness of life here than on the other planets. As an artist, that picture from space has to affect my view.

Question: I'm sure their reference is to worlds in other dimen-
sions, that the holy world is more real than this world.

Answer: Perhaps. But this world merited the Incarnation. If everything is a symbol of spiritual reality, then earth's beauty means
something. The classical orthodox definition of beauty is that
beauty is the splendor of truth. Beauty and goodness and truth are a
triad.

The beauty of this world can't be brushed away. It is true there is
sin and pain and suffering, but to call the earth a blot in the universe
is evasive. If you carry that through to its conclusion, then God
should never have created the world; it was all some horrible mistake.

Question: Lewis uses the analogy of Christ's incarnation as a diver plunging into the depths to rescue a pearl without a glimmer of light and pulling it back into the light.

Answer: Yes—I love that image of God's emptying himself.

Question: So we're really back to your own key question of time and eternity. Just how involved is God in this world?

Answer: I believe, often, that nature participates in the essence of God himself, and if he removed his loving attention from it for a fraction of a second, life would cease.

Question: You referred in *Pilgrim at Tinker Creek* to Heisenberg's Indeterminacy Principle in physics. If randomness is the rule, what part does God play? Isn't it true that this principle strengthens the concept of God the sustainer? If he weren't here, it could literally fall apart at any moment. There must be wisdom behind it.

Answer: And yet you have to be very careful how you state that, because it borders on superstition. I believe that ultimately the people praying in the monasteries are keeping the whole thing going—metaphorically, at least—but there's a huge danger within any religion that it will lapse into superstition.

Question: Do you believe in miracles of the supernatural, nature-interrupting sense?

Answer: Of course. I have no problem with them at all. I'm a long way from agnosticism. I can't imagine now how I could have had a problem with them at one time.

To me the real question is, How in the world can we *remember* God? I like that part of the Bible that ticks off kings as good and bad. Suddenly there comes this one, King Josiah, who orders the temple to be cleaned up and inadvertently discovers the law.

This happens after generations of rulers and following God through the Exodus. Somehow they had forgotten the whole thing, every piece of it. Recognizing that, the king tears his clothes and cries.

A whole nation simply forgot God. We think, how can we forget—we who have seen God? Is it right of God to insist that we wear string around our fingers to remember him?

This notion of recollection is a pressing spiritual problem—not only how can we remember God, but why does he let us forget? I'm always forgetting God—always, always. That famous prayer, "I will in the course of this day forget thee; forget thou not me" is sometimes thought of as a warm Christian joke. I don't think it is so funny. I think it's exactly what we should be asking.

The secret of seeing is, then, the pearl of great price. If I thought he could teach me to find it and keep it forever I would stagger barefoot across a hundred deserts after any lunatic at all. But although the pearl may be found, it may not be sought. The literature of illumination reveals this above all: although it comes to those who wait for it, it is always, even to the most practiced and adept, a gift and a total surprise. I return from one walk knowing where the killdeer nests in the field by the creek and the hour the laurel blooms. I return from the same walk a day later scarcely knowing my name. Litanies hum in my ears; my tongue flaps in my mouth Ailinon, alleluia! *I cannot cause light; the most I can do is try to put myself in the path of its beam. It is possible, in deep space, to sail on solar wind. Light, be it particle or wave, has force: you rig a giant sail and go. The secret of seeing is to sail on solar wind. Hone and spread your spirit till you yourself are a sail, whetted, translucent, broadside to the merest puff* (Pilgrim, *p. 33*).

Question: There is another side of God. One of the scenes in the Bible shows Jesus weeping over unreceptive Jerusalem. "Oh that I could gather you under my wings," he says. A very strange statement for an omnipotent God. He has limited his actions on earth; he refuses to coerce.

Answer: I often wonder why God didn't make things clearer, why he spoke in a still, small voice. And I get angry at God when I see so many good people who appear to lack an organ by which they can perceive God. I blame God for that; but that's just the way he chooses to go about things. I often think of God as a fireball—friendly—who just rolls by. If you're lucky, you get a slight glimpse of him.

Question: But if you actively look for the fireball he can be found. Nature can be one vehicle, as *Pilgrim* shows.

Answer: The sixteenth-century British mystic named Juliana of Norwich wrote *Revelations of Divine Love*, which I've only had the courage to read once. Its main idea, God's love, is the most threatening of all, because it demands such faith.

Question: You have described yourself as hanging onto the edge of a cliff, grappling. Yet I read a review of *Holy the Firm* that paints you as the predetermined Christian with pat answers. To the reviewer, you were not hanging on the cliff; you were still very much on solid ground and he was over the cliff, unbelieving.

Answer: That's the trouble. Agnostics don't know what in the world is going on. They think religion is safety when in fact *they* have the safety. To an agnostic you have to say over and over again that the fear of death doesn't lead you to love of God. Love of God leads you to fear of death.

Agnostics often think that people run to God because they are afraid of dying. On the contrary, the biblical religion is not a safe thing. People in the Bible understood the transitory nature—the risk—of life better than most people. They weren't using religion as an escape hatch. Faith forces you to a constant awareness of final things. Agnostics don't remember all the time that they're going to die. But Christians do remember. All our actions in this life must be affected by God's point of view.

What can any artist set on fire but his world? What can any people bring to the altar but all it has ever owned in the thin towns or over the desolate plains? What can an artist use but materials, such as they are? What can he light but the short string of his gut, and when that's burnt out, any muck ready to hand?

His face is flame like a seraph's, lighting the kingdom of God for the people to see; his life goes up in the works; his feet are waxen and salt. He is holy and he is firm, spanning all the long gap with the length of his love, in flawed imitation of Christ on the cross stretched both ways unbroken and thorned. So must the work be also, in touch with, in touch with, in touch with; spanning the gap, from here to eternity, home (Holy the Firm, *p. 72).*

I visited Francis Schaeffer in Rochester, Minnesota, during one of his treatments at the Mayo Clinic. In 1978, while filming Whatever Happened to the Human Race?, *Schaeffer had begun to feel extremely tired and to lose weight. Two days after completing the project, he went for a medical checkup, which revealed an advanced case of lymphatic cancer. Until 1984, he fought a steady battle, relying mainly on chemotherapy, and managed to stay productive until only a few months before his death, despite the debilitating disease and treatment.*

Unlike many Christian authors, Schaeffer was not "discovered" after death. His popularity billowed in his prime, and he soon fell subject to a blitz of media coverage and critical analysis as well as the normal accouterments of fame. He lived the last decade of his life under the glare of a spotlight.

After twenty-two books, what more did Francis Schaeffer have to say? Quite a lot, I discovered. His books typically focus on ideas. In three days I spent with Schaeffer, I found him to be remarkably candid in evaluating his own contributions and in addressing issues commonly avoided by most evangelical leaders.

3

The Legacy of Francis Schaeffer

There are two kinds of people in the world: those who divide things into two categories and those who don't. Francis Schaeffer built an impressive assemblage of books, speeches, films, and followers by being one of the best at bisecting the world and slapping on appropriate labels.

What kind of man was Francis Schaeffer? Many who knew him only through his writings expected a rigid, rationalistic personality. In fact, he was quite emotional. If you told him of an acquaintance suffering severely, he might begin to weep, or stop and pray aloud. His wife Edith claims that fame did not affect his sincere interest in people. "If we're in a big hotel," she said in 1978, "and we're on our way to a meeting of seven thousand people, he's just as interested in talking and praying with the girl who comes to clean up the room as he ever was. It's not an act. The same day he heard he had cancer, he prayed with two nurses who had come and told him about their lives. I've known him since I was seventeen, almost fifty years, and I can say he hasn't changed. Once when he came for a date, he apologized for being late. He had seen a drunk on the street and had taken him to the Salvation Army for a bed."

In some ways Schaeffer assumed the role of a modern prophet. His thinning hair was long, his goatee snow white, and he often appeared in knickers. He spoke with a sonorous timbre, sweepingly describing the pitfalls of our present day and the decline of Western civilization. Critics asserted that, like a prophet, he took himself too seriously. Schaeffer was not given to tentativeness about an issue. Answers came easily and quickly and were the direct product of his "antithetical" approach. Surrounded by an intensely loyal family and thousands of fans, he overestimated the impact of his thoughts.

Some who have worked with the Schaeffer family come away grumbling about their "Messiah complex."

But, unlike a prophet, Schaeffer lived among a vigorous intellectual community marked by love, forgiveness, and personal concern for the whole man. He was as interested in beauty as in order. And he spent as much time talking about the application of his message in personal, life-changing ways as he did defining the message itself.

Schaeffer's approach should be seen in the context of his own development. He became a Christian as a teenager; while reading Ovid he decided he should read the Bible also. "I saw that there were innumerable problems that nobody was giving answers for," he told me during our interview. "But in the Bible I began to find answers. Even though I was finite, it put a cable in my hand which bound all the problems together and gave a systematic answer to them."

"In about six months," he said, "I was flattened." He was impressed by the order and consistency of the Christian system as "beautiful beyond words."

After attending Hampden-Sydney College in Virginia, he enrolled in 1935 at Westminster Theological Seminary, which had splintered off from Princeton Theological Seminary in 1929 under the leadership of J. Gresham Machen in the Fundamentalist-Modernist controversy. A year after Schaeffer entered the seminary, Machen was suspended by his denomination for setting up an independent mission board, and he formed the Orthodox Presbyterian Church.

Carl McIntire and some others subsequently withdrew from the new denomination, forming the Bible Presbyterian Church and Faith Theological Seminary. Francis Schaeffer followed the McIntire forces, finishing up at Faith.

Later, of course, McIntire repudiated the direction Schaeffer took with L'Abri, the mission he founded in Switzerland. It is important to note that Schaeffer's early training took place amid controversy. Learned men were defining terms, drawing battle lines, splitting doctrinal hairs. Schaeffer survived it all, somehow learning how to listen compassionately to different viewpoints and to emphasize love and unity in the church.

For ten years Schaeffer was pastor of a church in St. Louis. Then, in 1947, a survey trip to thirteen European countries changed his life. He came away stimulated by the intellectual climate but deeply concerned about the spiritual state of Europe. Though some countries were experiencing a postwar resurgence in religious interest, Schaeffer concluded that the neo-orthodox roots of their message would doom the long-term impact of the renewal.

For the next five years, Schaeffer was an itinerant evangelist across the Continent and in Scandinavia. He lectured on church history, tracing Christian origins back to the first church in Acts and through the Reformation. He especially attacked the liberal trends personified by Karl Barth whose thoughts he labeled in a 1951 pamphlet as "insanity." Besides lecturing, he and Edith helped churches organize children's work.

L'Abri grew out of the Schaeffer's ministry in the Swiss town of Champery, where they summered. He held services in an unused chapel of the mostly Catholic town. Some girls at a cosmopolitan finishing school began to attend the church, then to frequent the Schaeffers' house. As he recalled, "I was amazed in those discussions to find that I could answer those girls' questions in a way that a lot of them actually became interested."

In 1955 Schaeffer formed L'Abri (French for "shelter") as an independent mission. Response in the United States was mixed. "You mean you're going to open your home to dropout sons and daughters of rich parents, without charging? What will you do all day? What is your ministry?" Edith's book *L'Abri* chronicles the turmoil of those first few years. Their son Franky contracted polio, a daughter battled rheumatic fever, and the whole family had a bout with food poisoning. Worse, their entire village was almost swept away by avalanches. At one point the Schaeffers were ordered to leave Switzerland for "having a religious influence on the town." Financial needs were also pressing. They had begun L'Abri with a vow that they would never directly solicit funds of students.

Word soon got out, among European students and American visitors, that "There's a man up there in the mountains who can answer your questions." The trickle of guests began.

Today the Swiss branch of L'Abri services some 110 people at a time. In addition, many people rent chalets and share in L'Abri activities. Smaller branches exist in France, England, Holland, and the United States.

L'Abri is a commendable example of the outworking of practical apologetics (although recent visitors there say the unity of the place sorely suffers from Schaeffer's absence). Even critics of Schaeffer's philosophical approach admit this. Professor Jack Rogers, after analyzing Schaeffer in a two-part article in *The Reformed Journal* concluded, "In reading their (Schaeffers') books I have found the inexactitude of the arguments exasperating, but the description of life at L'Abri exhilarating."

While L'Abri can affect only a few score people at a time, through books and films Francis Schaeffer's thoughts spread throughout the world so that he was hailed as one of evangelicalism's leading spokesmen. "Missionary to the intellectuals," *Time* called him. And *Eternity* said he had "more influence with today's youth—from members of the dropout world to the disillusioned heirs of evangelicalism—than any other man." Schaeffer's twenty-two books have sold well over three million copies, not to mention his wife's books and those of other L'Abri staff members. InterVarsity Press even printed a booklet called "Introduction to Francis Schaeffer" in which he explained how all the various books fit together. The books tend to be repetitious and didactic, but they cover a broad range of topics, and all are readable by the educated consumer.

His first book came about after Schaeffer had been touring colleges and universities in the United States delivering a lecture called "Speaking Historic Christianity into the Twentieth Century." He got an enthusiastic response at Wheaton College in 1968, in the midst of that era's student turmoil. Students were delighted with a man who believed orthodox doctrine and yet tried to interpret the "worldly" thought and art which surrounded them. Schaeffer then agreed to have his tapes edited into the first few books.

The only books Schaeffer wrote intentionally (as opposed to someone adapting his spoken material) were those two connected with his film series, *How Should We Then Live?* and *Whatever Happened to the Human Race?* and later *The Christian Manifesto*. The book *How Should We Then Live?* grew out of a challenge from Billy Zeoli of Gospel Films, who had seen Kenneth Clark's *Civilisation* and was convinced an evangelical reply was needed—either from Schaeffer or from Malcolm Muggeridge. *Whatever Happened to the Human Race?* was the brain child of Franky Schaeffer, not yet thirty, who produced and directed it. It dealt specifically with the three topics of abortion, euthanasia, and infanticide, and featured Schaeffer and Dr. C. Everett Koop of Philadelphia (who eventually became the United States Surgeon General).

Reflecting on his life, Schaeffer seemed to take most delight in pointing out the things he pioneered, such as his early fight against racism and his call for Christians to use their wealth compassionately. L'Abri spearheaded a model of community long before radical Christians took up the cause. There was considerable sacrifice involved in the early days of L'Abri: the Schaeffers' open-door policy resulted in ruined wedding presents, cigarette burns in the rug, torn sheets, and vomit stains.

As for his contributions to thought, Schaeffer spoke most proudly of two messages. First was his dual stress of orthodoxy and the need for love and community although he wished he had stressed specific applications in his arguments against racism and for distributing wealth. Second was his encouragement of Christians to operate as whole persons within all of culture, giving them a framework for interpreting books, painting, music, and movies.

Schaeffer's system of thought derived from the "antithesis" which he stressed so often: that if a statement is true, the opposite of that statement cannot be true. In personal contacts Schaeffer attempted to furrow backwards until a person's presuppositions were exposed. Then he developed them logically until the person saw the contradiction in his conclusions. To Schaeffer "no non-Christian can be consistent with the logic of his presuppositions."

In other words, start with a presupposition that the world came about by chance. Schaeffer would prod you, intellectually, to conclude that humans cannot have meaning and that none of our actions makes any difference in the world. There is no "outside force" to be accountable to. To Schaeffer, a person who starts with presuppositions that exclude God must become "an atheist in religion, an irrationalist in philosophy, and completely immoral in the wider sense." Schaeffer was at his best in finding contemporary examples of people who admit those presuppositions and conclusions but fail to live consistently with them. For example, Jean-Paul Sartre asserted there is no basis for ethical judgments of right and wrong, yet he broke his own principles by denouncing France's treatment of Algeria on moral grounds.

"Preevangelism" was the term Schaeffer used to describe this process of bringing a person to see the logical result of his or her own presuppositions. Thereafter Schaeffer presented the Christian alternative and showed how the Christian conception of a world created by an intelligent designer made more sense.

Schaeffer saw a huge rupture in the history of thought cracking open about the time of Hegel, who rejected the antithesis mode of thinking in favor of synthesis. Sören Kierkegaard took Hegel's synthetic approach and applied it to the realm of theology, thus becoming in Schaeffer's words, "the father of all modern existential thought, both secular and theological." The natural world of the visible and created began to swallow up the unseen world. We can only be sure, say the moderns, of the seen world. The unseen world is not known through reason: It is known through irrational "leaps of faith."

Schaeffer did not like leaps of faith, at least in doctrine. He believed doctrine must derive from a carefully reasoned, step-by-step approach based on the verbal revelation God has given in the Bible. Thus, he downplayed the nonrational (not irrational) aspects of the gospel. Schaeffer seemed to rely on the power of reasoning, as if the only way a person can come to Christ is by arguing himself into the Kingdom, even though many of the gospel's most salient features— unearned grace and unmerited sacrifice, for example—would not be arrived at on the basis of logic from natural revelation.

Where in Schaeffer's system was the *Sehnsucht*, the sense of longing that provided the motif for C.S. Lewis' conversion, or what of a person who came to an emotional, not propositional, awareness of good and evil through reading Tolkien or Tolstoy? Would his apprehension of a "first-order, existential" experience be rejected because of its weak epistemology? Or could it too lead him toward Christ? C.S. Lewis, certainly a rational thinker, startled the intellectual world with his premise that the Romantic movement (not Hegel's synthesis or the Renaissance) caused the most profound shift in recent history; yet Schaeffer seemed to sidestep that area entirely.

Unlike some apologetics, Schaeffer did not restrict his inquiry to the field of knowledge. He was a preacher and devoted equal time to the practical application of how the church could and should reveal the holiness and love of God. "I'm sick and tired of dusty apologetics," he said. "To my mind apologetics is not a safe system to live in. Apologetics should lead people to Christ and to a greater comprehension of the Lordship of Christ in the whole spectrum of life."

Schaeffer's main weaknesses resulted from this dual role of evangelist and apologist. He believed so sincerely in the force of what he presented that, to him, the arguments compelled agreement. He used phrases describing the Christian answer as being a "logically necessary conclusion" rather than a "probable conclusion" or "plausible conclusion." And, searching for illustrations from modern culture to demonstrate his points, he passed over hundreds of examples that wouldn't demonstrate the point. He was a dramatist. He spoke in italics. He made such statements as, "Picture the line between reason and nonreason as a solid concrete wall with barbed wire in the middle charged with ten thousand volts of electricity. Then you can begin to understand how there can be no interchange between the lower story with reason which leads to despair and the upper story of hope without reason."

Naturally, some Christian philosophers and theologians fidgeted when Schaeffer placed some of their favorite mentors, such as Barth and Kierkegaard, on the wrong side of the concrete wall. As Jack Rogers commented, "Schaeffer lumps Rosseau, Kant, Hegel, and Kierkegaard together. His characteristics of their thoughts are almost unrecognizable with reference to either their own works or standard textbook treatments of them.... One is soon tempted to defend a philosopher simply because he has been unfairly caricatured by Schaeffer, even when one is in reality as critical of him as Schaeffer is—but for quite different reasons."

Schaeffer's confident, panoramic assertions gained him both notability and notoriety. He had an incredible impact on young evangelicals who are now likely to confront their teachers with such befuddling questions as: "Let's see, did that composer write before or after the line of despair?"

Sometimes his prophet's mantle caused him to stumble, as in the late sixties when he predicted that the New Left in America would grow "stronger and more violent and more disruptive" and "society itself will move toward chaos."

Yet in many ways Schaeffer stayed consistent with his presuppositions about what his role should be. Sometimes he called himself an "old-fashioned evangelist," and one got the distinct impression that a child who accepted Christ in his little chapel in Switzerland gave him more pleasure than all the brilliant students whose theoretical discussions kept him up so late.

To some sophisticated non-Christians, who are not atheistic existentialists, and who live fulfilled, hopeful lives, oblivious to the line of despair, this strange man with the aura of the Alps about him appeared to be a relic. They continued to benefit from the moraine of Christian civilization, to read Dostoyevsky, and to listen to Mozart masses played by the Los Angeles Philharmonic. It was precisely those people who made Francis Schaeffer so intense, so pessimistic, so sober. They were living, he believed, an absolute lie to their presuppositions. They were teetering on the brink of cosmic choices, yet they refused to face the evidence. He spent his life trying to convince them.

Evangelical Prophet: Francis Schaeffer

Question: Many Christian leaders have tried unsuccessfully to maintain the respect and enthusiasm of young people over a long period of time. But you have succeeded. Why?

Answer: First of all, different people have different qualities and gifts from the Lord. Having said this, I think there are some human elements.

I have dealt with the questions of the developing contemporary scene and haven't gotten stuck back at the point of my own studies when I was a young man, the way some people seem to do. One reason for this is that I was not raised as a Christian and I went through a period when I was agnostic. I became a Christian at eighteen simply through reading my own Bible after reading a lot of philosophy. Therefore I think my own conversion is conducive to thinking in modern terms.

Also, I have had a continuing education, not just from the books that I have read but from many, many people that I talk to. So often Christians don't listen to what the other person says; they just present the Christian position. I've always tried to listen to people who have come from all over the world and from all kinds of disciplines. When young people come to me they find empathy for the simple reason that I don't write off their questions, intellectually or otherwise, and just give them a formula. I really try to deal with the questions.

Question: Some of your critics admit that what you've just said is true within the context of L'Abri. When you are with someone in person, you do understand and empathize with their questioning. On the other hand, they say, in your writings—on the cold, dispassionate black and white page—when you deal with people like Karl

Barth, for example, that same sort of true listening doesn't occur. There you have a tendency to categorize and typecast people. Do you agree?

Answer: No, I really don't. When you're not writing twenty-six books about Karl Barth, you have to make summaries and, in general, my summaries are correct. Now everybody makes mistakes— I'm sure I've made some—but I would say that I've tried to treat other thinkers compassionately.

In the type of writing I do, I must summarize; I can't possibly deal with all the nuances. So I try to find the central things they've said and present them. I always hold my breath because I know certain nuances would sound different if I were talking for two hours instead of writing on one page.

Question: When *How Should We Then Live?* was breaking sales records, your publisher took out a full-page ad in the *New York Times*, asking, "Why are the secular media ignoring this book?" Does it disappoint you that the secular media have not given coverage to your thought?

Answer: Yes, in a way, because I have tried to write my books for two audiences, Christians and non-Christians. The first publisher I offered a book to turned it down because, he said, it seemed directed at both audiences. I was sure books could be written and directed at both audiences, and this has proved to be true. Many non-Christians, whom Christianity wouldn't normally reach, have been touched and even changed.

I'm disappointed about the media, because I'd like to see a big impact for the Lord in that world. In order to be accepted in the secular media area, you generally have to be within their framework, and I'm outside of it. But I don't know anyone who has really taken a clear Christian position who has been more widely accepted in the secular area.

Question: In the evangelical world, at least, you became a media figure with people bidding for your book contracts and audiences of seven thousand packing auditoriums, when you were previously accustomed to a room of thirty people discussing issues. Was that a difficult adjustment for you?

Answer: It wasn't really, because I believe it is just an extension of my previous work. The Lord gave us something that none of us was sure could occur: atmosphere in the midst of those seven thousand which I found just as intimate as speaking to a hundred people in our chapel at L'Abri.

As far as the actual commercial side of it, you have to live in the world we live in, in the same way supermarkets are in our generation. You might wish that the Christian booksellers' business was a different business than it is in our present day. But if you're going to publish books, you have to publish them in a setting that exists and not one that doesn't exist.

Question: Do you think that you have been substantially changed by all that's happened?

Answer: I've thought and prayed about this. I don't see changes. Far more important than my own opinion is that of my friends who would be very honest, and they don't seem to find any change either. Now, who knows? I have to wait to talk to the Lord on Judgment Day to be sure.

Question: Your wife very vividly describes your compassion for people. You care for people, and you listen to them intently. Have you always had this quality?

Answer: I think it is a gift.

Question: Was it present before you were a Christian? Were you drawn toward people?

Answer: I don't think so. Neither was my intellectual interest. I got rotten grades until I became a Christian, and after that I always studied to try to excel. I graduated *magna cum laude* from Hampden-Sydney College even though in high school I barely made it.

I know I have an analytical mind, and one thing I've learned in a long lifetime is that you don't meet many people who have really analytical minds. This I had before I was a Christian. In fact, I became a Christian after analyzing the liberalism I was hearing preached on one side and the philosophy I was reading on the other.

But I really believe that my ability to sit and talk with one person or seven thousand and answer the questions the way I answer them, covering the intellectual spectrum, is as much a gift of God as anything, and I think the Lord can take it away. As long as that gift is useful in this world, I'm thankful to have it.

Since I've had cancer we've realized more than ever before how God has used our work. Professors in law write, "After all my law studies it was reading your books that made me understand the modern framework of law." Or people in medicine write, "The whole discussion of medical ethics fell into place."

Question: Could you summarize the crucial thinkers who've influenced you?

Answer: Literally hundreds of people have influenced my thought.

But certain key people made a real difference in my thinking. It goes all the way back to my junior high school days when I had just one art teacher. I came from a family which was not interested in art at all. She opened the door for me.

Then I had a professor in college, my philosophy professor, who was brilliant. I was his favorite student because, I think, I probably was the only student in the class who understood him and stimulated him. He used to invite me down at night to sit around his pot-bellied stove and just discuss. He became committed to neo-orthodox thinking, but he was very important in my intellectual development.

Question: What historical people?

Answer: I tried to study the whole spectrum of the historical Christian background, specifically out of the Reformation; so I come from a Reformed background by choice. Then I went to Westminster for two years and to Faith Seminary. Cornelius Van Til and Allan MacRae of Biblical Theological Seminary stirred my intellectual thought. Those who are trying to minimize me try to link my thinking only into the Princeton thinking of Hodge and Warfield, and so on. A careful reading of my works shows that, although I am very thankful for those men and their day of history, I don't believe they were facing the same problems we are facing in our day. My theological position would be similar to theirs, but our respective presentations are necessarily different.

Question: Because of the breadth of fields that you try to cover, are you mostly limited to secondary sources? There's no way you could encompass music, art, philosophy, literature, science, etc., through primary sources.

Answer: Secondary sources are very important to me, of course. On the other hand, I try to keep up on primary things I think are crucial, so that when I read a secondary source I have a sound basis of judgment.

Also, you must realize that I do not work in isolation. L'Abri is not myself; it is made up of a group of scholars. The outstanding example, I guess, is Hans Rookmaaker, whom I met first when he was still a student. Both he and I have kicked stuff around for so long that in large areas, including art, we would hesitate to say who thought of an idea first. So I haven't worked in isolation. I think anybody who searches for only one or two people to explain my positions and my attitudes is pursuing a hopeless task.

Question: Have any of your major views significantly changed in the last decade—I mean, really abrupt reversals?

Answer: If I thought for a couple of days, I might think of something. Not basic ones, I think. I've made tremendous shifts in details. But I think not in major views.

Question: At what point, then, was your basic framework developed?

Answer: Theologically, it was developed all the way back before I went to seminary. When I went to Hampden-Sydney College, the Bible professor, the college president, and the college chaplain were outstanding Christians. But I never would have had the equipment or the content to write the books I've written nor to deal with the people I deal with across such a wide area if I had remained in the United States. I think going to Europe was providential; it allowed a wider intellectual framework from people coming from all over the world.

People often say, "Why didn't you come and help your own country?" But Edith and I have often said we think we've been greater help to the United States by having gone to Europe.

Question: Do you read in other languages?

Answer: No. And it's been a limitation. My family is all bilingual (French), but I'm not.

Question: As your role has changed over the years, do you think you have been subjected to new, specific temptations?

Answer: Yes, a great danger of spiritual pride has arisen as I deal with large numbers and with so many people reading the books. But then I quickly counteract that by saying I've never seen greater spiritual pride in my life than when somebody was elected president of the Sunday school class with three people in it. Pride is something inside you; mere size doesn't change the danger of it. I believe Satan is playing chess against me and against you, and he is clever enough to play it on the existential board we're living on at the moment.

Question: Let's shift to politics. Your writings imply that democracy is the outgrowth of Christian principles of society. Are you committed to democracy as the ideal form of government, or are you just as comfortable in some cultures with very different forms of government?

Answer: When you talk about democracy, you have to define it. It doesn't mean you can't have a king. It doesn't have to take the form it takes in the United States. Switzerland doesn't have a strong president: a council of seven rotates, and most Swiss people don't even know who's the current president. So I'm not talking about a specific form of democracy. If you're asking about just the concept of democracy—responsibility being invested in the people, or checks and balances, or *lex rex* rather than *rex lex*—then, yes, I think this is an outgrowth of Christianity.

Question: Some Christians believe models of communism, though not classical Marxism, could be acceptable to Christians and could be adaptable forms of government for other cultures. Do you agree?

Answer: If by communism you mean somewhat more economic control by the state, then, sure, that would be acceptable in certain circumstances. But the word *communism* has a very strict definition today. The philosophy developed by Marx, Engels, and Lenin brings forth oppression as naturally as the Reformation of Christianity brought forth "law is king." The word *communism* means that specific materialistic philosophy.

If on the other hand you ask, "Is it necessary to equate democracy with the exact economic situation we have?"—absolutely not. A perfect example is Switzerland. When Switzerland socialized the railroads, did this mean it became a noncapitalistic country? Not at all. It is more capitalistic than the United States. When we socialized the postal system in the United States did this mean that we gave up capitalism or democracy? Absolutely not.

At the moment we are a very different kind of democracy than was visualized by Jefferson. Back then they visualized an elitist group, and our electoral college, for example, endures as a hangover from their ideas. But I believe Christianity leads increasingly away from that to the kind of thing we have now.

Question: Are you a pacifist?

Answer: No, very strenuously no. I hate war with all my heart. But we live in a fallen world, and I think you have to take this into account.

Question: Would you support any revolutionary movements, such as in Africa or in Indochina?

Answer: Oh, sure, I would in certain circumstances. To me, the right of revolution is a part of the democratic process. You must remember I am a radical in this sense. Most people don't realize that.

Question: Would you support armed intervention in a place like Cambodia, or Albania, for the purpose of bringing liberty?

Answer: We live in a very complex world. I'm not hedging. I'm really not. But I discuss this with congressmen and senators, and all kinds of people. And none of this is theoretical.

In this complicated world you have to realize that you can't do everything. But on the other hand, I do believe that at certain points of history it is an exhibition of non-Christian lack of love not to use what is at one's disposal to help other people in their extremities. The monstrous situation in Germany in World War II is an example of a need for outside force.

Question: Are any such monstrous situations facing us now?

Answer: Yes, and I'm worried, because I think the world is going to face the most monstrous situation ever in the role of modern Russian power. It's larger than Hitler's Germany.

I hate all forms of totalitarianism. The political liberals always look at the left with rose-colored glasses in contrast to the right. The biggest example of this tendency is the one that everybody ought to have recognized before Solzhenitsyn came on the scene. The liberals saw the monstrousness of what Hitler was doing almost immediately, but most of these people did not acknowledge what Stalin was doing until *thirty years later*. It's the same with China and Mao. People who are totally neutral have estimated that Mao probably killed more people in taking over power in China than Stalin and Hitler put together.

Now I would just say that in our present circumstances we're facing an obvious confrontation of power. And fortunately, some people are beginning to speak up.

Question: In the film series you draw parallels between our current crisis and the decline of previous civilizations, and you give a lot of warnings about trends in our own civilization. Doesn't the nuclear moat around the United States introduce a brand new element in this decline of civilization because, regardless of internal forces, we have the capacity to destroy the rest of the world?

Answer: Yes, we are now living with the possibility of blowing up the whole planet, which makes the whole situation more overwhelming.

Before I continue I must emphasize again that I could never be construed as right wing, so what I'm going to say mustn't be put in that context. I hate the loss of freedom whether it comes from the right or the left.

How Should We Then Live? built up to a climax against authoritarian government itself as such. I hate authoritarian structure in any form—in the church, in the state—and I haven't practiced it in my own family with my kids. I believe we are facing a perilous situation today. Churchill was right when he said, after the war, that the only reason the Russian armies were no longer advancing was because America had supremacy with the atom bomb.

Up through the Cuban crisis, the United States had the preponderance of power; so therefore the nuclear situation was a plus for us. At the present time it's a toss-up who has nuclear supremacy. If Russia gains the nuclear supremacy, whether America will be blasted off the face of the earth, I don't know, but certainly in this present alignment China will be.

I could be entirely wrong, but my own conclusion after talking to people in centers of power is that nuclear power now is overestimated. We've reached a stalemate, and I think what will come next will be determined not as much by nuclear weapons as by more conventional methods. I don't think the impetus is an outgrowth of communism as such; it's a blend of Lenin's concept of power and, behind that, "Mother Russia."

Question: It's enlightening to see how Russia capitalizes on that by using Cuba. They could not get away with intervention in Africa by their own soldiers. So they hired mercenaries, like their own French Foreign Legion.

Answer: Exactly right. I doubt they plan to invade Europe. I think they intend to use their military might as a political weapon to achieve their purpose without the necessity of armed intervention.

Question: You mean Western European countries will become communist through political means?

Answer: No, we'll come to a showdown and the result will be the reverse of the Cuban missile situation. The enormity of what would be involved for poor Europe will cause them to take a lesser stand politically. Then will come another political stand.

Question: In the same way the Arabs changed Europe's foreign policy toward Israel in 1973 with the threat of an oil embargo?

Answer: Yes! Overnight. To pursue this, I think Russia has a several-pronged program which shows great brilliance and is consistent with Lenin. The first prong is their armies; they've stalemated us with nuclear power. Then they have the hardcore of the political parties in Western Europe. And then they have the extension of military power with the Cuban and Vietnamese forces. And also, I am convinced that they support the terrorists in the West, even though the terrorists may be against the communistic parties. I think Russia supports anything that causes upheaval and chaos and breakdown in the West. So they have a many-pronged, yet united, program.

You asked originally if I saw any monstrous situation in the world today. Boy, oh, boy, do I! My brothers in Christ, whom I love very much, who are pacifists—I just think they're mistaken.

Question: Have you worked out theories about how the trends of civilization which you trace in your books and your own view of prophecy come together?

Answer: No. I take eschatology seriously, of course. But I think the Bible warns us that we can't be absolutely sure by any means that we live in any specific portion of that eschatological program. Let me state it another way. I believe I should live every day of my life as though Christ may come back before I die. But at the same time I don't believe I can ever say I know that I am watching the fulfillment of the eschatological situation. I'm curious, and holding the very strong views I do on eschatology, naturally I'm intrigued. But I don't allow it to shape my practical and political feelings.

Question: I get the impression that a lot of Christians would vote for the Antichrist if they knew who he was, just to hasten Christ's return. But in the Arab situation, the fact that Israel may in fact be God's chosen people and may eventually fit into some theories of eschatology really should have no bearing on the morality of how you treat the Arabs or Palestinians.

Answer: I quite agree. If I were President of the United States, I must say, I wouldn't make my decisions here in a certain historical situation on the basis that scriptural prophecy would make certain decisions mandatory.

Question: One of your more recent emphasis is the disparity of wealth and a Christian's responsibility in an affluent society. The theory and scriptural basis are fairly common in the Christian world today. But the practicality—how this affects me in my decision on what car to buy, what house to buy, how many pairs of pants to own, whether to have investments—is very complex. Do you have any practical advice?

Answer: When I was a pastor in western Pennsylvania, one of the big discussions was whether you could be spiritual and have life insurance. I emphasized then that the church cannot legislate you. The Bible doesn't and, therefore, we cannot give absolutes. All we can do is produce principles, and then the individual must decide under the leadership of the Holy Spirit how to apply those principles to the situation. Conceivably the Holy Spirit could lead one person to apply them one way, and another person to apply them slightly differently and they would be equally right.

I've stood for a compassionate use of accumulated wealth, and I get shot at by both sides. The people who want to have all the affluence and never think of compassion don't like my emphasis, but I also get shot at for using the term *accumulated wealth*, because radical Christians are drifting toward the position that any accumulation of wealth is wrong.

I believe the Bible teaches a right of private property. There are cautions: first, how we get it; second, how we use it. In the New Testament, it is quite clear that Christians had personal property, or they wouldn't have had anything to give when Paul appealed for funds.

I've stressed repeatedly that the church should have two orthodoxies—the orthodoxy of doctrine and the orthodoxy of community. L'Abri was an icebreaker among evangelicals in many senses, including a whole new emphasis on community. But we have made a very strenuous distinction between a commune and a community. The commune has more or less taken on the connotation of sharing all goods. L'Abri is not a commune, but a community of families living together in their own homes with their own personalities, their own property, their own direction of their children.

I cannot remember anybody preaching about community when I was younger. And I can't remember anything that would approximate what I would emphasize and what L'Abri would emphasize on the compassionate use of accumulated wealth.

Question: Do you give away a lot of your income?

Answer: Well, first of all, understand that Edith and I have turned all our earnings over to L'Abri. They control our royalties.

Question: Do they contribute heavily to underdeveloped countries?

Answer: Individuals do. But L'Abri is a very costly program because we take people in and charge them very little.

Question: Your book, *The New Super-Spirituality*, referred to Christian competitiveness. Isn't there a new danger among certain groups to build competitive pride about how cheaply they live and how much they give away? That's exactly what caused the downfall of Ananias and Sapphira, who were trying to be superspiritual.

Answer: I think we have to live consciously within two Christian realities: the fallen world and our finiteness. Nobody can give away everything. It's always proportionate. Now I would say the proportion must be left up to the Holy Spirit to lead.

We have no right to set absolutes unless they can be shown directly from Scripture. Nobody has a right to tell me that spirituality means that I should get four thousand dollars a year instead of five, or whether I should buy my children a bicycle. That's my business before the Lord.

Question: Looking back over all the things that you have done, which do you feel best about?

Answer: The first would be speaking historical Christianity in a way that can be understood by contemporary people and can be shown to be relevant to them, so that many of them become Christians.

The other thing would be the emphasis that being a Christian is not some obscure thing in the upper levels of spirituality but encompasses the whole of life. Christians have begun to realize that Christianity meant something in the arts and culture and law in a way that a lot of them had never thought of before.

I stand theologically in the stream of historical Christianity—the early church and the Reformation—so I haven't said anything new. But I seem, by the grace of God, to have been able to say these things to contemporary people in a way they have comprehended.

Question: Some Christians have come away from you confused about how they should relate to the arts. You refer to a "line of despair" which implies that the *form* used by modern artists and musicians and writers are somehow tainted or immoral. The only way I can function as a Christian artist, people have said to me, is to leapfrog back a century and pick up old forms.

Answer: Oh, no. Maybe I didn't protect myself sufficiently. The people who have been with me in L'Abri don't think this way—but I can see how the people who just come in contact with the books could think that.

Technique is neutral, and you can't say that a certain technique is godly or ungodly. But there is a form of the world's spirit for every generation, and this infiltrates all kinds of things, including Christian thinking, unless we consciously reject it.

In art, techniques have been born of the really brilliant people in those fields trying to find a vehicle to express their world view. I don't believe that these people necessarily sit down in the Cafe Voltaire in Zurich, where dadaism was born, for example, and construct these things. I would just say that a person's world view, consciously or unconsciously, naturally shows itself with some consistency in the totality of life. Be careful here, because they're still made in the image of God, whether they know it or not; so there are brakes. But in general what I've said is true.

Because modern forms of art were brought forth in order to express a certain world view, it therefore becomes very tricky for the young Christian artist or writer. The techniques are neutral, neither godly nor ungodly. But it's easier to produce a world view through the vehicle conceived to express it than it is to convey another world view. Therefore I am not opposed to modern form of art, but I think you do have to keep in mind why the form was produced.

Question: Can you think of any examples like that in music?

Answer: Music is the hardest of all to discuss, and it's the one which I always approach with the greatest hesitancy. You can't visualize music or examine it in the same way in which you can examine something on the printed page, or on a canvas. Yet nevertheless we see the same general things in music that are more easily pointed out in writing or poetry or painting.

Question: Of the various disciplines, I think the popular culture has been most resistant to new classical forms of music. When the New York Philharmonic plays John Cage the people boo. I don't know if they can ever get over that.

Answer: I don't think they should get over it. By the time you get to John Cage, in contrast to somebody like Stravinsky, he is writing a philosophical statement. One of my quarrels with modern art is that it's too philosophical. I have the same quarrel with it that I have with much evangelical art; It isn't art; it's a tract. Propaganda. People like Marcel du Champs and John Cage didn't set out to make works of art, they set out to make philosophic statements.

Question: You make specific interpretations of artists. For instance, when you criticize the Salvador Dali crucifixion painting as implying a lack of reality, have you researched that? Have you found a statement by Salvador Dali that says his technique was intended to imply historical questions about Jesus or are you just inferring that?

Answer: Curiously enough, in a *Playboy* interview, Salvador Dali said that he now was reading the modern scientists and coming to realize that the earth was basically made up not of mass, but of energy. Then he leaped to the fact that we should have a spiritual representation in our art. So *Playboy*, of all things, has been very helpful with Salvador Dali.

Question: That introduces an interesting subject: the philosophic movement within science for a view of the universe at its core being irrational rather than rational. You don't seem comfortable with these new findings, such as the Heisenberg Indeterminacy Principle.

Answer: Certainly I realize the older Newtonian concepts have to be modified. But even when we're dealing with the very small, say in a cyclotron, we are still dealing on a basis of cause and effect in the large area, regardless of what's happening in the smaller area. If we didn't deal with the basis of cause and effect, nobody could build the cyclotron.

There is a difference between not accepting the Cartesian concept that in our human finiteness we can plot every graph mathematically and jumping into the area of irrationality. The building of the cyclotron is an absolute proof that the very men who are producing it are denying irrationality by their own actions.

Question: What do they say to that when you confront them?

Answer: Nobody's ever answered me. There's sudden silence.

Question: You mean you have sat, one to one like this, with physicists and asked this question?

Answer: Yes, sure. Amazingly, a great number of them have never thought it through, perhaps because people are playing many, many games instead of thinking of big questions. Their game can be knocking one-tenth of one second off a downhill run in the Swiss Alps. It also can show up in a highly disciplined science where one focuses on a very small area of reality and then never thinks of the big question.

Question: I assume you're familiar with Niebuhr's principles of Christ and culture. How good is it for us to redeem culture? In some ways is it not better for Christians to be a minority, a counterculture?

Answer: The ideal would be if I could wave a wand and have a Christian consensus so that you wouldn't have a confusion of church and state. I believe that's what the founders of America hoped for. You wouldn't have a state church but you would have a Christian consensus. Therefore you really would be influencing the culture overwhelmingly.

Question: When in history has that occurred?

Answer: Never. There's no golden age. I'm tired of people who would try to make me say the Reformation was a golden age. It was anything but a golden age.

But the United States when I was young, through the twenties and thirties, basically showed a Christian consensus. It was, of course, poorly applied in certain areas, such as race or compassionate use of accumulated wealth.

Question: What has happened since that time? Has the Christian consensus shrunk in percentage? Has it grown less vocal? Or would you say the worldly philosophies have taken sway and leveled its impact?

Answer: All of those factors. Humanism has come to its natural conclusion and we now live in a secularized society. You can teach atheism in our schools but you can't sing Christmas carols. And secular presuppositions now control law, education, all these things.

The church follows the same curve slightly later. Most of our large denominations allow liberal theology to dominate the seminaries and the bureaucracies. They take on exactly the same thought forms as the secular world because, to my mind, liberal theology is only humanism in Christian terminology.

So those two trends have come together: secularism and a church dominated by the same basic philosophy.

Question: You are now introduced on stage as an intellectual muscle man and people come knowing that, ready to attack you. Your book jacket blurbs call you "the missionary to the intellectual" and other labels that probably embarrass you. How do these things affect your self-concept? Do you get nostalgic for those old, first days in Europe, thirty years ago?

Answer: It all seems very unreal to me, which I think is a protection that the Lord has given.

Question: I've heard people snipe at you by saying you feed the image of the wise man on the mountain—for example, by wearing knickers to go along with the role.

Answer: The reason I wear knickers is just because I have found them comfortable. I used them first for climbing and cross-country skiing and so I gradually got into the habit of wearing them.

Question: But when you go to a U.S. ministers' conference, it becomes a statement. Why are you standing apart from the norm?

Answer: I suppose I found it helpful the first times I came over in the sixties. I'd never thought of it before until you just asked me. When I went to a place like Wheaton, it gave me an edge by setting me off from the stereotype. So in a way I wasn't what they were used to, and of course in my thinking I wasn't.

Question: If I had asked you fifteen years ago, "Are you ever going to write a book?" what would you have said?

Answer: No. I'm interested in *talking* to people. But after lecturing, for example, at Harvard, suddenly these Harvard students, almost none of whom were Christians, gave me a standing ovation. One of the professors' wives turned to Edith and said, "I've been at Harvard for thirty years and have never seen a standing ovation." It was true at M.I.T., and other places. But I still wouldn't have thought of going beyond the individual conversation, the lectures with give-and-take afterwards. In those days I had more energy, so I'd stay up until two or three o'clock in the morning.

Question: One critic who observed you in Los Angeles said that probably most of the people in the auditorium did not understand what you were saying in the films or in person. The audience applauded your seeming expertise, but this critic really doubted that they went out with changed perceptions.

Answer: I would just say that he ought to read the letters that have come. If you preach a straight gospel sermon, part of the people aren't going to understand that. A remarkable number of people have understood remarkably much, to such an extent that it has changed their lives. I think the critic is mistaken.

Question: In the film series on Western civilization, at what point were you trying to do a respectable scholarly analysis of history and culture, couched in terms of objectivity, and at what point did you have the motivation of evangelism? Aren't those two motives dichotomous?

Answer: I believe that Christianity is true. And it's true in the totality of truth. Now it doesn't give you the answer to quantum physics. But I believe that the closer you can come to truth, objective truth, the more Christianity will be substantiated. I don't see any dichotomy.

In the beginning of the book *How Should We Then Live?* I say this is not an exhaustive study of Western history and culture. Nobody could write a book like that. It is selective, but every history book is selective. I am so convinced of the truth of Christianity that I see no inherent tension between objectivity and what I think is the purpose of apologetics (that is, getting people to become Christian and Christians to become more deeply endowed with the concept of the Lordship of Christ in our culture and in the whole spectrum of life).

Question: Why do you downplay many of the gross Christian errors throughout history? You do mention some of them, of course, but it surely seems that the Thirty Years' War, the Crusades, the Inquisitions, the squelching of science, and events like these had a comparatively lesser part in your film series than they had in history. Did you do that purposely?

Answer: Yes. In the first place there is the space limitation. Second, there are some things to which you must devote a huge number of pages or frames of a film, or you'd better not touch them. The Crusades are a perfect example. I think they were destructive. I don't think they had any place in a real Christian framework. But what are you going to do with them in a book or a film like this? If you ask me to discuss them, I'll spend half an hour talking to you about the Crusades.

Question: Your methodology, not in person, but in writing, can appear to be rationalistic. And yet, your concept of the Fall must include the fact that human reason also is fallen. How can you build on such a rationalistic base?

Answer: I'm convinced that the Bible teaches something between a natural theologian such as Aquinas and a materialist who cannot count on human reasons. We are fallen, and there's no way to start from the finite and move to the infinite—we'll draw the wrong conclusions. But human reason still functions and, as Paul argues in Romans 1, the evidence is adequate—so adequate that we can be called disobedient if we don't bow to it.

PART TWO

The Message

Journalism presents unique challenges to the committed Christian, who must balance the desire for full disclosure with biblical admonitions to be loving and compassionate. The impact of good reporting on a specific ministry may indeed be negative; the journalist must keep in mind his responsibilities to the broader public.

Christian television provides a fertile ground for good reporting today. Its personalities are larger than life and it thrives on visual images. In addition, Christian television stirs up issues that deserve careful scrutiny by the Christian church and the general public. The concentration of resources in Christian television, half a billion dollars a year, is unparalleled in church history.

I chose the Charlotte-based PTL Club *as an archetype of Christian television. It is flamboyant, colorful, and endlessly controversial. I went as a TV guest as well as a reporter, which allowed for unusual access to people and facilities.*

When a shorter version of this chapter appeared in Christianity Today, *the Jewish Defense League attacked Jim Bakker for his comment on "a Jewish Reporter." Bakker denied saying such a thing, implying that* Christianity Today *and I had manufactured the quote. I had seen Bakker respond too often by shoot-from-the-hip denials and, after careful thought, I played the tape recording of his quote for a Charlotte reporter. Bakker's apology appeared in the next day's paper.*

5

The Christian TV Machine

HE IS a skilled Assemblies of God pastor from Maine with a lyrical Irish accent. He begins calmly, "I just want to share a few verses of Scripture with you here, and then I'll be done." But, like a politician warming to his audience, he soon begins embellishing. The story, from 1 Kings, becomes less a retelling than a twenty-minute dramatic performance. His arms flail the air. He falls to his knees. "God will take your nothingness and through it do anything!" he shouts.

A crowd erupts into applause. In front of them a well-groomed, smiling man in a vested suit nods his head enthusiastically, holding his hands high and leading the applause, mouthing "Amen" and "Praise the Lord."

To the right, off camera, is a formal living room setting, with a plush blue carpet and baby blue walls accentuated by cream-colored Corinthian columns. Jim Bakker, host of television's *PTL Club* sits behind a desk there, shuffling through papers, studying the lineup of guests who will appear as soon as the preacher finishes. His wife Tammy sits off to the side, examining her caramel-colored fingernails and fluffing her hair, while sometimes offering aloud a "Praise the Lord."

Beyond them, to the left, singers dressed in pastel evening gowns are arranging themselves on risers, while stagehands are positioning huge, colorful geometric shapes into an attractive backdrop. Miss Illinois of 1959 is clearing her throat, waiting for her entry cue. Four cameras mounted on silent electric carts—$80,000 cameras, the best in the business—sweep over the scenes, focusing now on the preacher, now on an intense listener. Overhead, a bank of three hundred computer-controlled lights swivel and adjust. And rising up from the stage floor are five tiers of sixty telephone tables, with volunteers manning each phone. Behind them, a globe of the world displays PTL's ministry: flashing white lights radiate outward from Charlotte, North Carolina, across the world.

And I, propped on a stool amid the whirl of energy, am one of the waiting guests. "That man is our Bible speaker this week—I've never heard him so filled with the Spirit," one stagehand whispers to me, pointing to the pastor from Maine, as she rustles past.

Other people flutter around the studio, dodging cameras and stepping over electric cables thick as an arm. Beautiful, stylishly dressed women whisper instructions to the next guests while a make-up expert freshly powders their noses. The smell of perfume hangs like a low cloud in the air. A producer hurries around holding up placards, warning the musicians they have five minutes until singing time. He tries to catch the attention of the preacher, who is now wildly gesticulating and bringing his talk to an emotional climax.

Offstage, all this activity is fed into an audio control board which is rumored to be the most sophisticated in the country. Twelve videotape editing machines, worth $75,000 each, patch together the very best camera angles.

Later, at 7:30 A.M. in New York City, 3:00 P.M. in Manila, and 8:00 A.M. in Anchorage, people will sit down to listen to a jazzed-up Bible story from 1 Kings. It's as if an old-time Pentecostal church service has been captured intact, extruded through machines, monitors, microwaves, and satellites, and then magically synapsed into millions of homes simultaneously. No one went to church to hear that pastor preach on the widow's miraculous supply of oil. He came packaged into their bedrooms, living rooms, and kitchens.

Besides the normal tensions of live television, also present are unvoiced but crackling tensions about the future of PTL. For years Jim Bakker and his show have been attacked in the local press for shaky financial dealings, and a feelings of anxiety pervades the staff. An FCC investigation is underway. Executives have left; employees have been fired. And Jim has been more irritable than usual recently.

The studio audience is well aware of these tensions. Whenever a speaker makes allusion to "our current trials," or "Satan's attacks against this man and this program," wild applause and hearty amens break out. That morning the host of PTL in Africa flew in unexpectedly from Nigeria to deliver two encouraging "visions from the Lord" to Jim. He related them, appeared briefly on the show, and flew immediately back.

There are few signs of tension on Jim Bakker's face, however, after the preacher finishes and Jim begins chatting on camera with the show's guests. He is laughing, pleasant, easy-going. He wears his patented boyish grin—unique because he smiles broadly, but using almost exclusively the muscles of his lower lip. On the desk are meticulously prepared prep sheets on each guest, including a list of stimulating, relevant questions to ask them. But, as usual, he ignores the preparations and goes with his instincts. He talks about whatever he feels like, giving each guest as much time as he wants to, disregarding the prepared schedule. Sometimes guests flown in from far-away cities never get on the show—Jim Bakker didn't "feel led."

Those very instincts pulled Bakker to the very top in Christian television, first in starting *The 700 Club* and now at PTL. "It's not listed in the Bible," he says, "but my spiritual gift, my specific calling from God, is to be a television talk show host. That's what I'm here on earth to do. I love television. I eat, I sleep it." A good talk show host has the ability to make each viewer—not the masses of viewers, but each individual viewer—feel personally addressed. Somehow, to his loyal audience, Jim Bakker accomplishes that. As many as twenty thousand viewers contact PTL each day, either through letters or the phone. In a year thirty thousand call in to become born again through telephone counseling. And hundreds of thousands of PTL partners support Bakker monthly. Because of Bakker's impact, the *Atheist Journal* named him "the most dangerous Christian in America."

Despite his spectacular success and popularity, Jim Bakker feels misunderstood, persecuted, and unappreciated by the Christian community at large. Some criticize his down-home unsophistication, some the show's excessive emphasis on charismatic gifts and healing, and almost everybody criticizes his use of money. After the program, in a private lunch in the brick kitchen of the million-dollar mansion which serves as PTL's headquarters building, he vented some of those frustrations. He reacted with hurt and anger to an article in *Christianity Today*. "The Christian press picks up material that was in error when it went into the paper here—half truths mixed with lies—and then they go with the same spirit as this local pub-

lisher who is an atheist and whose reporter is Jewish. All that is repeated in a Christian magazine as being gospel truth. You have a
Christian magazine parroting stuff that has been published by one of
the most well known anti-Christian newspaper chains, and that's
disappointing to me."

Bakker is weary of answering questions and of bearing the incredible strain of the financial obligations he has committed PTL to. "I
feel like I've been pushing a railroad train up a mountain," he says.

He is a complex man, full of ironies. His book, *Move That Mountain*, tells of his youth: short of stature and insecure, he grew up
with an inferiority complex, in relative poverty as the son of a ma-
chinist at a piston ring plant. Bakker recalls being ashamed to invite
friends to his home, an ugly concrete block house, painted orange.
After he dropped out of North Central Bible College (in Minneapo-
lis) to marry his wife Tammy, the two traveled together as a gospel
team, sleeping in pastors' bedrooms, cheap motel rooms, and dusty
church attics, accepting whatever meager "love offering" their host
church offered. Those painful, struggling days are etched sharply
into Bakker's memory, and now he can't understand why people
censure his plush lifestyle. He has paid his dues.

It took a long time in the White House for Jimmy Carter to realize
that he was no longer a peanut farmer in Georgia, that every word he
spoke, every glint in his eye, every personal taste, no matter how
trivial, would be instantly noted, perhaps distorted, and then broad-
cast around the world. Jim and Tammy similarly made a difficult adjustment to seeing themselves as symbols in the public eye. For
example, they failed to understand the outcry that arose when, the
same month that Jim wrote a direct mail letter saying, "Tammy and
I are giving every penny of our life's savings to PTL," he bought a
$24,000 Drifter houseboat equipped with white shag carpeting, two
wood paneled bedrooms, a gas grill, television, and refrigerator. "I
paid for that boat just like anyone else," he protested defensively. "I
financed it with a bank—there was no PTL money involved."

The Bakkers also drew flak for moving into a $200,000 house
during one of PTL's financial crises, shortly after sixty employees
had been cut back to save money. Again Jim reacted to criticism
with confusion and hurt. A wealthy donor had provided the house
free of charge. "It was a trifle to her, worth less than the bracelet she
was wearing," he argues. "Yes, I live in a $200,000 home and I'm
not going to apologize for it. For seventeen years we prayed that

God would give us a home. We didn't really dream of one that expensive, but God gave it to us. Why should I be so foolish as to say I won't take it?"

Visiting reporters wax eloquent in describing the luxury of PTL headquarters. The mansion, obtained at a bargain-basement price by PTL, is tastefully decorated with chandeliers, a grandfather clock, and oriental rugs over solid mahogany floors. Bakker's office is paneled in mahogany with a black marble hearth on his fireplace. Outside, brick sidewalks lead to a Florida meditation garden and a reflecting pool lined with fifty flags. "I love architecture," says Bakker. "It's my hobby, you might say. This is one of the most beautiful examples of southern architecture in the southeast United States. I could have taken some hammers and beaten the walls and made it look like a poor place, but I'm not going to destroy it or tear it down because my critics want me to live a life of poverty."

For other buildings, Bakker insisted on importing real cedar shingles costing many times the price of local roofing materials. Expensive bricks were trucked in from Pennsylvania to preserve the authentic look of Heritage Village. The $3 million studio is one of the best in the world, and a television tower is cleverly concealed in the steeple of a giant replica of the Bruton parish church in Williamsburg.

Interviews with Bakker keep drifting toward financial questions, and with good reason. The electronic church, of which he is an impressive representative, has skyrocketed to a place of financial prominence in the evangelical world. The shift of power and resources is as abrupt and decisive as the recent shift of world resources to the Arab oil countries. The top five evangelical television personalities draw in $50 million in revenue a year—an amount that equals the annual budget of Vatican City, long criticized for its ostentation.

In 1974 PTL was started with sixty-five dollars in a bank account; five years later it could raise one million dollars in a single day. The large Christian publishers have for years been building up solid financial foundations with sales forces, retail outlets, and networks of distribution channels to consumers. Yet suddenly one man with a television ministry can easily beat their total annual income. The headquarters of established evangelistic organizations such as InterVarsity and Youth for Christ struggle to raise funds through banquets, direct mail appeals, and personal contacts, only to find that a television program gathers in their annual income *in a single week*.

Naturally, grumblings have emerged from certain Christian quarters, notably the evangelical denominations, who fear a siphoning off of needed revenue. Most television preachers, however, insist that they raise an awareness for giving among viewers and that giving to churches actually increases during their fund appeals.

What do PTL donors get in exchange for their money? First, of course, is the daily program aired throughout the United States and the English-speaking world. PTL must produce the show and then purchase air time from local stations. Another fifteen percent of PTL's income goes for literature expenses: Bibles, study guides, and follow-up pieces, mostly sent out free of charge. And, or course, there is the overhead of a payroll.

But Jim Bakker's dreams, like those of most television evangelists, extend far beyond the television ministry. He has what one Charlotte reporter calls "an edifice complex." In his autobiography he records that he got the idea for Heritage Village from direct revelation.

> "Lord," I questioned, "you've given us this property, what do you want us to do with it?"
> Sometime around three o'clock in the morning, the Lord began answering that question.
> "I've got it, I've got it," I shouted, forgetting Tammy was asleep beside me.
> "What in the world do you mean, you've got it?" she murmured drowsily. "Lay down and go to sleep."
> "But, Tammy, I've got it," I shouted again. "God wants us to build a village, a miniature version of colonial Williamsburg."
> God had imprinted a blueprint of the building in my head. I got out of bed and began drawing it just as I had seen it. With the Carters Grove mansion situated in the front, the building would be interconnected with walking paths and flower gardens.

Besides the mansion, the studio, and the well-equipped offices, the complex grew to include such amenities as a sauna, a massage room, and a remarkable $200,000 swimming pool. The pool, used by employees' families and visitors' children, is located in the studio basement in a setting of white Grecian columns, arched mirrors, and trailing plastic vines. Its filtering and chlorine systems are computer-controlled.

Even impressive Heritage Village was soon dwarfed by Bakker's most ambitious project. Fifteen miles down the road, just over the border in South Carolina, PTL developed a 1,400-acre tract of ground called "Heritage, USA." Hoping to provide a recreational mecca for Christians who had been blessed by PTL's ministry, Bakker built log chalets overlooking a lake, and tent and camper sites complete with cable television and phone hookups. Open-air tram vehicles shuttle guests along the winding asphalt drives to shady hiking spots, an Olympic-sized pool, eight lighted tennis courts, and a barn auditorium seating two thousand, where summer television programs are taped. The village includes an amusement park that has become the third most popular in the United States (behind Disney World and Disneyland).

A massive Polynesian-style pyramid, designed to house Heritage University, dominates the site. The university started off in grand style, boasting it would serve twelve thousand students in four years, and hiring Donald Barnhouse, Jr., son of Donald Grey Barnhouse, as its dean. Barnhouse later resigned, as did two successors, and soon the school closed down.

All facilities on the Heritage, USA property were completed in just one year, despite work stoppages when contractors insisted on cash payments. Bakker also plans a retirement center, a twelve-story Polynesian hotel, a clinic, an Old American Main Street, a condominium high-rise, and other developments exceeding one hundred million dollars. The entire grand scheme is called the "Total Living Center." Bakker defends the project: "I know some will say, 'You should not have built the Total Living Center,' but I know I heard from God."

In addition to its luxury, Heritage, USA also bears the downhome country stamp of PTL. It has as its symbol a twenty-five-foot plastic moose, the kind of advertising behemoth normally found in restaurant parking lots. Employees liked the moose so well that they bought a plastic pig to house the ticket concession stand and hid a giant plastic rooster in the woods to surprise unsuspecting hikers. Speed limit signs are marked in odd figures—17 or 33 mph—with the warning "Speed checked by God."

Such grandiose plans took their toll on the PTL ministry, however. In his telethon appeals Bakker often spoke darkly of the threat of PTL's going into receivership. On the air he tearfully warned viewers that he might have to sell the studio. "We're within days of this network ceasing." In fund-raising letters he pleaded, "Unless God performs a financial miracle, this could be the last letter you will receive from me." And, "It will be a sad Christmas for Tammy and me without your help." Bakker was caught in great pincers, however. As he cried and described the failing financial situation on television, more and more money poured in. Giving never sagged. But anxious creditors, scared by his pronouncements, demanded cash before resuming work; banks refused to make loans and creditors filed liens against PTL assets. Television stations bumped them off the air. Finally, PTL had to cut back from a two-hour to a one-hour format.

While Bakker has his edifice complex and his desire to make a splash with big, impressive monuments, he also has a compassionate side. One on one with a hurting person, he can be deeply touched. When a black church burned down in Charlotte, he helped rebuild the church at PTL expense with no fanfare. When visitors from such organizations as Wycliffe Bible Translators or Teen Challenge describe their needs on his show, Bakker will often weep, then on the spot promise them whatever amount they need.

In the midst of one financial crisis, he went on a five-week, round-the-world survey report to see firsthand the needs of other countries. Bakker hit Calcutta shortly after a disastrous flood. The sight devastated him. "As tears streamed down my face, I cried, 'O Lord, please make it possible for us to do more.' " Despite PTL's precarious position, he tripled the pledge in order for India to feed more children each day and to supply a new nurses' wing at a hospital.

Bakker urgently appealed to his supporters for personal sacrifice. It was a bizarre request: the mastermind of a multi-million dollar, first-class Total Living Center begging American Christians to give up money they waste on sweets and soft drinks to help the starving in India. The appeal went live via phone hookup through one of the most lavishly appointed studios in the world. Hearing her husband's pleading voice, Tammy turned to the cameras and said, "Moms in India love their babies just as much as you do. They're going through hell on earth because we in America don't care. Oh, people!..." Then the camera panned to the PTL Singers, swaying to music, dressed in lace-trimmed formals. Such are the anomalies of Jim Bakker and PTL.

After his trip, Bakker was so impressed by the needs of the world that he decided to commit 10 percent of PTL's gross income to overseas mission projects. He did, however, include a clause that allows PTL to use the fund for operating expenses if needs arise. The FCC soon began investigating complaints that funds designated for projects overseas never left Charlotte.

Charlotte newspapers delight in accusing PTL of profligate use of money, editorializing how their money could best be spent. Yet the impoverished people who read the papers rise in righteous anger to Bakker's defense. "If Jim Bakker got one million dollars a year, it wouldn't be too much," said one, "when you consider the marriages he's saved, the healings, the alcoholics, the dope addicts." Even when PTL's use of money was widely publicized, giving—most of it averaging fifteen dollars per gift—continued to climb. Bakker has tapped into his constituency. He understands their needs, and they, indentifying with his promises of hope, give him vicarious approval to obtain the best that money can buy.

When asked pointblank "If you had one million dollars to spend on implementing the gospel of Jesus in the world today, is a Total Living Center—with its chalets, campgrounds, and condominiums—the best way to do it?" Bakker responded first by describing the retirement section, then the nursing home and hospital. He concluded, "People talk like there's a lack somehow in God, like there's a shortage, and that if we build a Christian retreat center, we wouldn't have the money to do this or do that. There is no shortage in God, believe me."

Bakker's belief in God as a benevolent resource permeates his theology and the message he offers his viewers. His 182-page autobiography contains fifty-five specific instances where God responded to his pleas for material assistance or requests for healing. In two instances he "felt led" to write a check for twenty thousand dollars knowing there was no money in the bank to cover it, believing God would fill the account before the check was cashed.

He, like most of the popular Christian television personalities, consistently holds to a "health and wealth theology," believing God will bless Christians materially. If you turn to Christ, your life will work. India's problems, he says, are due to that country's rejection of Christian principles. "Theirs is a religious, not a political, problem." Religion locks them into a rigid caste system and an aversion to using their cattle. In Africa and India, he has observed, the Christians' homes are better and more comfortable than non-Christians'. Most ghettoes, he says, are ghettoes of the mind. "The gospel will bring people to a higher standard than they've known before. I'm convinced that Christianity is a lifestyle—a way of life—not a religious experience. And I believe the Bible says, 'Delight yourself in the Lord and he'll give you the desires of your heart.' " His book relates one prayer incident where a man who asked for a brown Winnebago got exactly that. "Specify the color of the camper you want God to give you!" Bakker urges.

When asked how this Christian lifestyle differed from the Positive Mental Attitude or Dale Carnegie lifestyle, Bakker replied, "It doesn't. They base about everything they do on scriptural principles. The Bible says, 'Give and it shall be given unto you.' " He flares up at people who blame America for oppressively contributing to the world's poverty, asserting that the original principles of America—such as the freedom of man and free enterprise—are biblical principles which naturally result in success.

Bakker's Christianity is not a counter-culture; it is a super-culture, a realization of the very best that the world has to offer. In that sense, it is paralleled by Oral Roberts' "seed faith" and Robert Schuller's "possibility thinking." Health and wealth theology permeates Christian television.

How does Bakker handle such passages as the one where Jesus tells the rich young ruler to sell all he has? "Keep reading," he says. "Later in that chapter Jesus says everything we give up will be returned to us. What would have happened if the rich young ruler had given all to serve Jesus? I sincerely believe he probably would have moved up in his ruling class. Everywhere we turn Jesus was preaching an abundant, full life."

In television Jim Bakker and his peers have found a perfect vehicle for promises of health and wealth. Television is made for packaged promises and easy-to-grasp answers. Shows resolve life situations in neat half-hour or hour-long segments. Commercials promise solutions, not problems. It is a miserable platform for discussing complexity and struggle, and hosts who try to represent life's complexity, such as Dick Cavett, are eventually relegated to the minority viewing audience of public television. Inevitably, a Christian faith tailored for a television audience comes across as scrubbed-up, incomplete.

A non-Christian friend, who has watched PTL faithfully, mainly out of curiosity, comes away puzzled. "If their God is so benevolent," he asks, "why does he allow death and suffering? Why did the Holocaust happen, or the floods in India, if he always wants the best possible lifestyle for us? After all, even Kathryn Kuhlman died. The Bible can't be as Polyanna-ish as it seems on PTL."

Indeed, Jesus did not paint a rosy picture for his disciples or for the early church. Most early church leaders ended up in jail, tortured, and often killed. Jesus warned the fledgling church against temptation, dissension, attacks from outside, lukewarmness, and painful persecutions. Discussing these aspects of the Christian life does not appeal to a large audience, though.

Many viewers are disturbed by the type of treatment given to another emphasis on such shows as *The 700 Club* and PTL: physical healing. Some accounts are downright tasteless. A man in PTL's studio audience described a wart on the end of his nose that developed into skin cancer. "After watching your show, I prayed, and it just bursted all open, running down my cheekbone. And then it completely disappeared!"

On one show Tammy Bakker recalled a bizarre episode of healing. She had a hernia and was scheduled for surgery to relieve it, but she believed God did not want her to have to endure the trauma of surgery. So, one Sunday during communion she felt moved to immerse a wart on her finger (she didn't explain the physiological connection) in the communion glass. She felt a sudden energy rushing through her and discovered the next day that her hernia had been healed and surgery was not necessary. In her autobiography, Tammy also records a sincere but unsuccessful prayer attempt to raise her dog Chi-chi from the dead.

A favorite guest on PTL is a Southern healer named Vicky Jamison. A gracious and attractive blonde, she reports that she discovered her healing powers quite by accident. She also claims the power to "slay people in the Spirit": when she touches them on the head, they fall backwards in a kind of swoon (with other guests catching them before they hit the floor, and some throwing blankets over beskirted ladies). She recalls that she was surprised the first time this gift manifested itself; as she lifted her hand, people in the audience fell over like wooden soldiers. Now, people can be slain in the Spirit without even being aware of her presence.

Jamison claims people in a fifty-mile radius of Charlotte are sometimes affected when she visits PTL. Ms. Jamison has added her own unique stamp to the healing process; she sings spontaneous words to familiar tunes. To "He Touched Me" she'll add words such as "If you believe, he'll make you whole," interjecting her music with such comments as "You out there to the left, you're cleansed of your colon. Where's the thyroid condition over in that section? There's a growth in someone's breast over there. Sir, if you'll stand up, that prostate condition is healed...I want to find that upper lip...."

PTL is flooded with accounts of healing from its viewers—twenty thousand in a single year. In addition, people describe in great detail marriages saved, families reunited, and miracles performed. Somehow the experience of hearing and seeing others' faith on television challenges many to seek new spiritual heights.

Critics, of course, point out certain dangers implicit in an experience-oriented Christianity. Grounding faith on a God who will make your lifestyle comfortable and take care of your health opens up several alarming possibilities. First is the confusion that arises when problems don't seem to work out. Christians such as Joni Eareckson (who was not healed despite fervent prayers) suddenly feel the implication that they are second-class citizens, somehow unworthy of God's best for them. Faith is tied to a money-back guarantee of God's protection—exactly the bargain Satan wrongly accused God of sealing with Job. And, if Christian faith does not produce the expected results, why not drop it?

Also, when people tie religious experience to a lifestyle experience, rather than grounding it in objective reality, they seem to make Christianity equal to other faiths that promise the same results. Mormons, Moonies, Christian Scientists—they all have impressive success records, complete with their own stories of healing and financial rewards. Where are the distinctives of Christianity which cost God the death of his Son? Exuberant Tammy on one show got carried away: "This life is so great—I just love it whether or not it's true!" To such a comment, orthodox Christians must reply that life is not always so great, at least in material terms, and it is worth loving precisely because it is true.

In spite of their background and certain emphases, it would be unfair to typecast the Bakkers as old-line Assembly of God Christians. They do host a parade of figures well-known within Pentecostal circles and unknown outside them. But PTL also has hosted Ruth Carter Stapleton, Art Linkletter, Dale Evans, Anita Bryant, Charles

Colson, Pat Boone, Lulu (of TV's *Hee Haw*), Senator Mark Hatfield, actor Dean Jones, and hundreds of others.

Although the show is not an effective forum for true dialogue or idea exchanges, it excels as a vehicle for expressing personal testimonies.

Bakker is unafraid to take courageous stands. He insisted on letting *Hustler* magazine's Larry Flynt appear on PTL, despite a swarm of local critics. One pastor took out a full page ad in the Charlotte paper denouncing Bakker for hosting a pornographer. He refused to endorse Anita Bryant's campaign against homosexuals, saying, "I'm not with Anita on this fight.... I think we ought to love them and welcome them into our churches."

Bakker's openness often surprises his closest advisers, who reflect a wide political spectrum. Even on a topic like healing he is capable of coming out with a statement like "Now all you healers out there who take credit for someone being healed in your ministry, why don't you also take credit for the ones who aren't healed—the ones who die?"

In his autobiography Bakker describes the effect of one image from his boyhood church: a large black-and-white picture of a human eye on the wall of his Sunday school classroom. To him, that eye was God himself, and it inspired a fear that "God was always looking and he would get you if you were bad." Somewhat in reaction, Bakker today grounds his approach on love, not on fear or appeals to hell. Though capable of brimstone preaching, he adapts to the "cool" medium of television, smiling, constantly assuring "God loves you, and we do too."

In short, PTL offers an affirming, upbeat brand of faith, free of many of the negative strictures of fundamentalism. In Charlotte, the staff seems to reflect this philosophy. Employees are warm and considerate, even to local critics of their organization.

The explosive growth of the electronic church, symbolized by PTL, is still being evaluated by the rest of the church. Certainly it expands the total outreach of evangelism, reaching into homes unaware, presenting the gospel to people who would never seek it out in a local church. The loyalty of PTL viewers demonstrates that there are millions of needy, lonely people whom the church is not reaching. They see Jim Bakker as a friend, someone they can count on to understand their problems. Scores of thousands of them write him personal letters and send in prayer requests. (PTL has a full-time person in charge of the prayer room, and other employees volunteer in shifts to pray for these requests.) Their effusive letters of how PTL has touched them are testaments to the power of electronic ministry.

In a sense, says Bakker, each of these letters is an accusing finger pointing to local churches that have let too many people "fall through the cracks." He freely admits his ministry and others like it are supplements to the church, not replacements for it. "To those pastors who feel like the media is draining from the churches," he says, "I would advise them to seek God for what they are feeding their sheep—the sheep will go where there is good food. If they are fed in churches, they probably won't need PTL or Oral Roberts or anyone—if the church does the job. If elders would come and pray for people's needs and the church was a place of prayer instead of a bingo game or a social club, then millions of people wouldn't call to these ministries for needs."

Television evangelists have not yet, however, sifted through the limitations that the electronic medium places on them and its resultant effect on their message. In television, the consumer is in control—at any moment he can reach up and turn the channel selector—so the emphasis of the message must be on what the viewer wants to see, more than what he should see. One can hardly imagine the Old Testament prophets with their stern messages from God capturing an acceptable viewing audience. Even Jesus, though he might arouse the curiosity of television documentary crews, would hardly fit the normal television format; his discussions were too slippery, not packaged right for a consumer society.

Bakker admits television ratings limit him from, for example, Bible exposition. Yet television can offer contributions not available to the local church. What local church could afford the weekly lineup of famous guests that parade before Robert Schuller's, Pat Robertson's, or Jim Bakker's cameras, as well as the music professionalism of Scott Wesley Brown, Paul Stookey, Johnny Cash, and Amy Grant?

To people on the fringes of Christianity, especially those with acute personal needs, Christian television opens up a whole new avenue of hope. The speakers and guests promise that their viewers' lives can have answers and fulfillment. To many lonely people those shows glow as the chief bright spots in an otherwise overwhelming existence.

For the mainline Christian, PTL and it companion shows offer an infusion of excitement about personal faith which is often lacking in the local church. Some viewers who strongly disagree with the philosophy of the show are nevertheless inspired by the fresh example of people who can articulate their faith in Christ. Many report their faith has been energized so that they become more active in Christian service.

The danger comes when viewers confuse the excitement of Christian television with the message and the work of the church incarnate. Compared to television glitter, the average local church is lackluster. Services are boring by contrast; the message seems complex and confusing. And perhaps most dangerous of all is the latent effect of television to create a dependence on vicarious experiences. The church on television is experienced, after all, not in a room that includes sniffling children, restless teen-agers, hard-of-hearing grandparents, and sleepy parishioners. It occurs in a much safer, more sterile environment: your own living room.

When you watch television church, no one asks you to participate in a visitation program. No one challenges you to hold the attention of a junior high Sunday school class. No one asks you to take meals to shut-ins. The only response PTL solicits is a monthly check of gratitude. What greater way is there to reach the world for Christ? A member of the electronic church may easily conclude the answer is his cash contribution to the newest satellite, never questioning whether his own personal involvement is of greater value. What can one solitary person's service accomplish, he may wonder, when dwarfed by the marvels of electronic evangelism?

The Bible presents a realistic picture of the Christian life, including long, dull marches through the wilderness, humiliating failures, pain, and struggle. These don't come off well on television—unless they're told as a quick, summarized prelude to the victorious conclusion. The resulting picture of the Christian life as being one of incessant joy and constant success can actually backfire instead. The viewer, whose experience is different, can begin to feel distressingly inferior, as if somehow he's missing out on the magic of faith.

In essence, the electronic church is the mouth of the body, but without the other parts. Individual Christians are linked to that mouthpiece by microwaves, television cables, and direct mail—tentative links at best. Corporate involvement in the electronic church tends to be of a vicarious nature.

Few Christians would question the potential of this mouthpiece, or the remarkable ability of electronic media to expand the gospel's outreach. But people can confuse the mouthpiece with the whole body. Occasionally people are so turned on by what they see on PTL that they pack up and leave their homes, spending their savings on a plane or bus ticket to the Charlotte headquarters. "Wouldn't it be better," they reason, "to visit Jim Bakker in person, to let him lay hands on my arthritis, to share in the financial success that seems so alluring on the television screen?"

Naturally PTL is not set up to handle pensions, senior citizens' housing, marriage counseling, healing clinics, food distribution outlets, and race relations centers. It disappoints many who come because it is not the church, but only a mouthpiece. It appeals to needs in humanity that can only be met on a local, corporate level. Despite compassion shown by individual PTL staffers, many of these vagrant people turn away, bitter.

In order to experience a direct link with the people PTL is reaching, on my last day there I volunteered as a phone counselor during the live TV show. I was given a book, *Speaking with God in the Unknown Tongue*, but cautioned not to exercise glossolalia on the telephone. I was quickly informed how to handle suicide and prank calls and was briefed on how to fill out the four basic telephone response forms. A blue form is used most commonly, for prayer requests, with a box to check off for each category (alcohol, anxiety, arthritis, asthma, etc.). The counselor prays with each person over the phone, "lifting up Jesus and claiming the promises of God."

A green form is a salvation report which details a conversation wherein the counselor takes the inquirer on a series of steps to become born again. It ends with a written prayer, which the caller should repeat word for word. Each person converted over the telephone receives a *Salvation Clear and Plain* book and a Bible course. A pink form is to record praise reports, especially healings, with such questions as "Duration of illness?" "Has doctor confirmed healing?" "Doctor's name and address?" and "Guests on program at time of prayer?" A yellow form is for miscellaneous requests for literature, desire for pastoral counseling, criticisms, schedules, and prank calls.

My first call came from a black boy in Arizona, age ten. "How do you stop bein' bad?" he asked, then giggled and hung up. Next was a New Jersey housewife trying to locate the song "In the Center of

His Will." Prayer requests followed, including one for "a fearful spirit and insecurity," two for heart conditions. Some more prank calls were sprinkled in among the requests: one said, "Merry Christmas," then hung up, and another said, "Hey, I need eight dollars." One lady wanted to become a Christian, she thought, but preferred to read the book *Salvation Clear and Plain* before deciding. And so it went.

The last call of the day was the most involved, and the most telling. A lady from California described in great detail a troublesome situation, which developed after her husband left her one year ago. Though she declined to give her name, she told me intimate accounts of fights with her husband. Her dilemma is basically a financial one. She has two sons, aged nine and three, and she must work to support them, since her husband sends no child support. The only jobs she can find require weekend work, and she has to hire baby sitters. She feels an obligation to be with her sons, who become mean and irresponsible when they're with baby sitters so much. Yet if she quits working, welfare money ($350 per month) is not enough to pay basic expenses.

Relating this on the phone between sobs, she sounded torn and confused. Her lack of skills confines her to low-paying jobs, and she hates herself for neglecting her children in a struggle for survival. She said she had accepted Christ, but was very disheartened because nothing seemed to work out right.

Who could help this woman? The government? They allotted $350 per month, but her apartment rent was over $200 and she couldn't pay her bills with the remainder.

Could PTL help her? Something about its guests with their easy, confident smiles and their suede sports coats and fancy dresses had attracted her. Even in her financial straits, she spent ten dollars on a desperation phone call. Yet the prayer I offered for her across three thousand miles of telephone transmission seemed puny in light of her problems. When PTL admirers pull into their campsite and plug into the phone hookups to counsel people like her, what hope can they offer?

Could the local church help? As a Catholic, she felt rejected because of her church's stand against divorce. No nearby church had extra funds to dole out to needy people; none had free baby sitting service.

This lady, eager to do right but unable to cope with the pressures of her world, represents millions of others with great needs. PTL and other programs like it tap into those needs, awakening in its viewers a thirst for justice and hope and joy. Yet television is limited; it is not the church, and so its help is incomplete. What the California woman needs is some old-fashioned, sacrificial Christian love— someone to be her friend, keep her sons sometimes, perhaps help out financially.

I couldn't help wondering how many of her Christian neighbors are too busy watching television to give her that love.

I often hear the question, "Why can't Christians write great books? Is it impossible to combine the message of faith with great fiction?" I can respond by citing numerous books written in this century by Christians such as J.R.R. Tolkien, Francois Mauriac, Alexander Solzhenitsyn, Graham Greene, Walker Percy, or Flannery O'Connor. All of them have written fine literature that, to varying degrees, incorporates a personal faith.

A great irony remains, however: the greatest fiction ever written, in virtually anyone's estimation, is explicitly and forthrightly Christian, and yet goes largely ignored except in college literature courses. I am referring to the novels by Tolstoy and Dostoyevsky. Who would not include Anna Karenina, War and Peace, *and* The Brothers Karamazov *in a "ten best novels of all time" list?*

Tolstoy's Resurrection *and Dostoyevsky's* The Idiot *express such moral force that in a modern climate they almost resemble gospel tracts. Most of the novels written by these two giants, in fact, begin with a Bible verse that encapsulates their message. The Brothers Karamazov begins with John 12:24, "Verily, verily, I say unto you, except a corn of wheat fall into the ground and die, it bringeth forth much fruit," a verse that reappears at a critical juncture in the novel. Anna Karenina cites Romans 12:19, "Vengeance is mine; I will repay, saith the Lord."*

Among the books produced by evangelical authors today, good fiction is as rare as a snowflake in Florida. Instead we are deluged by endless piles of self-help books that tell us "how to" straighten out our lives. For me, reading a book on how to overcome temptation or improve my marriage rarely makes a lasting difference. But the message of a classic novel that plumbs the reality of sin and depravity or love and fidelity can seep inside me and change me in a permanent way. That's why, when I decided to write a chapter on what it means to "find myself," I went back to Anna Karenina.

6

A Russian Mirror

NOT LONG ago, the Public Broadcasting System ran a weekly BBC series that popularized Tolstoy's monumental novel *Anna Karenina*, sometimes called the greatest novel ever written. Christian concepts underlie the structure and message of Tolstoy's major novels, so much so that Solzhenitsyn has concluded this is one of the main reasons Christianity survived among Russian intellectuals. After Bibles were confiscated, the novels of Tolstoy and Dostoyevsky lived on.

Tolstoy has, in fact, been criticized for writing "morality plays," an unpardonable sin today. It is true that he used his novels to express Christian ideas, and *Anna Karenina* expansively illustrates for me a puzzling statement of Jesus: "The person who finds his life will lose it; he who loses his life for my sake will find it." That statement made such an impression on the gospel writers that they recorded it more often (four times) than any other saying of his. Tolstoy certainly did not intend the novel to be a mere fleshing-out of his truth; nevertheless, because he wrote skillfully about life, from a Christian perspective, the lesson shines out powerfully.

Though it's difficult to apply, the truth Jesus intended has piercing relevance to our pop-psychology age, and specifically to me. But first, let's see how Tolstoy developed his epic.

After a few chapters of *Anna Karenina*, it becomes clear that the novel should more accurately be called *Anna and Levin*, for it contains the distinct stories of two characters. Anna moves to center stage because of her enchanting power and the web of intrigue and self-deception she spins around her adulterous affair. But always the camera shifts away to Konstantin Levin who is living out an entirely separate plot, most of which takes place on his country estate.

Two more unlike characters could not have been devised. Anna, a sophisticated, urbane princess, would sweep into a ballroom wearing a low-cut gown and reduce all talking to hushed whispers about her. She could carry on fascinating conversations on a range of subjects with guests while simultaneously sizing up the dress and hair styles of other women in the room. On a train ride from Moscow to Petersburg early in the story, Anna attracts a dashing young cavalry officer, Count Vronsky. Their affair, its effect on Anna's family, and ultimately its death grip on Anna herself consume most of the plot of the novel.

All the while Tolstoy provides a nearly comic relief to the passion of Anna's life by involving the country bumpkin Levin. We see him first as he's visiting Moscow, madly in love with Kitty Shcherbatsky, a flirtatious young belle. He blushingly stumbles through a crude marriage proposal which she politely turns down.

Crushed, Levin swears off city life and returns to his country world of hay and piglets and farm machinery and ignorant peasants. Yet he is never quite content. As Anna gets caught up in an upward spiral of romance, travel, gossip, and attention, Levin fidgets on the farm. He ought to be happy with his gentleman-farmer's life of hunting and forest hikes, but he's not. He worries too much about the peasants and whether it's right to perpetuate Russia's class distinctions. Christianity haunts him as he watches his brother die and observes the simple faith of the peasants and of Kitty, whom he eventually manages to marry. Why can't he believe?

In a social situation, Levin is like a large dog wagging his tail in a small room. He blunders, gets angry inopportunely, laughs at the wrong times, and expresses himself clumsily. While other wealthy landowners are enjoying the fruits of one of the greatest concentrations of wealth in history, Levin is off brooding about its philosophical and moral implications. Nothing can make him happy for more than a few days at a time.

It seems at first as though Anna will be eternally happy. Carefree, she tours Europe with chivalrous Vronsky, has a child by him, gardens at his estate in the country, and charms whomever she contacts. Everything she wants in life—social standing, attention, love, adventure—she gets. In contrast, if Levin does get what he wants, he's so melancholy that he fails to recognize it.

Tolstoy's powerful tale spotlights the activities of these two: Anna, who seems ecstatically to be finding her life, and Levin, who always seems to be losing his. If the two were alive today, I imagine Anna would be hailed as a competent, independent woman who has learned how to "look out for number one" and could qualify as an assertiveness-training leader. Levin, on the other hand, would sorely need a subscription to *Psychology Today* and *Esquire*, where he could perhaps learn how to take charge of his life. Obviously, he has a self-image problem.

Hardly a day goes by that I don't receive on my desk a magazine article or book which deals with the subject of self-image. Levin's problem has become the flagship of our age. I must get in touch with myself, I'm told, and I'm offered a variety of techniques (some of which are quite expensive and require trips to California mountain resorts) to do so. My childhood, I'm told, has been a singular process of burying the real me under layers of guilt, suppression, sublimation, and anger. Somehow I need to find myself. I take quizzes to find out my basic personality type. I follow the instructions on how to learn to love myself. As books like *How to Be Your Own Best Friend* climb to the top of the best-seller charts, they awaken in me a hunger for the secure fulfillment this self-knowledge will bring.

After dutifully obeying the advice of these masters, here is what I have found out about myself.

•I am a Southern fundamentalist by background, and that sloshes over into my attitudes toward people. I have shed many of the visible trappings of the fundamentalist milieu in which I was raised: I no longer oppose civil rights; I'm not a Republican; I don't believe dancing, smoking, drinking, and movies will keep a person out of heaven. Yet, some trappings of fundamentalism I have not shed. I find it hard to have an attitude of grace and forgiveness toward people. When I meet someone, I don't expect the best of him; I immediately start sizing him up, judging him. I am harsh on people who aren't good workers. I perceive value in people by what they contribute. I judge people by their actions.

•I have the personality of a writer. My idea of a fun evening is to sit in a great rounded chair, with stereo headphones blocking out the world, and read a book like *Anna Karenina*. I love to take hikes alone through forests or to waterfalls, where I sit and absorb the beauty around me. Having a group of friends on such an experience would detract from the experience. I'm improving with age, but I used to dread parties, and I still feel uncomfortable in any group larger than four. Whenever I attend a gathering, I relate to it by standing on the edges, as an observer, watching what's going on. This weakness turns into an advantage when I do my trade, because the writing process requires standing on the edge, objectively evaluating, sorting through observations.

•I react to new people with initial suspicion. When a guest speaker comes to my church or organization, I think, "Who does he think he is? What's he got to say that I haven't heard before? Why does he have that fake, phony smile?" People can win me over, but it is exactly that, a winning-over-process. Over the years I have developed an impenetrable resistance to sales pitches, and it carries over in some degree to my responses to people. I envy people who make others feel warm and at ease in the first meeting.

•I am a type-A worker. That is, I prefer working through lunch hours and sticking with a project until it's completely done. The most difficult activity in the world for me is to blankly relax. I love to make lists of tasks and exuberantly erase them one by one as I complete them. My idea of a vacation is to get out a map and draw a thousand-mile line in any direction, preferably west. Then, with the help of an AAA book, I circle any spot of scenic, historical, or cultural interest within two hundred miles of that line. Each day of the vacation, I get up about 6:30 A.M., zig and zag across the topography until 10:00 P.M., covering all the circled spots, filling my camera bag with rolls of exposed film. After returning, exhausted but exhilarated, I can develop the film and write articles based on my trip.

If I extended this list *ad infinitum*, I would have a complete profile of who I am. The unique thing about that profile, of course, is that it is only true of me. The definition of my *self* is that collection of quirks, traits, tastes, statistics, and preferences which are true only of me, out of the four billion people in the world. No one else possesses my exact height, weight, nose structure, and hair curl, as well as all these other things I have mentioned.

Now that I have found myself, what are the implications of Jesus' statement that I need to lose my life for his sake? What does he mean, specifically, when he says I should deny that self which I have been so carefully exploring, take up a cross, and follow him?

A young woman summarized the conundrum in a small group meeting as part of the Lenten series for my church. As we met together and discussed the Cross, it quickly became obvious that the Cross presents an enormous dilemma to modern men and women, mainly because it does cut directly against the message being taught by psychology. "The Bible says I'm supposed to give up myself," this woman said, with lines of anxiety creasing her face. "But I pay sixty dollars an hour to a Christian counselor who tells me I must *find* myself. He tells me I let people walk all over me, that I need to become more aggressive and not let others dominate me." Others in the group nodded assent. All of us had felt a Janus-like paradox in our faith.

Christians give cacophonous interpretations to what Jesus meant. Some would advise me to gouge out my guarded, introspective personality and replace it with one that smiles more often, relaxes easily, and trusts people more readily. I listen to them, but even if I did agree with them, I'm not equipped to make those changes. And reading the Bible has impressed me with the wide variety of misfits God uses to accomplish his will on earth—without forcing major personality overhauls upon them.

I don't think Jesus wants me to deny my role as a writer and editor and go into the pastoral ministry. I cannot annul the peculiarities that conspire inside me, and I've accepted that those patterns will probably never change. I doubt I'll ever choose a week's vacation on Miami Beach, for example.

Obviously, though, Jesus meant something important by those statements or the gospel writers would not have repeated them so often. After much reflection, I have come to these conclusions about what he meant.

Self-denial first strikes at my basic identity. I am by nature a selfish creature, and I spend my time inside a body and a personality which is unique in all the world. It inevitably follows that I begin viewing the world through a viewpoint, making value judgments based on how things align with my perspective, and imposing my likes and dislikes on others around me. In his essay, "The Trouble with X," C.S. Lewis points out that we spot a fatal flaw in almost everyone we meet, even our closest friends. We say about them, "He's a very fine fellow, and I enjoy his company. If only it weren't for his..." Yet we almost never see that fatal flaw in ourselves. We rationalize our weaknesses, explaining them away with references to our backgrounds or our good intentions.

Denying myself starts with a full and repentant acceptance of the fatal flaw within me. Regardless of all my accomplishments, all my sophistication, all my admirable traits, I must come to the humbling ground where I acknowledge I am no different from every person who has ever lived. I am a sinner.

I cannot imagine a more difficult stumbling block in Christianity. It is relatively easy to inspire people with the Christian ethic of love; much liberal humanism is built on similar feelings. But every mechanism of self-protection within me cries out against this painful, renouncing step of identifying myself as a sinner. In that act I lose all the collected aspects of my identity and am known simply as a rebel against God.

Fortunately, however, I do not remain in that state. "Christianity is strange," says Pascal. "It bids man recognize that he is vile, even abominable, and bids him desire to be like God. Without such a counterpoise, this dignity would make him terribly abject." Where sin abounded grace did much more abound.

After going through the humiliating act of losing myself by letting go of that protective pride, I suddenly find myself with a new identity—the exalted state that Paul describes as "in-Christness." No longer must I defend my thoughts, my values, my actions. I trade those in for the identity I am given as a son of God. I relinquish the responsibility for setting my ethical standards and my world view.

My sense of competition quickly fades. No longer do I have to bristle through life, racking up points to prove myself. My role has ideally become to prove God, to live my life in such a way that people around me recognize Jesus and his love, not the other set of qualities which separates me from the world. I have found this process to be healthy, relaxing, and wholly good. All of us will realize it incompletely, but I believe the extent to which we realize it will determine our psychological health. Tensions and anxieties flame within me the moment I forget I am living my life for the one-man audience of Christ and slip into living my life to assert myself in a competitive world.

Previously, my main motivation in life was to do a painting of myself, filled with bright colors and profound insights, so that all who looked upon it would be impressed. Now, however, I find that my role is to be a mirror, to brightly reflect the image of God through me. Or perhaps the metaphor of stained glass would serve better, for, after all, God will illumine through my personality and body.

Self-denial, then, initially involves a radical transformation in my basic identity. I no longer find my identity in my apartness from the rest of the world. Now, I find it in my sameness. I am exactly the same as everyone in the world in terms of my standing before God—I am a sinner. And yet I am breathlessly redeemed and now find my identity as a member of Christ's living body.

That is the general, overall way in which denying myself has changed my life. The theology is basic but indispensable. "You gotta *serve* somebody," Bob Dylan growls in his caveman voice. "It could be the devil or it could be the Lord." It could also be yourself. Redemption involves a conscious choice to serve the Lord, and that act is a denial.

The denial process, however, does not stop at conversion. Practically, it can affect me in hundreds of specific actions as I choose Christ and his way over my natural preferences. For me, losing my life has included working in a difficult management situation in a Christian organization when my natural bent would have kept me at home, earphones plugged in, writing articles and books. God called me at that time to do a specific task. It has also meant several hundred (should be thousand) incidents of willingly giving up my own desires for those of my wife. Self-denial for me has included acts of pain, such as seeking out a sick, whining friend in a hospital, and even firing an employee at work. It has meant spending time with emotionally needy people who want to ramble, while I want to get work done. It has meant a constant scrutiny of my use of money.

While Jesus' statement includes self-denial, it does not end with a spirit of martyrdom so that I'm left with a resigned sense of duty. The verse contains a remarkable, paradoxical promise. Jesus implied that if we lose our lives for his sake we will find them *in the very process of losing them.*

I understand this best by thinking of the various Christians I have interviewed for magazines. I lump them into two sets: Christian entertainers and Christian servants. The Christian entertainers—musicians, actors, speakers, comedians—fill our periodicals and television shows. We fawn over them, reward them with extravagant book contracts and fan mail. They have everything they want. Yet many whom I've interviewed express to me deep longings and self-doubts. They feel uncomfortable in the limelight, a terrible place for Christian growth, because they are unfairly being held up as examples. They are playing out their Christian lives before an audience.

On the other hand, most of the Christian servants I have interviewed are not in the spotlight. They toil unnoticed in remote parts of the country and the world. I think of Dr. Margaret Brand, a missionary eye surgeon who in India would perform fifty to one hundred cataract operations a day under the shade of a village tree. (I can spend thirty minutes in the local clinic getting a speck of dirt washed out.) Or of Mother Teresa who chooses life among the rejects of society. Or of the faithful pastors in communist lands. Or of John Perkins' workers in Mississippi. Or of the relief workers in Africa. These people have all impressed me with a profound wisdom and a deep-seated contentment which is strikingly absent from the entertainers. They work for low pay, long hours, no applause. They "waste" their talents and skills among the poor and uneducated. Yet somehow, in the process of losing their lives, they have found them. God has reserved rewards for them which are unattainable in any other way. (Strangely, we Christian publishers and media people are always trying to push the Christian servants up into the entertainers' category, tempting them with lucrative book contracts, TV appearances, movies.)

The Sermon on the Mount spells out in detail Jesus' list of practical ways in which our actions may be affected by our attitude of self-denial. Those he calls happy are the poor, the beggars in spirit, the humble, the unambitious, the unselfish, the persecuted. I once thought Jesus pronounced those Beatitudes as a sop thrown to the unfortunate: *Since you can't be rich, popular, and successful, the least I can do for you is to pronounce a blessing.* I have come to believe, however, that Jesus was revealing a central truth. Those of us who are poor and humble in the way he mentioned truly are blessed.

If self-sufficiency is the most fatal sin because it pulls us, as if by a magnet, from God, then indeed the suffering and the poor do have an advantage. Since their dependency and lack of self-sufficiency are obvious to them every day, they can turn more easily to God for strength. The enticing encumbrances of life—lust, pride, success, wealth, glamour—are too far from some to be striven for, and a tremendous roadblock to the kingdom is thus bulldozed. Without an inflated sense of self-importance, they have an easier time losing their lives in the sense Jesus described. The great and the humble, said Pascal, share the same passions and human natures, but the one is at the top of the wheel, and the other near the center, and so is less disturbed by the same revolutions.

If I find myself in the way pop psychology would have me do, I will someday find myself separated from all other people in the world. I will have myself, yes, but that is all.

If I lose my life in the way Jesus laid out as a model, the net result is a common binding, first with all humanity on the level ground before God and then with the common identity in Christ reserved for those in his body.

I want to cling to my life, to pamper it, make it secure, protected. I keep clamoring for uniqueness, attention, achievement. Jesus gently invites me to let go, to trust him with my life and to let the Father care for me.

In Frederick Buechner's words, "Inspection stickers used to have printed on the back 'Drive carefully—the life you save may be your own.' That is the wisdom of men in a nutshell.

"What God says, on the other hand, is 'The life you save is the life you lose.' In other words, the life you clutch, hoard, guard and play safe with is in the end a life worth little to anybody, including yourself; and only a life given away for love's sake is a life worth living. To bring his point home, God shows us a man who gave his life away to the extent of dying a national disgrace without a penny in the bank or a friend to his name. In terms of men's wisdom, he was a perfect fool, and anybody who thinks he can follow him without making something like the same kind of fool himself is laboring under not a cross but a delusion."

The PBS series on *Anna Karenina* ended with the famous scene of Anna's suicide. Though she had attained everything she wanted, Anna found herself tormented by greed, doubt, and jealousy. What if Vronsky only wanted her for her body, and if so, what if her body lost its appeal to him? How could she cling to those things she had fought for? Ultimately, she decided that death was "the only way of restoring his love for her in his heart, or punishing him, and of gaining the victory in the fight which an evil spirit was waging against him in her heart." She threw herself under the great iron wheels of a steam locomotive.

Though the PBS series ended with that scene, Tolstoy did not. He takes us back to the country, to Levin. Levin had been wrestling with love for his wife and his young son, Mitya. Why was it he did not feel intense caring for his young son? Was something wrong with him? He had decided to invest himself in his farm, in his family and neighbors and servants, but still he was torn by doubt. Was his decision a mistake?

One event cauterized his doubts and supplied for him the faith which had always eluded him. A sudden Russian summer thunderstorm came up and Levin discovered Kitty and Mitya were missing. He ran toward their favorite oak tree. "Suddenly there was a blinding flash and the whole earth seemed to have caught fire and overhead the vault of heaven seemed to crack. Opening his blinded eyes, he saw with horror through the curtain of rain the strangely altered position of the green crown of a familiar oak in the middle of the wood. 'Has it been struck?' The thought had barely time to cross his mind when, gathering speed, the top of the oak disappeared behind the other trees and he heard the crash of the great tree falling on the others.

"The flash of lightning, the peal of thunder, and the sudden sensation of cold that spread over his body merged for Levin into one feeling of horror.

" 'Dear Lord, dear Lord, not on them,' he said.

"And though he thought at once how senseless was his prayer that they should not be killed by the oak that had already fallen, he repeated it, for he knew that he could do nothing better than to utter that senseless prayer."

Kitty and Mitya were safe, but Levin remained deeply moved by the experience. In that moment of crisis, his true love for them had crashed down upon him. An instinctive, visceral surge of faith and dependency on God washed him with a consciousness that even he, troubled, doubting Levin, could believe. He tried to verbalize what he had experienced, but he could not. "I am asking about the universal revelation of God to the whole universe with all those nebulae. What am I doing? Knowledge unattainable by reasoning has been revealed to me personally, to my heart, openly and beyond a doubt, and I am obstinately trying to express that knowledge in words and by my reason."

Tolstoy ended his brilliant epic with two paragraphs which chronicle Levin's Christian awakening. They were missing from the PBS series, and in fact from the first publication of *Anna Karenina*, which was serialized in a literary magazine. Tolstoy had included them, but his editors decided the tragedy was the place to end, not this shift to Christian hope.

Fortunately, later versions of the novel reverted to Tolstoy's ending, though it still attracts a barrage of literary criticism. The structural merits may be debatable, but to me they finish the logical consequences of Anna's and Levin's lives. One found her life and discovered it lost: she was consumed by her own selfishness. Another lost his life in others and abruptly discovered he had found it:

" 'This new feeling has not changed me, has not made me happy and enlightened me all of a sudden as I had dreamed it would—just the same as with my feeling for my son. There was no surprise about either. But whether it is faith or not—I don't know what it is—but that feeling has entered just as imperceptibly into my soul through suffering and has lodged itself there firmly.

" 'I shall still get angry with my coachman Ivan, I shall still argue and express my thoughts inopportunely; there will still be a wall between the holy of holies of my soul and other people, even my wife, and I shall still blame her for my own fear and shall regret it; I shall still be unable to understand with my reason why I am praying, and I shall continue to pray—but my life, my whole life, independently of anything that may happen to me, every moment of it, is no longer meaningless but has an incontestable meaning of goodness, with which I have the power to invest it.' "

I debated a long time before writing this next chapter. A Christian author critiquing writing treads a treacherous path. On the one side are Christian writers, many of them friends, who may take offense; on the other side are fellow-critics who may justifiably use my ammunition to take shots at my own work.

And yet we have been too easy on ourselves for too long. Could the nonreligious press be ignoring Christian books partly because of our failure to take ourselves seriously enough? If we would police ourselves, and apply our own rigorous professional criteria, perhaps then skeptical onlookers would take notice. And perhaps a Chaim Potok or Saul Bellow or Philip Roth would arise from the evangelical subculture.

Christian writing is not simply a self-expression to further our own careers and egos, but rather an expression of Truth and an offering to the Father of lights. It's time for us writers to realize that the quality of our work becomes an integral part of its message. And, it's time for Christian readers to show concern when that message gets smudged.

7

The Pitfalls of Christian Writing

"THOU HAST conquered, O pale Galilean, and the world has grown gray with Thy breath." Thus concluded the poet Algernon Charles Swinburne about the wearisome effect of Christianity on culture at large.

I can speak comfortably only about the field of writing, and that indeed has grown gray in recent years. Walk into any Christian bookstore and thumb your way through the orderly, monochrome rows of self-help books, lifeless theological works, and personal testimonies. Very few seem interesting or appealing enough to attract readers from the general populace. Those who browse in the religious stores, surveys show, represent a scant 10 percent even of the forty million born-again Christians who supposedly live tucked away in the corners of America.

Fortunately for Christian publishing, that 10 percent is large enough to support a passel of evangelical publishers and a burgeoning industry of over six thousand Christian bookstores. The sales figures are indisputable: three evangelical books placed on the New York Times' top-twenty-of-the-decade list. And yet, is Christian literature penetrating culture, or is the fissure separating Christian readers from the broader public yawning ever wider?

I leave the consumer buying habits for marketers to worry over, but an underlying question haunts me as a Christian author: why should anyone read anything religious? Hundreds of Christian books have crossed my desk in the last decade and, I must admit, after a time they do seem to look and sound alike. I have watched literary sparks flare up in the Jewish and Catholic subcultures, but why have evangelicals produced such mediocrity?

Sales may well continue to double every five years but I care more about the quality of Christian writing. I have tried to analyze trends in the books I have seen in order to erect Caution! signs around the pitfalls of Christian writing. Below, I outline four criticisms of Christian writing, criticisms that I accept for myself, as a Christian author. I do not intend to point to specific negative examples and therefore must paint "Christian writing" with a very broad brush. Will high standards of quality improve sales? Who knows? I am convinced, however, that we Christian authors must strive for higher literary standards for our works to be taken seriously in the world at large. A captive audience will read indiscriminately; a skeptical or even hostile audience must be lured.

Thought Without Art

Too often Christian writing performs a kind of literary decapitation: it renders the head without the body, the thought without the art. We allow someone to speak to us from his or her brain only, and to conceal the background and context that produced those thoughts. For example, we will record Christian leaders' thoughts about lifestyles without delving into how they spend their own money and free time. In our profiles of Christian leaders, we give little regard to the stages of development and processes that contributed to form their opinions.

Numerous examples in the secular world should teach us how a person's head can be artfully connected to his body, and John McPhee is one of the best practitioners. McPhee resists the moniker of *nonfiction*. Why indeed should a category of writing be labeled by what it is not? Preferring "the literature of fact," he has led the way in showing how fact can be written as good literature.

I think especially of McPhee's book, *Encounters with the Archdruid*, in which he sets conservationist David Brower against the forces that would destroy his beloved natural environment. Of the scores of articles and books I have read analyzing the clash between industrial growth and natural resource conservation, none comes close to McPhee's artful presentation. He sets the stage by describing the adversaries.

Brower hardly resembles the stereotyped forest ranger or mountain hiker: he is balding and, except for a pot-belly, seems frail, with pale legs like toothpicks protruding from his shorts. But he has led the fight for conservation, first with the Sierra Club and then with the John Muir Institute. (Looks deceive: Bower has climbed nearly every mountain in America over 14,000 feet.)

Floyd Dominy is Brower's opposite: a tall, good-looking cowboy who wears a ten-gallon hat, smokes a fat cigar, and spins one yarn after another. Starting back in Dust Bowl days, Dominy devoted his life to building dams and eventually rose to the position of head of the Bureau of Land Management. He and Brower constantly lock horns, especially in courtrooms, as Brower seeks injunctions to halt Dominy's latest dam project. Everything you would want to know about the complex growth/no growth decisions confronting civilization is contained in McPhee's book, but embodied in an absorbing style. Entertaining personalities come to stand as archetypes for the philosophies they represent.

In one sequence, McPhee takes a rafting trip down the Colorado River with Brower and Dominy. There, in the surging rapids of the Colorado, between the gorges of the Grand Canyon, around a fire on the great river's banks, we get to know the two men and observe the collision of two powerful movements in Western civilization. Perhaps McPhee does not include as many histrionic facts about the clash as other reporters and journalists might have done, but no one I have read captures the conflict more graphically. McPhee gives us the ideas behind each movement in unforgettable narrative form.

George Plimpton accomplished the same result in a different arena with an article in *Harper's*. He wished to feature Marianne Moore, a demure Christian poet. But who today reads articles on poets, even if the poet is one of the greatest? In a stroke of great ingenuity, Plimpton succeeded by linking her with one of the worst poets, but most colorful characters, of our time. He set up a luncheon between Moore and Muhammad Ali and simply recorded what happened.

What happened was that Muhammad Ali decided to honor Marianne Moore by letting her participate with him in a joint effort. His topic: a fight with Ernie Terrell. Plimpton describes the hilarious interaction of Ali and the utterly intimidated Moore. The two finally do produce a "poem." Writes Plimpton, "While we waited, he told me that he was going to get the poem out over the Associated Press wire that afternoon. Mrs. Moore's eyes widened at the irony of all those years of struggling with *Broom* and all the other literary magazines, yet now to be with a fighter who promised instant publication over a ticker. It did not help the flow of inspiration. She was doubtless intimidated by Ali's presence, especially at his obvious concern that she, a distinguished poet, was having such a hard time holding up her side. To his mind speed of delivery was very much a qualification of a professional poet."

In his indirect way, Plimpton exposes American culture and its values and the role of art and entertainment in that culture. He achieves that in a holistic and incarnational manner. His treatment is memorable but not shrill; in fact, he never draws the moral for his readers. The article itself is the message—the implication of that bizarre lunch being the only way to gain national exposure for Marianne Moore.

In contrast to McPhee and Plimpton, Christian authors tend to give *only* the ideas and thoughts, without tracing the personalities involved and the context of how those thoughts developed. Too often religious books are organized and written like sermons, with an outlined structure superimposed on the content.

Many successful evangelical authors are not authors at all; they are speakers who make their living by speaking at churches and conferences. One can hardly blame them for organizing their written material in the same way as their spoken material, and often it sells well. But speakers who write books in the same style defy the basic rules of communication. Writers cannot merely list facts and hope to penetrate readers' brains. They must take readers on an emotional journey to hold their attention. People do not read the same way they listen, and a book-speech is effective only with an audience previously committed to agree with the material. It cannot reach out to a noncaptive audience such as a world skeptical of Christian ideas. That requires books created according to the rules of written communication.

Few authors can captivate an audience with their own personal magnetism the way a speaker can. Authors must use such techniques as a gripping narrative style, well-placed anecdotes, suspense, and a structure that compels a reader to follow the train of thought. To a diverse audience, ideas come across best when they are embodied by and live within a visual, imaginable context.

Of contemporary Christian writers working in the field of "nonfiction," I know of no one who finds more consistent artistic success than Frederick Buechner. He tackles formidable tasks in his choice of material: retold Bible stories (*Peculiar Treasures*); jazzed-up theology (*Wishful Thinking*); sermons (*Magnificent Defeat, The Hungering Dark*); and even a fictionalized biography of a saint (*Godric*). In each of these genres Buechner applies his sharply honed novelist's skills, and one cannot fault the books for didacticism or boredom.

In *Telling the Truth*, Buechner constructed a book around one thematic sentence: "The gospel is, in some ways, like a tragedy, a comedy and a fairy tale." The book covers old ground but, through wise use of images and allusions to literary sources as disparate as *King Lear* and *The Wizard of Oz*, Buechner makes the basic facts of the gospel glow as though he has just discovered the truth in a pottery jar in the Middle East.

Is it merely incidental that some of the most effective Christian apologists in this century—C. S. Lewis, Dorothy Sayers, George MacDonald, G. K. Chesterton—drank deeply at the well of fiction? There, they learned the need to construct even their theological works with the flair of a novelist.

Supernature Without Nature

G. K. Chesterton proposed a theory to explain the Dark Ages, that wasteland of painting, music, writing, and the other arts. Could they, he asked, be a necessary interlude after the Roman and Greek defilement and before the discovery of the true Romance? Nature had, in fact, been spoiled. "It was no good telling such people to have a natural religion full of stars and flowers. There was not even a flower or a star that had not been stained. They had to go into the desert, the monasteries, where they could find no flowers or even into the cavern where they could see no stars....Pan was nothing but panic. Venus was nothing but venereal vice."

Gradually, against this gray background, beauty began to appear, something fresh and delicate. In St. Francis of Assisi, the flowers and stars recovered their first innocence, fire and water were deemed worthy to be the brother and sister of a saint. The purge of paganism was complete at last, and Christians began to rediscover nature with a rush. The greatest blossoming of art in all of history, the Renaissance, immediately followed.

Several centuries later, however, the scientific revolution sent new shock waves throughout the church, from which we have not yet recovered. Nature and "supernature" split apart. The church abandoned nature to the physicists and geologists and biologists, retreating to the more limited purlieu of theological speculation. The scientists, in turn, abandoned the supernatural to the church and the paranormalists.

Too often today Christian writers tiptoe around God's creation; it is simply "matter," unworthy of the attention granted supernatural issues. (Similarly, says Jacques Ellul, science avoids questions of supernature to such an extent that it puts on blinders and severely restricts intellectual thought.) It is time for Christian writers to rediscover our natural environment and the characteristics of true humanity. By avoiding nature we divorce ourselves from the greatest images and carriers of supernature, and our writing loses its chief advantage, the ability to mimic creation. When Tolstoy describes spring in the wonder of tiny flowers poking through the thawing tundra, he invests in it the same exuberance and significance that he gives to a description of Christian conversion. It too is an expression of God's world. As a result, both passages stir up the feeling of longing in a sensitive reader. People live in the world of nature; we must first affirm that and plumb its meaning before leading them on to supernature.

Recently some fine authors have led the way in attempting to reveal nature as a carrier for supernature. Annie Dillard's *Pilgrim at Tinker Creek* was a landmark in that genre. Loren Eiseley and Lewis Thomas applied the same approach but from a less explicitly religious viewpoint. Response to these three authors demonstrates the hunger in readers for a more holistic approach to the world. Nature and supernature are not two separate worlds; they are different expressions of the same reality, and effective writing must deal with both.

In a brief passage, Pablo Neruda shows what can be done with the subject of writing itself, in the choice of words as carriers of expression:

> You can say anything you want, yessir, but it is the words that sing; they soar and descend. I bow to them, I love them, I cling to them, I run them down, I bite into them, I melt them down. I love words so much: the unexpected ones; the ones I wait for greedily are stalked until, suddenly, they drop. Vowels I love: they glitter like colored stones, they leap like silver fish. They are foam, thread, metal, dew. I run after certain words. They are so beautiful that I want to fit them all into my poem. I catch them in mid-flight as they buzz past. I trap them, clean them, peel them. I set myself in front of a dish: they have a crystalline texture to me: vibrant, ivory, vegetable, oily, like fruit, like algae, like agate, like olive. And then I stir them, I shake them, I drink them, I gulp them down, I garnish them, I let them go. I leave them in my poem like stalactites, like slivers of polished wood, like

coal, pickings from a ship wreck, gifts from the waves. Everything exists in the word.

Such enthusiasm for words should spill over into the whole process of presenting both the natural and supernatural. The concept of creation is, at heart, a Christian concept. That thought did not exist among the Greeks, who instead used the word *techna*, from which we derive our word "technological." The great Greek poets and playwrights thought in terms of arranging or manufacturing their works; they had no model of divine *creatio ex nihilo* to mimic. It staggers me to think that we Christians so blithely forfeit our opportunity to explore that magnificently created world. We fly, instead, to a supernatural world so far elevated from our fringe readers that they cannot possibly make the leap.

Conversely, when we discuss the realm of the supernatural, we must do so with unflinching realism. An article I read recently described a solemn vigil in which the author, standing before the Washington Monument, listened reverently as someone read aloud the names of thousands of those killed by the Hiroshima bomb. He was participating in some anniversary sponsored by an antiwar group. He described a terrible dilemma: while doing his very best to concentrate on the horrible immolation of Hiroshima's victims, his mind ineluctably dragged him back to the more immediate pain of his aching feet. His weak arches could not bear this vigil. Similarly, why cannot we be honest about such spiritual acts as praying and truly portray the dilemma of unholy people performing holy acts while contemplating fallen arches, twitching eyelids, and wobbly knees?

In short, we need a more supernatural awareness of the natural world and a deeper natural sensitivity to the supernatural world. In our art the two must come together, and fuse.

Action Without Tension

Sometimes when I read Christian books, especially in the fields of fiction and biography, I have a suspicion that characters have been strangely lobotomized. It's as if body snatchers have sucked out the humanity I know and replaced it with a sterilized imitation. Just as a lobotomy flattens out emotional peaks and valleys, Christian writers can safely tend to reduce life's tensions and strains to a more acceptable level.

A biblical book such as *Jeremiah* or *Hosea* spends a full chapter describing, in graphic terms, Israel's resemblance to a harlot who goes a-whoring, sleeping with every nation that comes down the street. We tend to take those same thoughts and express them as "God is mad at us," or "God is disappointed in Israel." Tragically, we also miss the emotional force of forgiveness that follows such gross adultery. We flatten the relationship between God and ourselves, and ourselves and other people.

We express theological concepts without emotion, drama, or tension. Old Testament Jews understood the full impact of words like *atonement* and *forgiveness*: they watched as the priest slid a knife across the spurting artery of a fear-stiffened lamb.

A perverse fear of overstatement keeps us confined to that flatland realm of "safe" emotions and tensions—a fear that seems incredible in light of the biblical model. Why is it that three-hundred-page novelizations of biblical characters somehow seem more stereotyped than the five-page description in the original source? As a beginning, we must turn to the masters of good writing and learn how tension and emotion can be expressed in print. Of modern authors, few surpass James Dickey, John Updike, and William Faulkner in ability to take the most ordinary event, say, a dinner conversation, and render it in a captivating manner. As for drama, Dickey can sustain a climb up a one-hundred-foot cliff for fifty pages, keeping the reader's heart pounding violently all the way. These skills can be acquired, but *only* through intense study and effort.

Far more difficult is the task of weaving morality into the fabric of the narrative. We Christian writers lapse into thinking of the world in terms of good or evil instead of the inseparable mixture of good *and* evil present in every person and nearly every action. Earlier times yearned for caricatured saints; they ascribed miracles when there were none. Our time scoffs at miracles and debunks saints. In order to communicate to a skeptical audience, Christian writers must temper their portrayal of good with a strong emphasis on realism.

Again, successful models abound. Consider Dostoyevsky, perhaps the greatest "interior" novelist, who displayed profound insight into the human psyche. His Christ figure, the protagonist of *The Idiot*, appears as a strange, unpredictable, epileptic prince. His goodness, though, is unquestioned, and *The Idiot's* final scene presents perhaps the most moving depiction of grace in all of literature: the "idiot" prince compassionately embracing the man who has just killed his lover. In *Crime and Punishment*, Dostoyevsky presents the darkest side of human nature, but even there the deranged murderer softens in the glow of Sonya's love. Somehow Dostoyevsky accomplishes both justice and forgiveness. In *The Brothers Karamazov* Dostoyevsky presents a truly good man but counterbalances that character with two brothers. How is it that, a hundred years after Dostoyevsky, Christian literature has, by and large, fallen back into a heroes-and-villains mentality?

A few novelists manage a believable blending of good and evil. Interestingly, these all present a badly flawed protagonist, seemingly a *sine qua non* of modern literature. Consider the whiskey priest in Graham Greene's *The Power and the Glory*, Mauriac's irascible curmudgeon in *Viper's Tangle*, Bernanos' frail saint in *Diary of a Country Priest*, and Buehner's tragicomic evangelist in the Leo Bebb series.

Light Without Darkness

Reading religious books sometimes reminds me of traveling through a mile-long mountain tunnel. Inside the tunnel, headlights provide the crucial illumination; without them I would drift dangerously toward the tunnel walls. But as I near the tunnel exit, a bright spot of light appears that soon engulfs my headlights and makes them useless. When I emerge from the tunnel, a "Check Headlights" sign reminds me that I still have them on. In comparison to the light of day they are so faint that I have lost awareness of them.

Christian books are normally written from a perspective outside the tunnel. The author's viewpoint is already so flooded with light that the author forgets the blank darkness inside the tunnel where many readers are journeying. We forget that, to someone in the middle of the mile-long tunnel, descriptions of blinding light can easily seem unreal.

When I pick up many Christian books, I get the same sensation as when I read the last page of a novel first. I know where it's going before I start. We desperately need authors with the skill to portray evolving viewpoints and marks of progression along the spiritual journey as accurately and sensitively as they show the light outside the tunnel.

I think of William Faulkner's *The Sound and the Fury* or Ken Kesey's *One Flew Over the Cuckoo's Nest* as examples of shifting points of view. Kesey tells his tale through the viewpoint of the mute Indian who, at the beginning, is thoroughly insane. As McMurphy weaves his liberating spell on twelve fellow inmates, however, the qualities of courage, hope, and self-confidence suddenly seep into the human prison. You can watch the Indian edge toward sanity as the book progresses; his own narrative begins to make more sense. Near the end of the book Kesey slips in an unexpected hint that perhaps there is only one truly insane person in the entire asylum—McMurphy is lobotomized and bought back to the ward strapped to a frame in a symbolic cruciform posture, and the captives (twelve) finally rebel. The movie version, of course, did not capture that subtlety; the medium cannot sustain it.

Kesey's book succeeds because he wrote as compellingly from the insane person's point of view as from the sane person's, just as Dostoyevsky in *Karamazov* argued the agnostic's views as strenuously as the believer's. Christian books should allow the reader to understand lack of faith as well as faith; if not, they will be read only by those predisposed to belief. The insanity must sound like insanity, not just glimmers of insanity as recalled by the sane. Doubt must sound like true doubt. In the middle of the tunnel, where one can barely fathom a headlight, pure daylight may blind.

These four criticisms of religious writing I accept for myself. Other Christian authors share my perceptions and are working hard to raise the standards of religious publishing.

Dorothy L. Sayers dedicated one of her books "In the name of One who assuredly never bored one in the thirty-three years He passed through the world like a flame." But we Christian authors must confess to having bored plenty of people. So far the evangelical reading public has been tolerant, buying millions of books of uneven quality each year. But a saturation point is inevitable. If Christian writing is not only to maintain interest in the forgiving Christian audience but also to arouse interest in the skeptical world beyond the Christian subculture, then it must grow up.

If we need models of how to do it well, we need only look as far as the Bible. Only 10 percent of the Bible's material, the epistles, is presented in a thought-organized format. The rest contains rollicking love stories, drama, history, poetry, and parables. There, humanity is presented as realistically as in any literature.

Why else do the paired books of Samuel, Kings, and Chronicles exist, if not to give a detailed context to the environment in which angry prophets deliver their messages? Can we imagine a more skillful weaving of nature and supernature than the great nature psalms, the theological high drama of Job, and the homespun parables of Jesus? What literary characters demonstrate a more subtle mixture of good and evil than David, or Jeremiah, or Jacob? And, from the despair of Ecclesiastes to the conversion narratives of Acts, is any wavelength on the spectrum of faith and doubt left unexpressed on the Bible's pages?

C. S. Lewis once likened his role as a Christian writer to an adjective humbly striving to point others to the Noun of truth. For people to believe that Noun, we Christian writers must improve as adjectives.

If I had to choose the single most decisive battleground for contemporary Christian writers, it would be the conflict between art and propaganda. For the nonfiction writer, the issue is how to express the Christian message in a structure and style that satisfies the demands of artistic integrity. The fiction writer struggles to include a nonintrusive, self-coherent message in his believable narrative.

Christian art has gained a reputation for erring on the side of propaganda. As a result, novels and especially films with an explicit Christian theme encounter mild condescension if not actual ridicule. Much secular resistance to propaganda appears hypocritical on close inspection, for Christians are not the only propagandists at work. Yet a baldly propagandistic film such as Mon Oncle d'Amerique *(My American Uncle), a gospel tract of behaviorism, somehow becomes the darling of film festivals. A film of that style with a traditional Christian message would be hooted off the screen. Clearly, some kinds of propaganda find wider acceptance than others.*

I include this chapter as a challenge to all Christians working in the arts, as well as Christian readers, viewers, and hearers who experience both good and bad Christian art. The church, once the dominant driving energy in artistic expression, now lags far behind, largely, I am convinced, because of an imbalance between art and propaganda.

8

Art and Propaganda

IF SOMEONE were to tell me that it lay in my power to write a novel explaining every social question from a particular viewpoint that I believed to be the correct one, I still wouldn't spend two hours on it. But if I were told that what I am writing will be read in twenty years' time by the children of today, and that those children will laugh, weep, and learn to love life as they read, why then I would devote the whole of my life and energy to it.

The man who wrote those words, Leo Tolstoy, vacillated continually between art and propaganda. Twenty years, even seventy years, after his death people are still laughing, weeping, and learning to love life as they read his books, but others are also reflecting on, arguing with, and reacting to his particular viewpoint on social, moral, and religious questions. Although in this quote Tolstoy claims to come down firmly on the side of art, veins of "propaganda" run throughout his novels, inspiring some readers and infuriating others. In nonfiction works like *What Is Art?* the great novelist leans toward propaganda, even, as some conclude, at the expense of true art.

Like a bipolar magnet, the Christian author today feels the pull of both forces: a fervent desire to communicate what gives life meaning counteracted by an artistic inclination toward self-expression, form, and structure that any "message" might interrupt. The result: a constant, dichotomous pull toward both propaganda and art. *Propaganda* is a word currently out of favor, connoting unfair manipulation or distortion of means to a particular end. I use it in a more acceptable sense, the original sense of the word as coined by Pope Urban VIII. He formed the College of Propaganda in the seventeenth century in order to disseminate the Christian faith. As a Christian writer, I must readily admit that I do strive for propaganda in this sense. Much of what I write is designed to convert or to cause others to consider a viewpoint I hold to be true.

Counterbalancing the literary tug away from propaganda, many evangelicals exert an insidious tug away from art. They would react to Tolstoy's statement with disbelief—to choose a novel that entertains and fosters a love for life over a treatise that solves every social (or, better, religious) question of mankind! How can a person "waste" time with mere aesthetics—soothing music, pleasing art, entertaining literature—when injustice rules the nations and the decadent world marches ineluctably to destruction? Is this not fiddling while Rome burns? Currently, novels written by evangelicals tend toward the propagandistic (even to the extent of fictionalizing Bible stories and foretelling the Second Coming) and away from the artful.

Somewhere in this magnetic field between art and propaganda the Christian author (or painter or musician) works. One force tempts us to lower artistic standards and preach an unadorned message; another tempts us to submerge or even alter the message for the sake of artistic sensibilities. Having lived in the midst of this tension for over a decade, I have come to recognize it as a healthy synthetical tension that should be affirmed. Success often lies with the extremes: an author may succeed in the evangelical world by erring on the side of propaganda. But ever so slowly, the fissure between the Christian and secular worlds will yawn wider. If we continue tilting toward propaganda, we will soon find ourselves writing and selling books to ourselves alone. On the other hand, the Christian author cannot simply absorb the literary standards of the larger world. Our ultimate goal cannot be a self-expression, but rather a God-expression.

C. S. Lewis explored the polarity in the address "Learning in Wartime," delivered to Oxford students who were trying to concentrate on academics while their friends fought in the trenches of Europe and staved off the German aerial assault on London. How, asked Lewis, can creatures who are advancing every moment either to heaven or hell spend any fraction of time on such comparative trivialities as art, math, or biology (let alone Lewis' field of medieval literature)? With great perception, Lewis noted that the condition of wartime did not change the underlying question, but merely accelerated the timing by making it more likely that any one person would advance *soon* to heaven or hell.

The most obvious answer to the dilemma is that God himself invested great energy in the natural world. In the Old Testament he created a distinct culture and experimented with a variety of literary forms which endure as masterpieces. As for biology and physics, everything we know about them derives from painstakingly tracing his creative activity. For a Christian, the natural world provides a medium to express and even to discover the image of God. Nevertheless, while Lewis affirms the need for good art and good science, he readily admits that Christianity knocks culture off its pedestal. The salvation of a single soul, he says, is worth more than all the poetry, drama, and tragedy ever written. (A committed Christian must acknowledge that intrinsic worth, and yet how many of us react with dismay when reading of such terrible tragedies as the burning of the library in Alexandria, the destruction of the Parthenon by gunpowder, and the bombing of cathedrals in World War II while scarcely giving a thought to the thousands of nameless civilians buried in the rubble of those edifices?)

The dilemma of art and propaganda is essentially a tremor of the seismic human dilemma of living in a divinely created but fallen world. Beauty abounds, and we are right to seek it and to seek to reproduce it. And yet tragedy and despair and meaninglessness also abound, and we must not neglect addressing ourselves to the human condition. That is why I affirm both art and propaganda. As an author, I experiment with different forms and I hope to express my propaganda (if the word offends you, read *message*) as artfully as possible and to imbue my art with a worthwhile message. I embrace both art and propaganda, rejecting the pressures to conform to one or the other.

In dealing with the tensions of art and propaganda over the years, I have learned a few guidelines that allow for a more natural wedding of the two. Whenever I have broken one of these guidelines, I have usually awakened to the abrupt and painful realization that I have tilted too far toward either art or propaganda. In either case my message gets lost, whether through pedantic communication or through a muddle of empty verbiage. Because Christian writers are mainly erring on the side of propaganda, not art, my guidelines speak primarily to that error.

1. An artful propagandist takes into account the ability of the audience to perceive.

For the Christian writer (or speaker) who wants to communicate to a secular audience, this caution cannot be emphasized too strongly. In effect, one must consider two different sets of vocabulary. Words which have a certain meaning to a Christian may have an entirely different, sometimes even antithetical, meaning to the secular listener. Consider a few examples of fine words which have had their meanings spoiled over time. *Pity* once derived from *piety*: a person dispensed pity in a godlike, compassionate sense. By responding to the poor and the needy, one was mimicking God, and therefore pietous, or full of pity. Similarly, as any reader of the King James Version knows, *charity* was an example of God's grace, a synonym for *love* (as in the oft-quoted 1 Corinthians 13 passage). Over the centuries, both those words lost their meaning until they ultimately became negatively charged. "I don't want pity!" or "Don't give me charity!" a needy person protests today. The theological significance has been sucked away.

Similarly, many words now used to express personal faith may miscommunicate rather than communicate. The word *God* may summon up all sorts of inappropriate images, unless the Christian goes on to explain what he or she means by God. *Love*, a vital theological word, has lost its meaning—for popular conceptions of it, merely flip a radio dial and listen to popular music stations. The word *redemption* most often relates to trading stamps, and few cultural analogies can adequately express that concept. Blood is as easily associated with death as with life.

As words change in meaning, Christian communicators must adapt accordingly, selecting words and metaphors which precisely fit the culture. Concepts, too, depend on the audience's ability to absorb them, and often one must adapt downward to a more basic level. If I see a three-year-old girl endangering herself, I must warn her in terms she can understand. For example, what if the child decides to stick her finger first into her mouth and then into an electrical outlet? I would not respond by searching out my *Reader's Digest Home Handyman Encyclopedia* and launching into an elaborate monologue on amps, volts, and electrical resistance. Rather, I will more likely slap her hand and say something like "There's fire in there! You'll be burned!" Although, strictly speaking, the outlet box contains no literal fire, I will choose concepts that communicate to the comprehension level of a three-year-old.

Andrew Young reports that he learned an essential principle of survival during the civil rights struggle. "Don't judge the adversary by how you think," he says. "Learn to think like the adversary." He voiced that principle in the days of the Iran hostage crisis when news accounts were using such adjectives as "insane, crazed, demonic" to describe Iranian leaders. Those labels, said Young, do nothing to facilitate communication. To understand the Iranians, we must first consider their viewpoint. To the militants, the Shah was as brutal and vicious as Adolf Hitler; therefore, they were reacting to the United States as we would respond to a country that sheltered a mass murderer like Hitler.

In a parallel way, when Christians attempt to communicate to non-Christians, we must first think through their assumptions and imagine how they will likely receive the message we are conveying. That process will affect the words we choose, the form and, most importantly, the content we can get across. If we err on the side of too much content, as Christians often do, the net effect is the same as if we had included no content.

Alexander Solzhenitsyn, who has walked a tightrope between art and propaganda all his life, learned this principle after being released from concentration camp when his writing finally began to find acceptance in Soviet literary journals. In *The Oak and the Calf* he recalls, "Later, when I popped up from the underground and began lightening my works for the outside world, lightening them of all that my fellow countrymen could hardly be expected to accept at once, I discovered to my surprise that a piece only gained, that its effect was heightened, as the harsher tones were softened."

(We must use caution here, as Solzhenitsyn learned. A new danger may seep in: the subtle tendency to lighten too much and thus change the message. *Just drop this one offensive word*, the Soviet censors coaxed Solzhenitsyn. *There's really no need to capitalize God—that's archaic. If you want us to publish* One Day in the Life of Ivan Denisovich, *merely cross out this one problematic line.* Solzhenitsyn resisted those last two requests; he capitalized God and left the controversial sentence, "I crossed myself, and said to God: 'Thou are there in heaven after all, O creator. Thy patience is long, but thy blows are heavy.' " Acceding to such pressure would efface his whole message, he decided.)

A Christian addressing a secular audience must maintain a balance between leaving the message intact and adapting it to that audience. We who are Christians stumble across God everywhere. We ascribe daily events to his activity. We see his hand in nature and the

Bible. He seems fully evident to us. But the secular mind can hardly see God at all in the maze of cults, religions, and television mountebanks, all clamoring for attention against the background of a starving, war-torn planet. Unless we truly understand that viewpoint and speak in terms the secular mind can understand, our words will have the quaint and useless ring of a foreign language.

2. Artful propaganda works like a deduction rather than a rationalization.

Recently, psychologists have begun to define an instinctual process of rationalization in the human mind, sometimes labeled the theory of Cognitive Dissonance. Basically, it means that the human mind, intolerant of a state of tension and disharmony, works to patch up inconsistencies with a self-affirming process of rationalization.

I am late to a luncheon with a publisher. Obviously, according to this theory, it cannot be my fault—I start with that assumption. It must be the traffic. Or my wife. Or the others at the meeting who showed up on time.

My article is rejected. Instantly I start consoling myself with the knowledge that hundreds of manuscripts were rejected that day. The editor could have had a bad breakfast. Perhaps no one even read my manuscript. Any number of factors arise to explain my rejection. My mind tries to quiet the jarring cacophony caused by this bit of news.

I define the process of rationalization very simply: it occurs when a person knows the end result first and reasons backward. The conclusion is a given; I merely need to find a way to support that conclusion. I ran headlong into an example of the process of rationalization while working on an article about Wycliffe Bible translators for *Christianity Today*. Since rumors of Wycliffe's CIA involvement proliferate, I felt it essential to try to track them down. I telephoned outspoken critics of Wycliffe all over the country. One, a professor in a New York university, insisted that Wycliffe was definitely subsidized by the CIA. I asked for proof. "It's quite obvious," he replied. "They claim to raise their thirty million dollars annual budget from fundamentalist churches. You and I both know there's not thirty million dollars available from that source. Obviously, they're getting it from somewhere else." Had that professor done a little research, he would have discovered that each of the five top television evangelists pulls in over fifty million dollars annually from religious sympathizers. Certainly the pool of resources in the United States is large enough to account for Wycliffe's contributions. But he started from a foregone conclusion and reasoned backward.

Solzhenitsyn encountered a startling case of rationalization when the Soviet editor Lebedev said to him, "If Tolstoy were alive now and wrote as he did then (meaning against the government) he wouldn't be Tolstoy." Lebedev's opinion about his government was so firmly set that he could not allow a plausible threat to it and so he rationalized that Tolstoy would be a different man under a new regime.

Sadly, much of what I read in Christian literature has an echo of rationalization. I get the sense that the author starts with an unshakable conclusion and merely sets out to discover whatever logical course could support that conclusion. Much of what I read on depression, on suicide, on homosexuality, seems written by people who begin with a Christian conclusion, who have never been through the anguished steps that are the familiar path to a person struggling with depression, suicide, or homosexuality. No wonder the "how-to" articles and books do not ring true. No conclusions could be so flip and matter-of-fact to a person who has actually endured such a journey.

A conclusion has impact only if the reader has been primed for it by moving along the steps that lead to it before being confronted with the conclusion. It must be the logical outgrowth, the consummation of what went before, not the starting place.

C. S. Lewis, Charles Williams, and J. R. R. Tolkien struggled with these issues intensely as they worked on fiction that revealed an underlying layer of Christianity. Lewis and Tolkien particularly reacted with fire against well-meaning Christians who slavishly pointed to all symbolism in their books, such as labeling the characters of Aslan and Gandalf as Christ-figures. Even though the parallels were obvious, both authors vigorously resisted admitting that had been their intent. Those characters may indeed point to Christ, but by shadowing forth a deeper, underlying cosmic truth, they said. One cannot argue backward and describe the characters as mere symbolic representations—that would shatter their individuality and literary impact. (I sometimes wonder if Lewis erred on the side of propaganda with Aslan and thus limited his non-Christian audience, whereas Tolkien's greater subtlety may last for centuries.)

In chapter five I alluded to several novels by Tolstoy and Dostoyevsky which begin with poignant quotations from Scripture. Their authors selected those verses because they summarize a central message. Yet are the novels *Anna Karenina, Resurrection, The Idiot,* and *The Brothers Karamazov* propaganda? Only a hardened cynic would say so. The novels, rather, incarnate the concept behind the Bible references so compellingly and convincingly that the reader must acknowledge the truth of what he or she reads. To be effective, a Christian communicator must make the point inside the reader before the reader consciously acknowledges it.

3. Artful propaganda must be "sincere."

I put the word *sincere* in quotes because I refer to its original meaning only. Like so many words, *sincere* has been preempted by modern advertising and twisted so badly that it ends up meaning its opposite.

Consider, for example, a shy, timid salesman, who doesn't mix well at parties and cannot be assertive on sales calls. He is sent by his manager to a Dale Carnegie course to improve his self-confidence. "You must be *sincere* to be a successful salesman," he is told, and he practices various techniques for sincerity. *Start with the handshake—it must be firm, confident, steady. Here, try it a few times. Now that you have that down, let's work on eye contact. See, when you shake my hand, you should be staring me right in the eye. Don't look away or even waver. Stare straight at me—that's a mark of sincerity. Your customer must feel you really care about him.*

For a fee of several hundred dollars, our insecure salesman learns techniques of sincerity. His next customers are impressed by his conscientiousness, his confidence in his product, and his concern for them, all because he has learned a body language. Actually, an acquired technique to communicate something not already present is the opposite of the true meaning of sincere. According to some language experts, the word was originally a sculptor's term, deriving from two Latin words, *sin cere,* "without wax." Even the best of sculptors makes an occasional slip of the chisel, causing an unsightly gouge. Sculptors who work with marble know that wax mixed to the proper color can fill in that gouge so perfectly that few observers can ever spot the flaw. A truly perfect piece, however, one that needs no artificial touch-up, is *sin cere,* without wax. What you see is what you get—there are no embellishments or cover-ups.

Propaganda becomes bad propaganda because of the touchup wax that authors apply to their work. If we can truly write in a sincere way, reflecting reality, then our work will reflect truth and reinforce our central message. If not, readers will spot the flaws and judge our work accordingly.

When I read *The Oak and the Calf*, I laughed aloud as I read the Soviet censors' advice to Solzhenitsyn, because their script could have been written by an evangelical magazine editor. Three things must not appear in Russian literature, they solemnly warned Solzhenitsyn: pessimism, denigration, surreptitious sniping. Cover up your tendencies to realism with a layer that might soften the over-all effect, they seemed to be saying.

Biography and fiction written by evangelicals too often show wax badly gaumed over obvious flaws. We leave out details of struggle and realism that do not fit neatly into our propaganda. Or, we include scenes that have no realism just to reinforce our point. Even the untrained observer can spot the flaws, and slight bulges here and there can ruin a work of art.

All three of these temptations to propagandize in the bad sense increase with a captive, supportive audience. When we no longer have to win people over to our point of view, for example, realism can become an impediment. The Christian public will applaud books in which every prayer is answered and every disease is healed; but to the degree those books do not reflect reality, they will become meaningless to a skeptical audience. Too often our evangelical literature appears to the larger world as strange and unconvincing as a Moonie tract or *Daily Worker* newspaper.

For models of these three guidelines of artful communication, we can look to the Creator himself. He took into account the audience's ability to perceive in the ultimate sense—by flinging aside his deity and becoming the Word, one of us, living in our cramped planet within the limitations of a human body. In his communication through creation, through his Son, and through the Bible, he gave only enough evidence for those with faith to follow the deductions to truth about him, yet without defying human freedom. And as for being sincere, has a more earthy, realistic book ever been written than the Bible?

A friend of mine, a hand surgeon, was awakened from a thick sleep by a 3:00 A.M. telephone call and summoned to emergency surgery. He specializes in microsurgery, reconnecting nerves and blood vessels finer than human hairs, performing meticulous twelve-hour procedures with no breaks. As he tried to overcome his grogginess, he realized he needed extra motivation to endure this marathon surgery. On impulse he called a close friend, also awakening him. "I have a very arduous surgery ahead of me, and I need something extra to concentrate on this time," he said. "I'd like to dedicate this surgery to you. If I think about you while I'm performing it, that will help me get through."

Should not that be the Christian author's response to God—an offering of our work in dedication to him? If so, how dare we possibly produce propaganda without art, or art without meaning?

To those few who succeed and become models of artistic excellence, the Christian message takes on a new glow. Looking back on T.S. Eliot's life, Russell Kirk said, "He made the poet's voice heard again, and thereby triumphed; knowing the community of souls, he freed others from captivity to time and the lonely ego; in the teeth of winds of doctrine, he attested the permanent things. And his communication is tongued with fire beyond the language of the living."

PART THREE

Our Bent World

My personal introduction to concentration camps came during a late-night conversation in the Albany, New York, home of a Jewish photographer. Many of his relatives had perished under Hilter's "Final Solution," and he was then experiencing the second-generation symptoms later explored by Helen Epstein in Children of the Holocaust. *The scenes he described, passed down from great-aunts and uncles, horrified me.*

Later the laconic prose of Elie Wiesel and the angry blasts of Solzhenitsyn pulled me into the great body of literature that spun out centrifugally from the camps. What I found in the accounts surprised me. The enslaved millions formed a separate civilization, a compression of basic humanity stripped of its normal trappings. Survivors teach us as much about life outside the camps as about life inside.

An appalling number of people today have no knowledge of (or interest in) the lessons from the concentration camps. To me, this sense of polite apathy is the worst injustice we can grant the few survivors. We owe them far more.

9

Lessons from the Camps

NEWSCASTER Edward R. Murrow, covering the Allied troops' liberation of Germany, accompanied one of the first contingents to take over a German concentration camp. No American was prepared for the horrible scene within the gates: emaciated, bony corpses stacked like cordwood and the awful stench of burning flesh. Worst of all were the living corpses, the *Muselmanner*, or walking dead. One man, a human skeleton with skin draped over him like loose-fitting leather, stared at Murrow with haunting, empty eyes. Finally he spoke in a raspy, wheezing voice: "Mr. Murrow...Mr. Murrow...do you remember me?"

Edward R. Murrow glanced at the man and quickly shook his head. But the man persisted. He grabbed Murrow's arm in his clawlike fingers and said, "Don't you remember? You interviewed me in Prague. I was the mayor then, of Prague, Czechoslovakia."

Six years after that liberation, thousands of miles away in the desolate Siberian wasteland, Alexander Solzhenitsyn was serving out his term for making a disparaging reference to Stalin in a letter. After six gloomy years he suddenly discovered the joy of writing. "Sometimes in a sullen work party with Tommy-gunners barking about me, lines and images crowded in so urgently that I felt myself borne through the air, overleaping the column in my hurry to reach the work site and find a corner to write. At such moments I was both free and happy" (*Gulag III*, p. 99).

But how could he write? Any scrap of paper would be confiscated and cause suspicion against him, no matter how innocent the writings were. After all, the lines could be in code or perhaps contain the membership list of some organization. Solzhenitsyn learned that

115

a prisoner's memory, cleansed of superfluous knowledge, was surprisingly capacious. He would write down snatches of twelve to twenty lines at a time, polish them, learn them by heart, and burn them. Then to keep count, he started breaking matches into little pieces and arranging them in two rows of ten each. As he recited the verses to himself, he would remove one bit of broken match from each row, first counting units, then tens of lines. Even this had to be done with care, for the regular moving of match bits along with the whispering movements of lips could have aroused stool pigeons' suspicions. Every fiftieth and hundredth line Solzhenitsyn memorized with special care, to help him keep count. Once a month he recited everything he had written. If the fiftieth or hundredth lines came out wrong, he would painstakingly go over and over the lines until he had them right.

Later, observing Lithuanian Catholics with their rosaries, Solzhenitsyn decided their counting technique would be more practical. He made a rosary of one hundred colored pieces of hardened bread, every tenth piece cubic. Amazing the Lithuanians with his religious zeal (devout ones possessed only forty beads) he happily fingered and counted beads inside his wide mittens—standing in lineups, marching to work, at all waiting times. Warders who discovered the beads assumed they were for praying and let him keep the necklace.

By the end of his sentence Solzhenitsyn had accumulated twelve thousand lines, which upon release he eagerly committed to paper.

As does every generation, ours is haltingly trying to come to terms with its recent past. The concentration camps, notably those erected by Hitler and Stalin ("Little Moustache" and "Big Moustache," as Solzhenitsyn calls them), caused such a moral crater in the history of humanity that only now are we beginning to absorb and assess their impact. In recent years events such as the television series *The Holocaust* and the publication of Solzhenitsyn's monumental three-volume work *The Gulag Archipelago* have stirred the consciousness of the general public.

The psychic effect of German concentration camps has been well documented by psychologist-survivors Viktor Frankl, Bruno Bettelheim, and Elie Cohen and powerfully retold by such novelists as Elie Wiesel and John Hersey. Because of strict censorship, accounts of Soviet camps have been more sporadic and deficient, and until

Solzhenitsyn no one had been able to compile any kind of a thorough history. If Germany's genocidal camps left a scar across the body of all humanity, Stalin's camps inflicted a near-fatal wound stretching across the breadth of the Soviet Union. Best estimates are that sixty million were killed or incarcerated by Stalin. Of these, fifteen million died in the great plague of enforced starvation or of disease in the Ukraine. That means one in three Soviet citizens lost a family member to the terror of Stalin's reign.

Why spotlight attention on concentration camps? Though it may cause discomfort and even anguish, such attention serves several useful functions. The primary function is chiseled into stone at the Dachau memorial, as articulated by philosopher Santayana, "Those who cannot remember the past are condemned to repeat it." We who have been reared in a climate of existential despair cannot fathom the optimistic belief in human progress that crescendoed before World War I and was finally put to death in Germany and in Russia. The two great fonts of culture and civilization (*Christian* civilization) gave birth to demonic forces. The camps became the central metaphor of evil in all history, so much so that George Bernard Shaw reluctantly concluded, "There is only one empirically verifiable doctrine of theology—original sin."

There is no way to exaggerate the impact of the camps on the modern view of humanity. Deliberate cruelty had become institutionalized as official state policy. Predictions that the world is "getting better and better every day in every way" abruptly stopped.

Historians sorting through the archives of the Third Reich came across such words as these, spoken by Heinrich Himmler to SS generals at Posen in 1943: "I also want to talk to you quite frankly on a very grave matter. Among ourselves it should be mentioned quite frankly, and yet we will never speak of it publicly...I mean...the extermination of the Jewish race....Most of *you* know what it means when 100 corpses are lying side by side, or 500, or 1000. To have stuck it out and at the same time—apart from exceptions caused by human weakness—to have remained decent fellows, that is what has made us hard. This is a page of glory in our history which has never been written and is never to be written..." (*Rise and Fall of the Third Reich*, p. 1259).

Words like *inhuman* and *unconscionable* were voided of meaning by the SS programs, which had, in fact, been carried out by humans who claimed their consciences were unaffected.

Anyone who has been sheltered from such horrors need only visit one of the preserved death camps, such as Auschwitz. There, in an open field, one can see flowers and grasses growing with unusual lushness. Bending down, one notices the white, powdery character of the soil that allows such fecund growth. The top twelve inches of that soil is fine bone loam—the remains of sixty thousand humans destroyed in the ovens of a single camp.

Jewish groups who worked for the preservation of such camps adopted the slogan "Never Again." Today the camps, cleaned up, well planted, seeming almost like state parks to the modern visitor, stand as an ineradicable testimony to the basic tragic flaw in humanity and as a terrifying warning to all of us who may underestimate the evil bent of power.

The iron commitment of "Never Again" is the primary function of looking at the camps. They should have seared all humanity against the promises of totalitarianism. The long litany of evil which followed has proved the world's memory to be short indeed.

Yet the memory of the camps and of the men who created them is not the only lesson for us to learn. There are also the survivors: Solzhenitsyn, methodically laying his bricks in Siberian winters while thousands of lines swirled in his head, the mayor of Prague, the psychologists Bettelheim and Frankl, the concert violinists—of the millions a few have endured to tell us about ourselves. Their voices are sometimes loud and screechy, even strident. Flannery O'Connor was once asked why she chose to write about odd, abnormal characters. Her reply: "To the near blind I write large. To the deaf I shout." Similarly, the survivors are caricatures of humanity forced to live in unbearable conditions; yet in such circumstances they reveal much about our ground of being. For there, in the camps, all distinguishing marks between prisoners were obliterated. To his captors Solzhenitsyn was just one more *zek* (Russian word for "prisoner") with his head shaven and a number painted across his chest; to all the rest he was merely a competitor for food and space. Taken together, the prisoners, stripped of their individual identities, teach us about the nature of humanity.

At first glance, the lesson from the survivors seems predictable. On one side of the fence was an indistinguishable herd of prisoners, thrown together like animals in pens, every detail of their lives determined for them. On the other side were the guards, individuals free to attend concerts, work at their hobbies, practice their sports, and read books. As Terrence Des Pres has pointed out, the aim of the camps was "to reduce inmates to mindless creatures whose behavior could be predicted and controlled absolutely. The camps have so far been the closest thing on earth to a perfect [B. F.] Skinner Box. They were a closed, completely regulated environment, a 'total' world in the strict sense. Pain and death were the 'negative reinforcers,' food and life the 'positive reinforcers,' and all these forces were pulling and shoving twenty-four hours a day at the deepest stratum of human need" (*The Survivor*, p. 162).

The experiment failed. A "rehabilitated" Solzhenitsyn cried out so loudly he was expelled from his homeland. Many men and women who survived the German camps resumed their normal lives, scarred and bruised by the experience, yes, but far from becoming the mindless robots wished for by their captors. If you visit a dinner held by survivors of the camps in memory of their experience, you will find doctors, lawyers, businessmen—nearly a cross section of humanity in general. They include children who were raised under a regime that approached absolute evil; yet even within them one often finds a highly developed morality and compassion for humanity.

Writings of the survivors sing with detailed character studies of individuals. A simple, brief book like Solzhenitsyn's *One Day in the Life of Ivan Denisovich*, which limits its scope to one sixteen-hour period in one camp, contains a wealth of three-dimensional portraits of inmates.

In one sense the camps reduce people to purely materialistic beings. The only things that matter, really, are the bowl of warm soup with the greasy fishbones floating in it and the pair of felt boots and warm mittens. Eight ounces of bread is the minimum—more for those who work hard. However, it soon becomes obvious to anyone who reads the survivors' accounts that they are not the accounts of materialistic beings. Though every vestige of food for the human spirit has been carefully removed, still, the spirit surges up. Within the malnourished bodies of the inmates there is a highly developed sense of *morality, art*, and *hope*. None of those qualities is to be expected in such a place. Yet they spring up like geysers out of granite.

Of course there was also crude violence, inhumanity, conniving, and cruelty among the inmates. There was mindless obedience, in many cases. These are to be expected. What is remarkable, however, is that in an environment designed to breed such responses, other, more lofty signs of humanity appeared. I should note that I am mostly talking of concentration camps, not death camps. The death camps, where each new entrant knew he or she had only days to live, produced an extraordinary set of pressures. As Elie Wiesel has tragically described in his remembrances, death camps included such scenes as sons beating their fathers to death for a piece of bread. Even there, however, glimpses of compassion and self-sacrifice existed, as Wiesel himself showed in his loving concern for his father.

If the victims reveal a surprising degree of individuality and resilience, their captors in almost all accounts blur together into an amorphous, indistinguishable clot. Solzhenitsyn realized this when he arose to address a special committee inquiring into certain prisoners' complaints. "All that is written in these pages, all that we had gone through, all that we had brooded over in all those years and all those days on hunger strike—I might as well try telling it to orangutans as to them. They were still in some formal sense Russians, still more or less capable of understanding fairly simple Russian phrases, such as 'Permission to enter!', 'Permission to speak, sir!' But as they sat there all in a row at the long table, exhibiting their sleek, white, complacent, uniformly blank physiognomies, it was plain that they had long ago degenerated into a distinct biological type, that verbal communication between us had broken down beyond repair, and that we could exchange only...bullets" (*Gulag III*, p. 267).

Another witness, George Mangakis, described the process of his torturer becoming the real victim after he was imprisoned by the Greek junta in the late 1960s.

> I have experienced the fate of a victim. I have seen the torturer's face at close quarters. It was in a worse condition than my own bleeding, livid face. The torturer's face was distorted by a kind of twitching that had nothing human about it...In this situation, I turned out to be the lucky one. I was humiliated. I did not humiliate others. I was simply bearing a profoundly unhappy humanity in my aching entrails. Whereas the men who humiliate you must first humiliate the notion of humanity within themselves. Never mind if they strut around in their uniforms, swollen with the knowledge that they can control the suffering, sleeplessness, hunger, and despair of their fellow human beings, intoxicated with the power in their hands. Their intoxication is nothing other than the degradation of humanity. The

ultimate degradation. They have had to pay very dearly for my torments.

I wasn't the one in the worst position. I was simply a man who moaned because he was in great pain. I prefer that. At this moment I am deprived of the joy of seeing children going to school or playing in the parks. Whereas they have to look their own children in the face.

Morality

Among the prisoners, a sense of morality persisted even in an environment of near absolute evil. It is true, some survivors lost their faith in God. Jews, especially, were susceptible: raised to believe they had been chosen people, they suddenly discovered that, as one Jew poignantly expressed, "Hitler is the only one who has kept his promises, all his promises, to the Jewish people."

Elie Wiesel records a true and profoundly moving episode which occurred while he, at age fifteen, was imprisoned at Buna. In one scene it expresses the horror of the camps perhaps more potently than all the camp statistics ever published.

A cache of arms had been discovered at the camp, belonging to a Dutchman, who was promptly shipped to Auschwitz. But the Dutchman had a young boy who served him, a *pipel* as they were called, a child with a refined and beautiful face, unheard of in the camps. He had the face of a sad angel.

The little servant, like his Dutch master, was cruelly tortured but would not reveal any information. So the SS sentenced him to death, along with two other prisoners who had been discovered with arms.

One day when we came back from work, we saw three gallows rearing up in the assembly place, three black crows. Roll call. SS all round us, machine guns trained: the traditional ceremony. Three victims in chains—and one of them, the little servant, the sad-eyed angel.

The SS seemed more preoccupied, more disturbed than usual. To hang a young boy in front of thousands of spectators was no light matter. The head of the camp read the verdict. All eyes were on the child. He was lividly pale, almost calm, biting his lips. The gallows threw its shadow over him.

This time the Lagerkapo refused to act as executioner. Three SS replaced him.

The three victims mounted together onto the chairs.

The three necks were placed at the same moment within the nooses.

"Long live liberty!" cried the two adults.

But the child was silent.

"Where is God? Where is He?" someone behind me asked.

At a sign from the head of the camp, the three chairs tipped over.

Total silence throughout the camp. On the horizon, the sun was setting.

"Bare your heads!" yelled the head of the camp. His voice was raucous. We were weeping.

"Cover your heads!"

Then the march past began. The two adults were no longer alive. Their tongues hung swollen, blue-tinged. But the third rope was still moving; being so light, the child was still alive....

For more than half an hour he stayed there, struggling between life and death, dying in slow agony under our eyes. And we had to look him full in the face. He was still alive when I passed in front of him. His tongue was still red, his eyes were not yet glazed.

Behind me, I heard the same man asking: "Where is God now?"

And I heard a voice within me answer him: "Where is He? Here He is—He is hanging here on this gallows...."

That night the soup tasted of corpses (*Night*, pp. 75-76).

Wiesel lost his faith in God at that concentration camp. But not because he lost belief in morality—for the opposite reason. He believed in morality so deeply that he could no longer worship a God who would allow children to be strung up at the gallows and tossed into the ovens.

The lesson intended by the SS guards at Buna was to reinforce their imposed justice: cooperate, and you may live; resist, and you will surely die. But the effect on the prisoners was just the opposite. Hardened as they were by viewing thousands of deaths, the prisoners convulsed before this one. The object lesson did nothing to break the spirit of resistance; it merely stiffened the will of those who were determined somehow to strike out against their tormentors.

Who survived the camps? The people who cooperated with guards, informing on fellow prisoners? Not in Germany. According to Bruno Bettelheim, "Those who...made common cause with the enemy, the camp commander, thus sacrificing the lives of others to gain advantages for themselves, were not likely to remain alive. There prisoners, to survive, had to help one another."

In Russia, too, prisoners constructed their own scheme of morality. Some of it was brutal. Stool pigeons, for example, were not tolerated—their throats were slit in the night. But when prisoners succeeded in taking over an entire camp at Kengir for six weeks, they set up humane and workable rules to govern themselves—far more sensible than those rules imposed by the guards. They did not disintegrate into anarchy and greed even when power and a measure of freedom were suddenly thrust upon them.

Psychologists who have studied concentration camp survivors universally affirm that guilt is one of the chief residual effects. Guilt over why they, and not others, survived. Guilt over whether they did enough to protest. As Bettelheim confesses, "The survivor as a thinking being knows very well that he is not guilty, as I, for one, know about myself, but this does not change the fact that the humanity of such a person, as a feeling being, requires that he *feel* guilty, and he does. This is a most significant aspect of survivorship." Elie Wiesel writes, "I live and therefore I am guilty. I am still here, because a friend, a comrade, an unknown, died in my place."

It is perhaps the ultimate irony that German after German calmly marched to the stand at Nuremburg to report that he felt no guilt about what had been done to the Jews, that he was "just following orders." Meanwhile scores of thousands of innocent people inherited an intolerable burden of guilt because their sense of morality would not dissolve inside the camps.

From his experience in the camps, Solzhenitsyn did not conclude that all inmates were pure and just, or even that all guards were viciously evil. But, as he records in the second volume of *Gulag*, his view of humanity was profoundly altered by what he saw in the camps: "It was only when I lay there on rotting prison straw that I sensed within myself the first stirrings of good. Gradually it was disclosed to me that the line separating good and evil passes not through states, nor between classes, nor between political parties either—but right through every human heart—and through all human hearts....*Bless you, prison*, for having been in my life" (p. 615).

The image of God in human beings is inescapable. In the depths of depraved human hell, in the presence of absolute evil, even there glimpses of his image can be found. The concentration camps teach us the depravity of humankind, surely. But they also hint at our immortality.

Art

Although nearly every element of what is generally known as art or culture had been dismantled within the camps, this human expression, too, kept asserting itself. There were fewer reminders of art, to be sure—no concerts or ballets, and few books allowed. But the inmates carried within them memories and a highly developed aesthetic sense. Even when life was reduced to its raw basics, when art required an exertion that might rob from the more pressing needs of survival, it surfaced.

Eugenie Ginzburg, a Communist Party activist who fell into disfavor and spent two decades in one of the worst Gulag camps, remembered it this way: "During those years I experienced many conflicting feelings, but the dominant one was that of amazement.... We still took pleasure in the fugitive mists of morning, the violet sunsets that blazed over us as we returned from the quarry, the proximity of ocean-going ships which we felt by some sixth sense—and in poetry, which we still repeated to one another at night.... I felt instinctively that as long as I could be stirred to emotion by the sea breeze, by the brilliance of the stars, and by poetry, I would still be alive, however much my legs might tremble and my back bend under the load of burning stones."

For Solzhenitsyn, as has been mentioned, writing became the single force which allowed him to leap over the walls of the camp. His body, still stuffed into a *zek* uniform, went through the exhausting daily regimen of wake-up calls, hard labor, food lines. But in the pause between wheelbarrow loads of mortar, in the winter warming-up shack, on the scaffolding, he would furtively scribble down new verses which filled his head.

"I lived in a dream," he says, "I sat in the mess hall over the ritual gruel sometimes not even noticing its taste, deaf to those around me—feeling my way about my verses and trimming them to fit like bricks in a wall. I was searched, and counted, and herded over the steppe—and all the time I saw the sets for my play, the color of the curtains, the placing of the furniture, the spotlights, every movement of the actors across the stage.

"Some of the lads broke through the wire in a lorry, others crawled under it, others walked up a snowdrift and over it—but for me the wire might not have existed; all this time I was making my own long and distant escape journey, and this was something the warders could not discover when they counted heads" (*Gulag III*, p. 104).

Across the Gulag, and in the camps in Germany, how many count-less others were stirred like Solzhenitsyn? How many invented their own secret codes and elaborate techniques for hiding their writings from the guards and took those codes to the grave with them, si-lently?

The prisoners, cramped into unimaginably small spaces, given barely enough calories a day to subsist, even under such conditions found the energy for writing, for music, for art.

Sometimes books were available, and the prisoners paged through those precious objects as if each one were made of priceless parch-ment. Eugen Kogon, an author and survivor of Buchenwald, found a rare opportunity for quiet reading. In the winter of 1942 a series of bread thefts at Buchenwald made it necessary to establish a night watch. For months he volunteered for the extra shift, sitting alone from three to six o'clock in the morning. The only sounds were the snores of sleeping comrades. "What an experience it was," he re-ports, "to sit quietly by a shaded lamp, delving into the pages of Plato's *Dialogues*, Galsworthy's *Swan Song*, or the works of Heine, Klabund, Mehring!"

Elie Wiesel records a poignant scene that occurred when he and hundreds of other Jews were barracked for three days at Gleiwitz, pressed into a room so tightly that many smothered because the sheer mass of human bodies cut off all sources of air. Twisted among the bodies was an emaciated young Warsaw Jew named Ju-liek. Somehow, incredibly, Juliek had clutched his violin to him dur-ing the forced death march through snowstorms to Gleiwitz. That night, crammed among the hundreds of dead and nearly suffocating humans, Juliek struggled free and began to play a fragment from Beethoven's concerto. The sounds were pure, eldritch, misplaced in such a setting.

Wiesel recalls, "It was pitch dark. I could hear only the violin, and it was as though Juliek's soul were the bow. He was playing his life. The whole of his life was gliding on the strings—his lost hopes, his charred past, his extinguished future. He played as he would never play again.... To this day, whenever I hear Beethoven played my eyes close and out of the dark rises the sad, pale face of my Pol-ish friend, as he said farewell on his violin to an audience of dying men.

"I do not know for how long he played. I was overcome by sleep. When I awoke, in the daylight, I could see Juliek, opposite me, slumped over, dead. Near him lay his violin, smashed, trampled, a strange overwhelming little corpse" (*Night*, pp. 107-108).

To me, the scene Wiesel describes stands as a parable of the role of art in the camps. There, death rules. All that is beautiful, joyful, and worthy is removed. Yet the camps contain people, not animals. And amid the shoving and scratching for existence there emerges a rumor of transcendence: the pure, otherworldly tone of a Beethoven violin concerto. From a pragmatic viewpoint, music, art, and poetry seem almost a mockery of the black despair that weighed so heavily on the camps. Yet their existence proves that the human spirit dies as stubbornly as does the body.

The most unexpectedly powerful lesson from the camps is the immortality they reveal. The candle of the image of God implanted within us cannot be snuffed out—not even in the cold, dreadful vacuum of evil where God himself seemed absent.

Hope

Pandora, the mythical first mortal to enter the world, brought with her a box containing all the mortal ills. The last ill remaining after she opened the box was hope. Yes, hope can be a mortal ill.

To the victims of concentration camps, on whom all mortal evils seemed focused as if by the lens of a magnifying glass, hope was sometimes the great destroyer. Why were there not more Jewish uprisings such as the one in Warsaw? Partly because the Jews had too much hope. They could not believe that such inhumanities as the gas chambers existed, despite the rumors sweeping through the Jewish settlements. Elie Wiesel in *Night* tells the story of Moche, an old Jew who miraculously escaped the machine-gun slaughter of Jews near Kolomaye, Poland. He returned to Wiesel's small town in Hungary and went from house to house warning his friends and neighbors of the coming terror.

No one believed Moche. " 'They take me for a madman,' he would whisper, and tears, like drops of wax, flowed from his eyes."

Later, when Wiesel and his town's Jews were jammed into railroad cars and hauled through blizzards toward Poland and Germany, another tried to warn them. Madame Schachter, a woman gone mad, would startle the boxcar occupants by standing at the window and shrieking, " 'Fire! Fire!...Jews, listen to me! I can see a fire! There are huge flames! It is a furnace!' "

No one listened to Madame Schachter either. Four different times she erupted with awful screams. Finally she was tied up in a corner and clubbed. The passengers could not stand the fear and tensions her outbursts caused. They had too much hope to believe the threats of a mad woman—until they pulled into Auschwitz and saw the chthonic flames for themselves.

Yet to the victims of the camps in Germany and Russia, hope was also the daily bread of survival. How can a man condemned to face twenty-five years of hard labor in Siberia make it through a day? He lowers his expectations, sets small goals and achievements for himself, anxiously searches for objects of hope. As Alyosha the Christian explained to Ivan Denisovich, he did not pray for packages or for extra stew or fur mittens. "Of all earthly and mortal things our Lord commanded us to pray only for our daily bread. 'Give us this day our daily bread.' "

Solzhenitsyn's account of one day in the prisoner's life ends with Ivan falling asleep fully content. "He'd had many strokes of luck that day: they hadn't put him in the cells; they hadn't sent his squad to the settlement; he'd swiped a bowl of kasha at dinner; the squad leader had fixed the rates well; he'd built a wall and enjoyed doing it; he'd smuggled that bit of hacksaw blade through; he'd earned a favor from Tsezar that evening; he'd bought that tobacco. And he hadn't fallen ill....

"A day without a dark cloud. Almost a happy day" (*One Day in the Life of Ivan Denisovich*, p. 158).

To those of us who spend our days worrying about excessive static on our car's FM radio, the worn pile on living-room carpets, and the decision of whether to add an extra layer of insulation in the attic, those hopes seem elemental indeed. But such is the nature of the human spirit. It adapts. And the great Solzhenitsyn, as well as the concert violinists, mayors, and artists shipped off to German and Russian camps, adapted downward. Their hopes became visceral and primordial.

Some survivors speak of "the puzzling potential of inner strength" which permitted their bodies to keep warm though the penetrating chill froze the soil and which allowed them to keep a cheerfulness of spirit while surrounded by death and extermination. Virtually all survivors firmly believed the Germans would lose the war, though they were surrounded by evidences of the Germans' strength.

The daily hope is not a foolish, Pollyanna belief that tables will soon be turned and all will be right. It is simply a decision, a mechanism of survival, which feeds a will to live. Solzhenitsyn concludes, "All that the downtrodden can do is go on hoping. *After every disappointment they must find fresh reason for hope.*" And they did.

In addition to this daily hope, however, there surfaced a deeper, more mysteriously uplifting hope—a hope for freedom.

How can any of us in America embrace the deep lust for freedom that fuels the inmates of concentration camps? We can read a thousand pages of Solzhenitsyn's accounts within the gray walls and then stumble upon his descriptions of those first few days outside. We can watch freedom-crazed Papillon, old and hobbled, as he dives off the one-hundred-foot cliff into the raging ocean. Or perhaps, we can gaze on the freeze-frame on which the movie *Midnight Express* ends: Billy Hayes in his stolen guard uniform leaping for joy as he steps into the bright sunlight outside the brutal Turkish prison.

Freedom. To those visionaries who have felt it drained from them, freedom is worth all enduring. To a committed escaper, two days outside the camp are worth any quantity of torture and beatings back inside.

Embarrassed, we wonder why Solzhenitsyn wags his finger at us, as he did at Harvard, for flaunting our freedom to the world and not caring enough to bring it to people who have been deprived.

Solzhenitsyn participated in one strangely defiant act of freedom: a hunger strike. That freedom was a self-inflicted punishment, but it was the only form of protest that could not be stopped. At least a man has control over whether he opens his mouth to keep alive.

"This was a hunger strike called not by well-fed people with reserves of subcutaneous fat, but by gaunt, emaciated men, who had felt the whip of hunger daily for years on end, who had achieved with difficulty some sort of physical equilibrium, and who suffered acute distress if they were deprived of a single 100-gram ration. Even the goners starved with the rest, although a three-day fast might tip them into irreversible and fatal decline. The food which we had refused, and which we had always thought so beggarly, was a mirage of plenty in the feverish dreams of famished men....

"But there was a sort of satisfaction in this feeling of hopelessness. We had taken a futile, a desperate step; it could only end badly—and that was good. Our bellies were empty, our hearts were in our boots—*but some higher need was being satisfied*" (*Gulag III*, pp. 258-259).

Much later Solzhenitsyn participated in a new kind of freedom. He walked outside, his sentence completed.

"And off I *walk*! I wonder whether everybody knows the meaning of this great free world. I am walking along *by myself!* With no automatic rifles threatening me, from either flank or from the rear. I look behind me: no one there! If I like, I can take the right-hand side, past the school fence, where a big pig is rooting in a puddle. And if I like, I can walk on the left, where hens are strutting and scratching immediately in front of the District Education Department....

"I cannot sleep! I walk and walk and walk in the moonlight. The donkeys sing their song. The camels sing. Every fiber in me sings: I am free! I am free!" (*Gulag III*, pp. 417, 20).

What is it that allows an Ivan Denisovich to go to bed fully content at night? What sparks a hunger strike by three hundred gaunt and starving men?

The experience of hope beyond all hoping, pregnant with symbolism, and the lust for freedom that burns inside the victims of the camp are further rumors of transcendence, evidences of the image of God stamped indelibly upon the human spirit. For God invested in humans such a potent dose of freedom that they ultimately perverted it to create the very camps which try to eliminate it.

Freedom has its abuses, of course. As C. S. Lewis said about democracy, we should seek it not because it is a romanticized ideal, but because we cannot entrust one person or a few with the precious gifts of power and freedom; we must spread them among the many.

One step beyond even the hope that expresses itself in a zeal for freedom is the religious hope that prevails among victims of the camps. "When things are bad," Solzhenitsyn said, "we are not ashamed of our God. We are only ashamed of Him when things go well."

Bruno Bettelheim, a psychologist and survivor of the camps, states flatly, "It is a well-known fact of the concentration camps that those who had strong religious and moral convictions managed life there much better than the rest. Their beliefs, including belief in an afterlife, gave them a strength to endure which was far above that of most others."

Demonstrating the same phenomenon, Terrence Des Pres quotes an unnamed survivor in his book *The Survivor*.

> Pain and...fear...kept us awake. A cloudless sky, thickly set with glittering stars, looked in upon our grief-filled prison. The moon shone through the window. Its light was dazzling that night and gave

the pale, wasted faces of the prisoners a ghostly appearance. It was as if all the life had ebbed out of them. I shuddered with dread, for it suddenly occurred to me that I was the only living man among corpses.

All at once the oppressive silence was broken by a mournful tune. It was the plaintive tones of the ancient "Kol Nidre" prayer. I raised myself up to see whence it came. There, close to the wall, the moonlight caught the uplifted face of an old man, who, in self-forgetful, pious absorption, was singing softly to himself.... His prayer brought the ghostly group of seemingly insensible human beings back to life. Little by little, they all roused themselves and all eyes were fixed on the moonlight-flooded face.

We sat up very quietly, so as not to disturb the old man, and he did not notice that we were listening.... When at last he was silent, there was exaltation among us, an exaltation which men can experience only when they have fallen as low as we had fallen and then, through the mystic power of a deathless prayer, have awakened once more the world of the spirit (*The Survivor*, pp. 92-93).

Religious hope did not survive for everyone. To some, the tragedy of the camps was final proof that God did not care about the human plight. But to others, in Stalin's Russia and Hitler's Germany, religious faith was a hope that could not be extinguished. Rumors of freedom and amnesties came and went: God could be hoped for forever, even though he seemed very distant at the time.

Resisting

We have surveyed some of the more remarkable effects of concentration camps on their victims. Contrary to expectations, the victims did not lose their identities and become faceless, docile automatons. Many showed individual acts of courage and self-sacrifice. Within them a highly developed sense of morality continued, so much so that they emerged with more of a gnawing sense of guilt than did their oppressors. Also, an appreciation for art and beauty flourished, even in the drab grayness of the camps.

Finally, a deep expression of hope and a lust for freedom characterized the victims. All of these point to the immortal human spirit. Unlike animals bred in a zoo, people never lose sight of their higher destiny. They never learn to *belong* to the camps.

Yet, that uplifting conclusion is far from satisfying. Solzhenitsyn emerged a stronger man—but what of his fellow *zeks* who died? Elie Wiesel today stirs the world's emotions with his memories of suffering—but what of the dead ones Wiesel describes? Six million Jews were killed; only 1 percent of that number were liberated from the camps.

And what of those who are permanently scarred? Some live with terror in their eyes, unable to cope with the outside world, incapable of trust. The sight of a German shepherd dog reduces them to trembling.

The message of *One Day in the Life of Ivan Denisovich* is that an iron will, some luck, and perhaps God can get you through one day in the concentration camps. But a larger question resounds. *Who will get you out?*

In the spring of 1978, while the TV series *The Holocaust* was being shown, my church introduced a service of identification for the Jews who suffered, a Yom HaShoah liturgy for Christians. Various members of the congregation, including children, read us voices from the survivors: Chaim Kaplan's diary in the Warsaw ghetto, a child's poem about the absence of butterflies in the ghetto, Viktor Frankl's observations as a prison doctor, Elie Wiesel's poignant tales, Nelly Sach's poem about the crematorium chimneys, and a selection called "Why Do the Christians Hate Us?" from André Schwarz-Bart's novel *The Last of the Just*.

The congregation sat quietly while each of the readings was given. A few people had to leave when the descriptions became too graphic. A friend thoughtfully absorbed all that was said, and after the service gave me this reaction: "Something pains me more than all the agony and guilt I feel hearing those voices of the Jews. All I can do for them is empathize and feel sorry. What really bothers me is how many situations like that we are ignoring now. It's easy to blame the Christians in World War II for not acting quicker, more decisively. But are we reacting today—what about recent situations such as in Cambodia and Uganda? Should we be having services about those places instead?"

The facts of the Jewish concentration camps were published in great detail in advertisements in the *New York Times* as early as 1939. Yet few believed them, no one responded, and the United States did not even enter the war until two years later, after a direct attack by the Japanese.

Outside of Auschwitz, I have said, there is a field covered with twelve inches of fine bone loam, the remains of sixty thousand Jews burned there. Yet three million Cambodians were killed in our own day. How did we respond?

A tormenting question echoes and re-echoes throughout the third volume of Solzhenitsyn's *Gulag Archipelago*: "Did I do enough to resist?" Survivors of the camps seem tortured with that issue. Yet to those of us on the outside, our attitude is seen in the fact that Solzhenitsyn's publisher delayed publication of volume three for almost two years, because American readers had grown bored with Solzhenitsyn's descriptions of the camps, and volume two was not proving profitable.

Appeals for direct intervention in places like Uganda and Cambodia by the radical right, or even by people like Senator George McGovern, evoke either self-righteous indignation ("Didn't you learn from the experience of Vietnam?") or a prolonged yawn. Who cares?

Yet an unavoidable conclusion from the camps seems to be that one lesson is more important than all others: justice must come from the outside. All victims of a camp are apocalyptic—they can only wait for relief from an outside force. No amount of morality or courage, no sense of beauty or infection of hope, will assure their survival apart from the outside force. For the overwhelming majority, survival depends on the destruction of the concentration camp world. The main issue is not what the prisoners can do—they are impotent—but the need to overcome in some way the perpetrators of the camp.

Until the Allied liberation, of all the millions of Jews imprisoned, only three had managed to escape—the German camps were that efficient.

Solzhenitsyn uses the example of the Kengir camp rebellion as the dramatic keystone of his third volume. Did they do enough to resist? They took over the camp at Kengir for six weeks, tearing down walls, marrying one another, establishing their own government and laws—all, of course, within the confines of the barbed-wire borders. Yet even Kengir lasted for just six weeks. Tanks and machine guns moved in, manifesting in a few tragic hours just how puny and futile that stirring attempt had been.

The cries of the survivors—Solzhenitsyn, Bettelheim, and the others—are so compelling one would expect them to unite a free world against tyranny of all forms. And yet the opposite is true. Jimmy Carter was scorned for foolishly trying to inject morality into foreign policy, daring to let issues of torture and human rights interfere with the more weighty matters of trade.

If today we uncovered genocide on the scale of the persecution of Jews by Nazi Germany, would we respond? Should we? To me, this is the complex, but inescapable, issue that rises like a flame from the ruins of the concentration camps. And it is an issue we are politely ignoring. After reading dozens of accounts of the German and Russian tragedies, I have recoiled with indignation against the evil they comprise. Yet almost immediately, subtle forces enter in to soften the anger, soothe it away, ease me back to complacency. I have tried to identify those forces.

1. First, there is the simple fact that a person who is warm finds it hard to understand one who is cold. Solzhenitsyn himself, a bulwark of unflagging resistance against oppression, found this process seep into his consciousness after he gained respectability in the Khrushchev era and his novel *One Day in the Life of Ivan Denisovich* was printed by the national magazines. He was called into the opulent bureaucratic headquarters in Red Square to testify about the injustices he had seen and felt. He gave his report to understanding technocrats who had reasonable answers to all his protests. "And indeed," he records, "seen from this bright, festive room, from these comfortable armchairs, to the accompaniment of their smoothly flowing eloquence, the camps look not horrible but quite rational. . . . Well, would *you* let these terrible people loose on the community?" (*Gulag III*, p. 500).

Wary of the dangers of forgetting, Solzhenitsyn started an annual ritual on the anniversary of his arrest. He established "a *zek's* day": in the morning he cut off 650 grams of bread for his daily ration and for lunch fixed himself some broth and a ladleful of thin mush. And, he reported, by the end of the day he "was already picking up crumbs to put in my mouth, and licking the bowl. The old sensations start up vividly."

This phenomenon of numbness to suffering showed itself shortly before World War II, as Joe Bayly pointed out in an *Eternity* magazine column. President Roosevelt and other world leaders met at Evian-les-Bains, France, in July of 1938 to discuss Hitler's encroachments on Austria and his maltreatment of Jews in Germany. Their efforts were futile. "More than any other factor," wrote one correspondent, the conference "underwrote the death warrant for six million European Jews."

That same correspondent, the Manchester *Guardian's* Peggy Mann, recently visited the resort area and talked to one employee who remembered the conference well. He recalled, "Very important people were here and all the delegates had a nice time. They took pleasure cruises on the lake. They gambled at night in the casino. They took mineral baths and massages at the *Establissement Thermal*. Some of them took the excursion to Chamonix to go summer skiing. Some went riding; we have, you know, one of the finest stables in France. Some played golf. We have a beautiful course overlooking the lake.

"Meetings? Yes, some attended the meetings. But, of course, it is difficult to sit indoors hearing speeches when all the pleasures that Evian offers are waiting outside."

The conference ended: immigration quotas were not changed to allow more Jews to escape to freedom, and Hitler was not censured.

And, I might add, it is difficult to sit indoors reading about the suffering and oppressed of the world when all the pleasures that America offers are waiting right outside.

2. Our resistance to fury at oppression has been aided, I think, by a mostly healthy reaction to our bumbling in Vietnam. Most people admit our policy there was mistaken in some way—either in conception or technique. Combining that experience with the one in Korea, we learned our nation cannot be policeman to the world. And now, as conflagrations flare around the world, especially in Central America and the Middle East, America takes a strident but muscleless posture. (The Soviet Union, of course, has cleverly gotten around the problem by paying our Cuban neighbors to the south to help carry out its foreign policy.)

Solzhenitsyn dares to hammer home at what he sees is the logical consequence of this reaction. In his Harvard speech he thundered,

> The most cruel mistake occurred with the failure to understand the Vietnam War. Some people sincerely wanted all wars to stop just as soon as possible; others believed that there should be room for national, or Communist, self-determination in Vietnam, or in Cambodia, as we see today with particular clarity. But members of the U.S. anti-war movement wound up being involved in the betrayal of Far Eastern nations, in a genocide and in the suffering today imposed on 30 million people there. Do these convinced pacifists hear the moans coming from there? Do they understand their responsibility today? Or do they prefer not to hear? The American intelligentsia lost its nerve, and as a consequence thereof danger has come much closer to the United States. But there is no awareness of this. Your short-

sighted politicians who signed the hasty Vietnam capitulation seemingly gave America a carefree breathing spell; however, a hundred-fold Vietnam now looms over you.

Solzhenitsyn drew those conclusions; I am not ready to. But I admit to being affected by a reaction against our country's failures in the past. A dog bitten by a snake is less apt to chase snakes again.

3. A latent pacifism has gained ground in Christian circles, especially in Europe but increasingly now in America also.

In September of 1978, *Sojourners* magazine ran an article entitled "Security in a Nuclear World," by the Rev. Gordon Cosby. In it Cosby argued that our dependence on spending billions for national defense is "a negation of biblical faith."

"One thing history confirms," he continues. "The nation who trusts in anything other than God is abandoned by God. Every attempt at security fails because God abandons that people. We feel that the danger of extinction is being held back by 9,500 missiles. They are not holding anything back. God in his mercy is holding it back. The missiles are the vials of his wrath waiting to be overturned. We would be safer without them."

I wondered why Mr. Cosby didn't apply the same logic to other areas of life. Am I mocking God and showing my lack of faith by locking my door at night? Am I mocking God by putting a new roof over my house? Should I instead trust him to send the weather that is best to me? Do our fire departments, police departments, and laws mock God? Would we be safer without them? Or do these means assist us in coping with a fallen world?

Christians who support the military do not support it, one would hope, for a great love of bloodshed and violence. They do so, sadly, as an expression of the restraints needed to contain the forces of evil which, unchecked, can create such monstrosities as the concentration camps. The term *just war* is a misnomer. No war is just, but Christians through the centuries have concluded that the results of fighting some wars are more just than the injustices the war is waged to overcome.

Today the trend is to emphasize the injustices of wars. Author Kurt Vonnegut dwells on the Dresden bombing of World War II rather than the liberation aspects. In the film *Seven Beauties*, Lina Wertmuller states her case superbly. By interspersing scenes from the concentration camps with scenes of American soldiers a-whoring through the streets of Naples, she seems to imply that those Americans who fought fascism were as bad, really, as the forces they defeated. She seems to say that nothing makes any difference— Hitler or his demise, the camps or their liberation. Tragedy, comedy, and injustice are found equally in all of them.

Bruno Bettelheim, a survivor of the camps, wrote a stinging denunciation of *Seven Beauties* in his lengthy *New Yorker* essay "Surviving," later published in *Surviving and Other Essays*. He concluded the piece with this paragraph:

> Our experience did not teach us that life is meaningless, that the world of the living is but a whorehouse, that one ought to live by the body's crude claims, disregarding the compulsions of culture. It taught us that, miserable though the world in which we live may be, the difference between it and the world of the concentration camps is as great as that between night and day, hell and salvation, death and life. It taught us that there is meaning to life, difficult though that meaning may be to fathom—a much deeper meaning than we had thought possible before we became survivors. And our feeling of guilt for having been so lucky as to survive the hell of the concentration camp is a most significant part of this meaning—testimony to a humanity that not even the abomination of the concentration camp can destroy (*Surviving*, pp. 313-4).

Christ came into the Gulag of earth to release the captives and to bring freedom to the enslaved, and he left us with the charge to make that our mission. The survivors of the concentration camps show the worthiness of the project Jesus left with us. Their morality, art, and sense of hope are glimmers of the immortal soul within them, souls worth freeing and redeeming, even when it sometimes involves great cost.

A passive watching of the diminution of freedom is far easier than a committed protest. The lesson of the camps teaches me that we dare not to abrogate our responsibility and pretend that the lessons from the camps are mere history lessons.

They came printed on direct mail appeals, sometimes indiscreetly staring out from the cover envelopes—the babies with distended stomachs, runny eyes, and pencil-thin arms and legs. At first East Asian children filled our mailboxes, then Indochinese, now African. One-third of the world goes to bed hungry each night, we're told, and a cloud of guilt hangs over sensitive Americans.

In 1981, a relief organization invited me to see the relief work in Somalia, which was then being described as a basket-case country comprising the worst human suffering in the world. I expected to return from Somalia with a visceral knot of despair. Instead, I came away encouraged by the commitment and efficiency of relief agencies, yet simultaneously nonplused by the unsolvable problems of development. Because relief work is such a booming business in the evangelical world, it's time we all became more aware of how our money is being used.

Just This Side of Hell

THE ROAD from Mogadishu to Halba Camp begins as a strip of macadam laid incongruously across the vacant Somalian desert. A flat, sere landscape is interrupted by occasional stands of acacia trees and giant red ant hills that jut abruptly upward like impressionistic sand castles. Few animals cross the road. Giraffes and elephants were killed off long ago. Now only the ugly and the fleet remain: cartoonish warthogs with their sinister tusks and a peculiar style of running with tails held vertically erect, and the diminutive dik-diks, antelope measuring only fourteen inches high.

Along this road ten marabou storks, four to five feet tall, were standing in a characteristic cross-legged posture. Unlike the beautiful, elegant creatures of legends, the marabou is more of a vulture poorly disguised as a stork. Its plumage is indeed a lush turquoise, displayed in the stork's odd practice of facing the sun with both wings spread, like a fully-robed pope blessing the masses. But the head attached to that hunchbacked trunk of feathers is all vulture: red, wrinkled, bug-eyed, and bald, with a protruding bill designed to rip apart carrion.

These marabou had gathered around a pool of water with a diameter of maybe twenty feet. We stopped the Land Cruiser and walked toward the water, where the fetid stench of death hung heavy. The evaporating pool contained two kinds of fish: a nondescript silvery variety and shiny black catfish—thousands of fish in all, piled together so densely that the top layer was completely out of the water. Thousands more, dead and dying, lined the muddy sides of the pool. As the land-locked fish near the edges scrabbled desperately back toward the water, the incessant flapping of thousands of fins gave an eerie background accompaniment to the smell and sight of

139

death. The storks stood by quietly, waiting. They had eaten their fill and would do so for many days until the pool dried up and no fish were left to die.

That water hole was the only one we passed on an eight-hour trip, and I thought of it often as I observed what was happening in the African nation of Somalia. An ancient and handsome people were nearly marooned in a land of vanishing resources. For three straight years in the late seventies it did not rain in Somalia, and potholes, lakes, and even the two significant rivers dried up. (Somali children count their birthdays only in years when it rains, and today if you ask an eight-year-old girl her age she will likely reply "three.") Water is only one of the endangered resources. Trees are disappearing too, at an alarming rate. The ones that remain are being cut for firewood, and few new trees are growing. They stopped propagating after the elephants were killed off by the ivory hunters. Before then, the elephants would munch vegetation, digest it, and deposit the seeds in moist clumps of fertilizer all over Somalia. No longer.

Somalia can barely feed its people in the best of years. Only 15 percent of the land is arable, and that consists of a terribly thin layer of topsoil that must be carefully cultivated. But now the scourges of drought, famine, and war have placed the country on the edge of disaster. Because of a war with Ethiopia, a million and a half penniless refugees streamed into the country, many of them a few days away from starvation. No one knows the nonrefugee population of Somalia, but estimates range between four and five million. Any nation would find it difficult to absorb a sudden 30 percent irruption of population, but for Somalia it is impossible. Somalia ranks as the fourth or fifth poorest country in the world, depending on the list, with an average annual income of $115.

When I visited, Somalia contained the greatest concentration of refugees in the world, and as a result it is the center of a great flurry of relief activity. The familiar ones are prominent: the Red Cross, Church World Service, the Swiss government—logos that follow disasters across the globe. The United Nations High Commission on Refugees, recipient of the 1981 Nobel Peace Prize, coordinates the forty refugee camps. But the most visible relief activity involves a new breed of Christian organizations, mostly evangelical: World Vision, the Mennonite Central Committee, World Concern, American Friends' Service Committee, International Christian Aid, MAP International, Seventh-Day Adventist World Service, Food for the

Hungry, Tear Fund, the Assemblies of God, and the Southern Baptist Convention.

Muslim Somalia might seem an unlikely place to find such a hum of Christian activity, since estimates of the Somali Christian population range from fourteen to fifty people. (Precise numbers are difficult to determine since "closet Christians" exist and some avowed Christians are probably secret police.) The presence of so many organizations reflects a remarkable development in the giving habits of American Christians. While the media have eagerly chronicled the rise of the Moral Majority and television evangelists in the United States, few observers have noticed a simultaneous explosion in growth among organizations committed to Christian relief and development work overseas. Two examples: World Vision, based in Monrovia, California, has seen its income zoom from $30 million in 1975 to $150 million in 1982. World Concern, headquartered in Seattle, started with a $67,000 budget in 1975, which now exceeds $15 million. It's boom time for relief work, and nonprofit agencies descend on ailing countries such as Somalia, Ethiopia, and Sudan with the same enthusiasm that multinational companies show toward economically healthy Third World countries.

The new wave of Christian relief agencies got valuable experience in the refugee camps of Indochina. Fund-raising departments were amazed at how much money flowed in to support their efforts as photos of sad-eyed Vietnamese, Cambodian, and Laotian children filled the pages of news magazines, newspapers, and direct mail appeals, touching the raw nerve of a nation haunted by Vietnam. The horrible drama of the boat people began, and refugee camps were quickly set up in Malaysia, the Philippines, Singapore, Hong Kong, and Thailand. There, the Christian agencies demonstrated that their personnel had at least as much stamina, motivation, and sensitivity as the old pros at the United Nations and Red Cross. When Somalia slid toward chaos, the United Nations readily agreed to coordinate efforts of the full spectrum of Christian relief agencies.

Initially, Somalia appeared to be a disturbingly familiar mirror image of the Indochina problem: hundreds of thousands of starving and malnourished refugees trudging, homeless, into a country ill-equipped to receive them. But the relief agencies quickly discovered that Somalia, unlike Indochina, lacked the basic infrastructure to support a major refugee operation. In Thailand, if an agency wanted fifty trucks to transport food, a few calls to Bangkok would secure them. In Somalia, fifty trucks were hardly available in the entire country, and there would probably be no gasoline to power them. There were no rice fields nearby, no abundant fruit trees, no roads to many of the refugee camps, no building materials, no warehouses full of medicine. Everything had to be brought in from the outside.

The situation demanded immediate action and the logistics required a massive infusion of outside aid, but one major hurdle remained. The leaders of relief organizations all knew that Americans did not normally contribute to projects in Africa. Some professionals warned of an intrinsic racism that could not be overcome. To complicate matters, the Somalian government followed a rigidly Marxist line of "scientific socialism." How could organizations plunge into one of the most expensive relief projects in history with no guarantee of proper support?

Somalia itself provided the answer, with a spectacular political somersault. For almost a decade after a military coup in 1969, Somalia had operated as a client state of the Soviet Union, welcoming Soviet advisers and giving them vital military bases positioned on the horn of Africa, which guards the oil fields of the Arabian Peninsula. In 1977–1978 Somalia engaged Ethiopia in a vicious war over the Ogaden Desert, homeland of ethnic Somali nomads. In carving up Africa, colonial powers had ceded the Ogaden to Ethiopia, and Somalia was breaking a golden rule of Africa by tampering with existing borders to consolidate its land.

A bloody military coup in Ethiopia, however, ushered in a heavy Soviet presence in that country also, and soon the Soviet Union found itself in the untenable position of propping up two antagonists. Moscow chose to back the larger and more populous country of Ethiopia, and Somalia promptly expelled Soviets from its soil. As Cuban troops and Soviet MIGs mopped up pockets of resistance in the Ogaden, Somalia resigned itself to a guerrilla war and performed a diplomatic about-face. It offered the United States access to military bases that had been built to Soviet specifications in return for forty-two million dollars in military aid. Somalia also became the only member of the Arab League to defend Egypt and support the Camp David peace treaty. Fund-raising for Somalia was given an obvious boost by its sudden emergence as "our strategic ally on the vital Horn of Africa." Money for relief work poured in.

The sudden plunge into relief work in countries like Somalia has altered the nature of Christian mission overseas. World Vision, the largest evangelical relief agency, had intended to include proclamation of the Christian message as a major thrust in all of its programs. But recent political events forced directors to amend that policy. In 1975, for example, World Vision built a seventy-five-bed children's hospital in Cambodia, fully equipped with state-of-the-art medical technology. Days before its scheduled opening, the Cambodian government was overthrown, and Phnom Penh became a deserted wasteland. Eventually, of course, Pol Pot's government also fell after an unprecedented reign of terror. And, while most of the world community, including the United States, was harshly condemning Vietnam for its occupation of Cambodia (now Kampuchea), in 1979 World Vision negotiated an agreement to return to Phnom Penh. It took an additional $1.1 million to finally open the hospital. In order to work in such countries as Kampuchea, World Vision had to agree not to attempt any proselytism or promulgation of the Christian faith.

Each of the Christian agencies in Somalia must similarly restrict its activities—the Somalian constitution forbids Christian evangelism. Somehow the Somalian government obtained an internal memo of one U.S.-based relief agency which reported that staff "have had extra time recently to witness for Christ." The organization was very nearly thrown out of the country. Christians sharing food and medicines is one thing; ideas are an entirely different matter.

The leaders of evangelical agencies who agree to such conditions justify it in two ways. Some talk in hushed tones about a grand strategy to "soften up" the Moslem (or Communist) world for future Christian penetration. "After all," the president of one group commented, "nothing has worked for those people in the entire history of missions. At least we are allowed into those countries which are sealed off from traditional missionaries."

Others, however, profess no ulterior motives, viewing their activities as a natural expression of Christian love and mercy. The president of World Concern, Arthur Beals, credits the boom in relief work to a raised consciousness among evangelical Christians. "In the early part of this century, when the fundamentalists split with liberals, they rejected not only liberal theology but also the liberal commitment to social action for the poor and oppressed. Somehow those actions seemed less Christian than direct evangelism. Fortunately, that has changed in recent years. People have come to realize that when Jesus fed the five thousand or healed ten lepers he did not first distribute questionnaires to determine the beliefs of his audience. In fact, 75 percent of Jesus' recorded ministry was to meet physical and material needs. Relief work is not a question of being a liberal or conservative, but rather of being faithful to Christ's example."

Beals traces his own enlightenment in the sixties to the influence of his son Mark, who participated in rousing antiwar demonstrations and headed a group called Evangelicals for Social Action. While working as a Baptist pastor in Portland, Beals was also affected by Oregon's Senator Mark Hatfield, who has become something of a guru to the followers of Christian humanism.

World Concern, a mid-sized but rapidly expanding Christian relief agency, was one of those called upon to respond to the refugees' plight in Somalia. In April 1981 World Concern workers agreed to administer medical aid at one particular camp, Halba 1, just forty miles inside the Ethiopian border. In many ways their experience serves as a microcosm of relief work in Somalia, the type of work that lurches into action whenever a major disaster strikes.

While visiting a project in Kenya in April 1981, Arthur Beals received an emergency message from his coordinator for Somalia. Come quickly, the message said. Morale is scraping bottom. The staff is on the verge of quitting in despair. Beals flew to Mogadishu and took the road to Halba, some 250 miles long, which is paved only halfway. The remainder follows a back-wrenching, rutted trail through unmarked wilderness. In 1981, in contrast to recent years, the rains came to Somalia and the ruts disappeared. Simply getting to the Halba camp was an arduous ordeal. Beals' trip from Mogadishu took eleven hours, including an unscheduled one-hour stop when the Land Cruiser became trapped in a mud pit. Fortunately, a Somalian bus got stuck also, and Beals mustered forty Somalis to help pull his Land Cruiser from the mud.

At Halba, Beals met with his staff of seven who were at the point of frenzy. They had contracted to administer medical help only; another organization was to handle food distribution. But medical supplies ordered months before had not yet arrived, and no food had reached Halba in five days. Sixty thousand refugees were ready to mutiny. When Beals was shown the site where World Concern staffers hoped to erect a makeshift clinic, an old man rushed up to the group, shaking a stick, and screamed, "We don't need a clinic! We need food. Can't you see our babies are starving?" As if to support his words, several Somali women silently pulled out their breasts to show how flat and milkless they were. Other women begged the Americans to take their children away to another country where they would have a chance to survive.

The seven people from World Concern insisted to Beals that they could not possibly provide medical care for sixty thousand people, 70 percent of whom were suffering from severe malnutrition. At least thirty babies were dying each day in the Halba camp. Cut off from supplies, the relief workers had even less hope for solutions than the refugees themselves.

The rain had brought a plague of flies and mosquitoes. Scores of flies swarmed over every refugee child's face, clogging up nasal passages and crawling across the surfaces of unblinking eyes. Dazed and lethargic, the children did not react. The camp doctor, an American, had to take care when sewing up cuts to assure that no flies were caught under his patients' skin flaps before he pulled them together for the stitches. During the daylight hours, when flies were worst, the relief workers could hardly eat without getting a mouthful of flies. The doctor would hold a peanut butter cracker in one hand, between his shirt and bare skin, then stuff his head inside the shirt for a quick bite.

Medically, Halba Camp was hell on earth. Dysentery, whooping cough, measles, diphtheria, and tuberculosis were breaking out everywhere, their symptoms complicated by the malnutrition. Supplies were hopelessly inadequate.

Beals acted quickly upon returning to Mogadishu. Despite gnawing reservations, he accepted the Somalian government's request that World Concern take over food distribution in addition to medical care and also supervise Halba 2, the refugee camp directly adjacent to Halba 1. It did not take long to track down the mystery of missing food shipments. In those days, corrupt distributors were siphoning off up to 60 percent of all food supplies. Trucks would pull off Somalian highways and openly sell food intended for refugee camps. After numerous complaints, the United Nations Commission appointed a responsible agency to supervise distribution and restore integrity to that system.

Medical supplies and equipment for workers were harder to come by. The most convenient, quickest source was South Africa, but getting anything from South Africa into another African country was problematic. In view of the desperate conditions, World Concern took the risk and ordered $17,000 in supplies. But the Somalian government refused to allow the shipments in, and $17,000 of life-saving supplies ended up in warehouses in Rome. At great expense Beals had the supplies shipped from Rome to London, where the labels of origination were changed, and then back to Somalia. When the shipment arrived in Mogadishu, however, one-half the boxes still bore a damning "Product of South Africa" stamp. The government confiscated those boxes; the others finally made it to Halba.

Back in the United States, Beals put together an emergency team of ten medical workers, by seconding some from a Dutch organization and recruiting two American nurses. He instructed all World Concern workers entering Somalia to carry in one thousand pounds of supplies as overweight baggage, at exorbitant prices. Within four weeks a vital supply link from the West to Halba Camp was in place. World Concern headquarters in Seattle packed a forty-foot steel trailer with medicines, food, furniture, a refrigerator and stove and an automobile. Two Toyota Land Cruisers were shipped through the free port of Djbouti.

After just six months of intense effort a remarkable transformation took place at Halba. Soon, the refugee camp appeared as a series of igloo shapes that hugged the horizon and stretched out in hummocky rows for miles in every direction. In Somalia, fortunately, the refugees provide their own housing. Many come with a bundle of sticks lashed to a camel or donkey. Refugees without animals simply wander off until they find enough sticks and brush to make a home. After selecting a site, the refugees bend the sticks toward the center of a circle and fashion a dome by wattling other vines through the supporting sticks. Grass, burlap, plastic, or paper is woven through the sticks or thrown over the top, as protection from the elements. From the distance, all the clustered huts appear identical, like some Boy Scout Jamboree with standard-issue shelters, but up close they are seen as custom-made.

A plume of dust announces a visitor's presence miles in advance. Upon the arrival of any vehicle, scores of children, dressed in rags, fill the dirt paths that wind among the huts. Drivers thread their way carefully through the camp, alert for children who dart out without warning; striking one of them could start a riot. The children clamber around the vehicles, chasing them and giggling loudly. This, says a World Concern worker, is the most noticeable change—six months earlier those malnourished children lived a torpid, almost motionless existence. Now the visible signs of malnutrition have disappeared, and Halba children are as active and exuberant as any on a playground in the United States.

The refugee women stand by their huts to watch the commotion. They have a striking beauty—visitors to Ethiopia and Somalia often remark that women there are the most beautiful in the world. They are tall, often over six feet, and elegantly slim. Years of balancing loads of firewood and buckets of water on their heads have given them perfect posture. A diet of milk and a twig that, when chewed, provides the same benefits as brushing and flossing give them perfect teeth. When Somalis smile, their teeth offer a gleaming contrast to their dark, fine-featured faces. Most refugee women have only one "dress," a brilliantly colored cloth slung over one shoulder and wrapped around the waist. Six months before, they wore colorless rags; the bright cloths indicate a thriving black market in the refugee community, most likely supported by stolen food supplies.

Not much happens in the daily routine of a refugee woman. Gathering firewood and collecting water consume almost all her daylight hours. But every few nights sounds of celebration come from the camp as small clusters of Somalis snake through its labyrinthine paths. Deeply reverbrating drums beat a monotonous rhythm, punctuated by the piercing wail of ululating women (a sound made by trilling the tongue against the roof of the mouth while holding a single high-pitched note). At Halba, such celebrations seldom signify a marriage, because so few men are available to marry. More commonly those sounds mark a circumcision ritual about to be performed on an eight-year-old girl. The camp doctor and nurses frequently treat young girls damaged for life by the effects of an unclean knife which cut off more than the clitoris. To assure chastity until marriage, the women also practice infibulation, in which the vagina is sewn shut with a thorn and thread. Sometimes the thread is pulled so tightly that urination is impeded, and a serious infection results. Relief workers do not even try to interfere with these more gruesome aspects of Somali culture, except by repairing the damage afterwards.

Women and children make up 85 percent of Halba. The scarcity of healthy men is a poignant reminder that Somalia is at war. Some relief workers suspect a high percentage of the men are carrying on a nomadic existence nearby, hiding from the guerrilla recruiters who make unannounced visits and forcibly conscript all males. But some of the men who remain bear unmistakable proof of their involvement in the war. The camp commander, a thin, shifty-eyed soldier in his early twenties, is missing two fingers. Veterans often gather in his tent, fill their metal mugs with Somali tea, and swap war stories. One shows off scars where machine gun bullets hit his thigh, arm, and side. Cuban soldiers gunned down over one hundred people in his village, he says. A hunchbacked old man wearing a turban tells of an atrocity in his village. In it, he lost his two sons, fifteen and seventeen, and therefore his security in old age. "What will happen to me now?" he wonders aloud, his rheumy eyes filling with tears. The other men shake their heads and do not respond.

The war rumbles uncomfortably close to Halba, which lies just forty miles inside the Ethiopian border. Sometimes at night workers at Halba can hear artillery fire. A vital bridge at nearby Lugh links the camp with the rest of Somalia and if that bridge were destroyed, Halba would sit defenseless on the Ethiopian side of the Juba River. Two Russian MIGs made low bombing passes over the bridge one summer, and to everyone's surprise the Somalis scored direct hits on both of them with SAM missiles. One of the MIGs, trailing smoke, banked and headed back toward Ethiopia. The other crash-landed with its Soviet pilot just outside a refugee camp in Lugh. The Soviet pilot held off the curious and hostile refugees with his machine gun for several hours until a helicopter arrived to carry him to safety. But no one worries seriously about the threat of invasion—what would the Cubans or Ethiopians want with a sprawling refugee camp?

In spite of occasional reminders of a lingering war and its recent history of death and despair, Halba camp today seems peaceful and calm. There are no more children with orange hair and bloated bellies, no more old men with wasted flesh clinging to their bones, no more despairing mothers with empty breasts. The women devotedly care for their children, who play games and chase each other through the winding paths of Halba. Older children receive instruction in the Koran at makeshift schools in the camp. One relief worker confided to me his belief that now one-third of the refugees are not primarily victims of war or famine, but rather local nomads who have settled down to enjoy the free services of the stable camp.

In America and Europe, television reports and relief agencies may still depict Somalia as a disaster area with diseases decimating the masses of starving refugees. But those photos and images are mostly dated. They are used because of the sad truth that hope does not raise money. The fact that people are now receiving food and medicine is not a sufficient stimulus for a giving country; crisis appeals to fear and guilt work far better. Therefore, the remarkable improvements made by the relief agencies in Somalia must go largely unreported to donors. Their own success would kill them.

The expatriate staff responsible for such transformations at Halba consists of seven nurses from Holland, a Dutch mechanic nicknamed "Golden Hands," a Finnish midwife and medical director, and twelve Americans (a doctor, four nurses, two community development workers, two cooks, and three support persons). Although living conditions have drastically improved with restored supplies, Halba presents several obstacles to comfort not normally encountered in Finland, Holland, and the United States. First, there is the heat. Somalia has two seasons, rainy and dry, better know as the "mud season" and the "dust season." Since Halba is barely a hundred miles from the Equator, both are mercilessly hot: one, a steamy heat, and the other, a searing heat.

The rainy season brings the flies and mosquitoes. Later, as the rains drift out to sea, strong winds, stirring up choking clouds of dust, dry up most breeding grounds and offer respite from those insects. But in the dry season scorpions emerge from hiding, usually on moonless nights. Sometimes at night the relief workers at Halba hear an eerie, howling sound, like that of a wounded wolf, carrying across the thin desert air. The sound gets louder and louder as its source becomes clear: a nomad, stung by a scorpion, has come to the camp for pain medicine.

After a scorpion stung her arm, one Halba nurse was incapacitated for three days and required a Novocain shot every four hours. She described the pain as "childbirth multiplied by twelve." Halba's only doctor, John Wilson from North Carolina, was stung in the face while sleeping one night. A baby scorpion had crawled up the slope of his tent and then dropped onto his face. He awoke in searing pain, fumbled around for his shoes and flashlight, and went outside to find the nurse for an injection. Just outside the tent he stepped on a squirming five-foot-long poisonous snake. On the path to the nurse's tent he spotted four more scorpions glowing phosphorescently in the darkness. Halba is a far cry from North Carolina. Dr. Wilson gets revenge by collecting scorpion specimens, preserving them in formaldehyde and mounting them. He is proudest of his collection of camel spiders: huge, hairy creatures larger than a man's hand that can inflict a wound as painful as a scorpion's but with toxic side-effects.

Relief workers must also avoid the dangerous crocodiles lurking in the Juba River. African crocodiles grow as long as eighteen feet and weigh up to two tons, yet can maneuver with surprising agility on land. One refugee, a pregnant woman, met her death while bathing in the Juba. Onlookers saw the flash of a horny snout, heard a cry of terror, and watched helplessly as a trail of bubbles disappeared downstream.

The relief workers live on a bluff overlooking the Juba, in an area cordoned off by a crude fence of piled-up thorn bushes. Their canvas tents have been so battered by the wind that zippers and mosquito nets no longer function. A small but thriving vegetable garden grows along the bank of the Juba, a project designed to interest the Somalis in agriculture. Camp workers also have a kitchen, well-stocked with boxed and canned foods, which includes one refrigerator and two stoves. Two roofless latrines stand some distance away.

Even in remote Somalia, a refugee camp is energy-dependent: kerosene for the lamps, propane for the stove, diesel for the water pump. All food is donated by the West, as are medical supplies. The usual nomad/visitor relationship has been reversed. Under normal conditions, nomads would have the advantage over Westerners of being able to live off the land. Now the war and drought and resultant overcrowding have made refugees totally dependent on the relief workers and their steady stream of supplies—an umbilical cord to the West sustains them. "If our supplies were interrupted for a week or ten days," said the Somali camp commander, "people would begin to die."

The daily routine of relief workers begins early, since clinics and food distribution stations open at seven o'clock. From noon until four in the afternoon everyone in the camp, refugee and relief worker alike, withdraws to shade or indoors to avoid the afternoon sun. Another round of work starts at four and lasts until dinnertime at seven. There are few diversions for the relief workers. Except for reading the few well-thumbed books and magazines at Halba, there is little to do. At night they often gather around a campfire, discuss the day, and reminisce about their respective countries. Most also served in Indochina and reflect nostalgically on those days in a less primitive setting. Once every three months the workers get a week in Mogadishu, and after six months, a partially paid vacation in the Seychelles or Nairobi.

What attracts people to a daily regimen of low-paid work under the equatorial sun with few of the amenities of modern life? Dr. John Wilson, a soft-spoken, silver-haired pediatrician from Black Mountain, North Carolina, mentions a sense of duty. "Sometimes I feel like Jonah out here—I came because I thought I should, whether or not I felt like it. My father was a missionary doctor in Korea, beginning in 1907, the only doctor serving five million people. I have worked in Korea also, among ten thousand leprosy patients after the war. Professionally, I've tried a little of everything—a busy private practice, teaching at a university, and working with coal miners. Over the years I've come to believe I ought to tithe not just my money but also my time to God. My wife's health keeps us from living overseas for long periods, so I accept short-term assignments and spend the rest of the year with my practice in North Carolina."

Among other factors, Dr. Wilson refers to the attraction of medical pioneering. "After seeing hundreds of children all year who may have nothing more than a runny nose or a sore throat, it does something to me to come over here and have a part in saving lives." The doctor who preceded Dr. Wilson performed one memorable appendectomy by flashlight inside a tent during a driving rainstorm. He used two tablespoons as retractors and dish towels as sponges. In Somalia, a dental hygienist pulls teeth and performs basic oral surgery. There are no insurance bills to pay, no malpractice suits to worry about. Most relief workers, in fact, are surprised by the resigned fatalism of the Muslim patients, who do not cast blame or complain if a treatment fails. If a baby dies, Allah has willed it.

Dr. Wilson's age is an exception among the relief workers in Somalia. The vast majority are in their early twenties—idealistic, fresh-faced youth who could be posing for a Peace Corps poster. Jeans and T-shirts have become the national uniform of relief work overseas. Lois Kelsey, a twenty-one-year-old blonde who wears her hair in pigtails because Somalis consider it modest, shrugs off the hardships of life in a camp. "How could anyone feel sorry for me?" she says. "Six months ago I was studying nursing in the tree-lined suburb of Oak Park, Illinois. Most of my friends from class are now grinding out the three-to-eleven shift at some hospital. They're the losers. I'm having the adventure of a lifetime—my perspective on the world will never be the same."

Lois grew up in Jordan among Palestinians. "Nomads are wonderful to work with because they are so fiercely independent. They aren't even tempted by a life of material luxuries. They take pride in being able to walk for two days without food and feel no hunger. In Jordan, I saw the tragedy of such people uprooted from their lifestyle and herded into camps. Their families and culture began to disintegrate. I decided back then that I wanted to spend my life trying to interrupt that process of decay in a beautiful culture." At a very early age she took on the goal of working among displaced persons, Muslims, and nomads. In Somalia, she has all three. Lois has high praise for two hundred Somali "health auxiliaries" whom she and the other relief workers supervise.

The government of Somalia observed health care in the refugee camps of Thailand, Bangladesh, Malaysia, and the Philippines and concluded they were too dependent on a Western mode of treatment. Therefore it decreed that most of the health work in the camps be carried out by volunteer Somalis trained to treat the most common ailments. Twenty diseases are officially recognized and posted in bold print in all the clinics. (A category, number twenty-one, is labeled "other".)

Perhaps 10 percent of the refugees, mostly late arrivals, are still affected by malnutrition, and their weakened states make them more susceptible to disease. Sixty thousand people living in close quarters, with poor sanitation, and a breeding ground for flies and mosquitoes nearby, combine in what one camp worker calls "a timebomb of communicable disease." Diseases like measles and whooping cough hit the camp in waves, taking the weak. Nearly every refugee in the camp has some latent form of malaria. Expatriate relief workers drill their Somali volunteers in the symptoms and treatment of those top twenty diseases. The health workers get no pay or special treatment, and they, too, must roam for water and firewood and care for their families. Yet most take their training so seriously that Lois estimates 90 percent of the health work could continue if all expatriates left. "They're the best thing we have going," she says. "We'll all be gone someday, but they will stay. If we do our training right, they can permanently change the culture for good."

In just six months, relief workers have moved Halba Camp from a flashpoint of disaster into an organized community with basic food and medical needs supplied. Short-term emergency goals have been met. A far greater challenge lies ahead: dealing with the long-term implications of the refugee crisis. Indochinese refugee camps were holding stations where refugees waited until Western host countries could absorb them. In contrast, no one is lobbying to relocate Somali refugees in other countries. And yet few observers there judge the nation of Somalia capable of absorbing them. As long as the war drags on, refugees cannot return to their homelands.

Some cynics believe the government of Somalia itself is not overly anxious to solve the refugee problem. Relief work is now the leading source of foreign exchange in the country—business has never been so good in downtown Mogadishu. On one occasion Somalia devalued its currency by fifty percent, which ordinarily would greatly strengthen the dollar there. But the government callously exempted all foreign organizations, so that relief agencies began paying a 100 percent markup on Somali goods.

While Somalia has extended an open hand to scores of relief agencies, which in turn have made giant strides toward stabilizing the refugee problem, every outside interference brings its own long-term consequence. Refugee camps, for example, ruin the grazing capacity of the land. As nomads, Somalis never stayed in one place long enough to cause irreversible damage to vegetation. But drilling a borehole or providing a water supply at a stationary camp allows the livestock and goats to trample the ground until the root systems of vegetation are destroyed. A seeming improvement, a well, actually proves destructive.

The communal search for firewood also denudes the landscape. Halba Camp was first located in the shade of a forest, an unheard-of luxury among Somalia's camps. Each month, however, the number of trees shrinks as refugees ignore rules and tear down remaining trees. Refugees must now walk eight miles for firewood. Soon they will walk ten, then twelve. Goats and donkeys will eat the new green shoots of trees, and in a few years the forest will vanish forever, replaced by the desert. For the people at Halba to survive, massive changes must come. But no one seems very sure what those changes should be.

The camp director has one idea: he is now teaching Halba's children to fish in the Juba, where a fast-growing species called *talapia* abounds. Somalis in the camp have never tasted fish—hundreds starved to death within sight of a river glutted with them. The children are trying the new idea, to the disdain of their parents. Agriculture faces even greater resistance. Before returning to the United States, Dr. Wilson sketched out a crude design for a passive flow irrigation system. The Juba falls sharply near Halba, and a pipe buried in the river upstream could follow a downward slant and provide energy-free water for irrigation. If money can be found, the Halba workers may install such a system. But there is no guarantee that the Somalis will use it. Their abhorrence of the settled agricultural life runs very deep. None of them has shown any interest in the camp garden.

"Water is the best feature of Halba Camp," says Dr. Wilson, "but it is also the biggest health problem. We could probably prevent half the illnesses in this camp if we could just teach the refugees not to drink the river water. We have a German-built filtration system that pumps river water through three treatment tanks. It's not totally pure—if we purify it completely, then the infants will grow accustomed to distilled water and will build up no resistance to the germs they'll find in water when they leave the camp. But the refugees at the extremities face a difficult choice. Should they take our advice and walk three or five miles for filtered water, carrying a heavy load back to their huts? Or should they do as they have always done and scoop it from the river a few hundred yards from their homes? So far, only a few of our Somali health workers have been effective in warning them against drinking the river water."

Relief workers don't talk much about another problem that, to their executive officers back in the United States, looms as the largest long-term problem of all. Will fickle American givers, who underwrite all their salaries and life-giving supplies, grow tired of Somalia? The Ethiopian crisis brought in a new unprecedented flood of contributions. But will interest last? Relief organizations are at the mercy of the cruel realities of fund-raising. They need a crisis atmosphere to sustain interest in their project.

Fund-raising techniques vary across continental lines. In Europe, an anti-Communist appeal brings in millions of dollars. Underground Evangelism supports a relief agency in Somalia called International Christian Aid by telling of exploits of smuggling Bibles behind the Iron Curtain. Australia and New Zealand have the most demanding donors, say the experts. They want hard, discriminating facts about specific relief projects. But Americans require emotional heat: tearful white bwanas holding dying infants in their arms and looking pleadingly into the camera lenses. European photographers don't usually perform well for American fund-raisers—their photos are too "pretty" and landscapy, not emotionally gripping enough.

Fund-raising, like any fifty-billion-dollar industry, operates according to scientifically measured principles. The Preview House in Hollywood can judge the relative appeal of a fund-raising approach. There, 450 carefully selected people sit in chairs and react to visual clips by moving a response dial from "low interest" to "high interest." Computers in adjacent rooms integrate the response data, combine it with demographic information, and read out exactly what slant appeals to each category of person. Children are the biggest draw, which is why so many of them stare out from the pages of slick magazines appealing for funds. A bona fide celebrity also helps. Commercials are measured in that room, as are soap opera segments and television quiz shows. And there America's fund-raisers keep confirming the inescapable reality that emotional appeals based on guilt sell, not development projects based on hope and an improved lifestyle.

The executive director of one major relief organization, who asked not to be identified, expressed his dilemma this way. "I tell you, the temptation is very strong for me to start up an 'Adopt a Child' program, whether it is needed or not. Those adoption programs are guaranteed fund-raisers, although they are bureaucratic nightmares. Since the government started scrutinizing them several years ago, some agencies now spend twelve dollars of each seventeen dollars they take in on the overhead, just to keep track of the children and communicate the specifics to the donors. I can't justify that.

"We got talked into Guatemala by another relief agency, and I'll always regret it. So much food was dumped down there after an earthquake that it put the local entrepreneurs out of business. I have vowed to stop ambulance-chasing. I won't go into a country that suddenly appears in news headlines just to clean up on the fund-raising dollars that are sure to follow. But to do any kind of meaningful development, I must feature the crisis aspects of a place like Somalia. I admit it, our film footage is six months old. But people will give money on that emotional appeal. About half the donors will specify their gift for emergency food or medicine supplies. The other half will check 'Use as needed,' and that's all the money I have to work with for true development activities."

The field of health services provides the most striking example of the conundrum of relief work. People will eagerly donate drugs and medical supplies to combat outbreaks of diseases. Mission hospitals readily attract donors. And yet, as wise health professionals know, those responses to health problems do not attack the underlying cause of disease. Civilized countries experienced steep declines in the incidences of bronchitis, pneumonia, influenza, tuberculosis, whooping cough, measles, and scarlet fever long *before* any effective immunization or therapy became available. Improved nutrition and sanitation did far more to disarm those diseases than any treatment devised by medical science. Parisian sewers were more effective than a hundred hospitals. The World Health Organization estimates that 80 percent of all health problems in the Third World relate to polluted water supplies. But try to raise money to clean up a river, or install a passive irrigation system, and you won't cover the cost of the mailing.

"A million people are plunging like lemmings off a cliff," muses one relief worker. "We can easily raise money to pick up the survivors and nurse them back to health. But there are no funds at all to set up prevention and warning programs at the top of the cliff."

For the present, it seems, relief agencies need situations like Somalia as bad as Somalia needs relief help. The experience of that country summarizes everything right and wrong with relief work. For the short term, relief agencies have worked miracles. Masses of people have been kept alive, fed, and medically treated in an extraordinarily brief period of time. The logistics of a poor country with no infrastructure absorbing a 30 percent increase in population have somehow been overcome. For the moment, the crisis in Somalia is no longer a life-or-death matter, as long as the tenuous thread of help from the West stays intact.

No one knows, though, what might happen in the long term as the focus changes from relief work to development. Money itself is no guarantee of success in development. Africa's greatest previous crisis was a devastating drought in the Sahel Desert that killed up to one hundred thousand people and twenty million cattle. In the past ten years a consortium of European agencies spent eight billion dollars to "drought-proof the Sahel." Realists admit that the Sahel is no better off now. Mismanagement and ecological complexities have undermined any hope for substantial change. The Sahel continues to encroach on fertile land. Some relief workers predict that in a decade or two there may not be a single surviving tree left in the entire region.

The Somalian government is just beginning to adjust to the fact that the camps—forty cities spread across Somalia—may turn into permanent settlements of squalor, somewhat like the Palestinian camps. Yet the land simply cannot support that kind of concentration; finite water and firewood resources will not allow it. Will the Somali nomads forfeit an entire cultural history and embrace agriculture or industry or fishing? Will the West continue the massive outpouring of aid required to support such a change?

The relief workers in Somalia are just now beginning to consider such questions. Their experience there vividly illustrates a universal principle of relief work: in relief, as in wars, it is far easier to get in than to get out.

I am sitting in an airplane returning from a trip to the Pacific Northwest. In four days, I interviewed three people. One woman was in an auto accident. As she was driving across a desert with her best friend, a drunken driver missed a stop sign and rammed her car. Her friend and the drunk died instantly; the woman survived with a shattered jaw, broken arm, collapsed lung, lacerated face, and various internal injuries. She has recovered now, except for haunting memories and the prospect of plastic surgery.

A young man had a story with a happier ending. He and his fiancee were hiking in a ravine of the Cascade Mountains when an ice bridge collapsed, burying them under tons of ice. The boy chipped his way out with a rock and went for rescuers. A helicopter lifted the girl out and, after spending five months in a body cast, she healed perfectly.

The third victim was an eighteen-year-old athlete from Anchorage, Alaska. In high school he lettered in football, basketball, and baseball. But during his junior year he noticed a bothersome lump above his ankle and had it diagnosed: cancer. He lost his leg below the knee.

In the past decade I've interviewed scores of people like these who have undergone extreme pain: a grandmother in a nursing home with two weeks to live; a race car driver in a burn ward. Every time I return from such a trip, I mull over their stories and their responses to pain. I can often read their reaction with one look into their piercing, sunken eyes. Each victim plods through similar stages: questioning, anger, self-pity, adjustment, gratitude, hope, more anger. Some wear this pain like a badge of courage. Others spend years wrestling with God.

Encounters like these led me on a personal quest into the problem of pain that culminated in the book Where Is God When It Hurts? *I readily confess that in that book I did not present a neatly packaged solution. I cannot say to each sufferer, "Praise God anyhow!" or "Pray for healing and it will come." And yet scores of letters from readers have convinced me of the need to face the problem of pain honestly and without flinching. "How can a good God permit a suffering world?" is the perennial question rustling through the pages of theology.*

11

In Defense of Pain

THE WELL-KNOWN German pastor and theologian Helmut Thielicke was once asked what was the greatest problem he had observed in the United States. He replied, "They have an inadequate view of suffering."

Ask any group of college students what they have against Christianity, and they'll likely echo variations on the theme of suffering: "I can't believe in a God who would allow Auschwitz and Vietnam"; "My teen-age sister died of leukemia despite all the Christians' prayers"; "One-third of the world went to bed hungry last night—how does that fit in with your Christianity?"

The problem of pain keeps popping up. Like Hercules' battle against the hydra, all our attempts to chop down arguments are met with writhing new examples of suffering. And the Christian's defense usually sounds like an apology (not in the classic theological sense of a well-reasoned defense, but in the red-faced, foot-shuffling, lowered-head sense of embarrassment).

I have never read a poem extolling the virtues of pain, nor seen a statue erected in its honor, nor heard a hymn dedicated to it. Pain is usually defined as "unpleasantness." In a dark, secret moment, many Christians would probably concede that pain was God's mistake. He really should have worked harder and invented a better way of alerting us to the world's dangers. I am convinced that pain gets a bad press. Perhaps we *should* see statues, hymns, and poems to pain. Up close, under a microscope, the pain network is seen in an entirely different dimension.

In our embarrassment over the problem of pain, we seem to have forgotten a central fact which has been repeatedly brought to my attention by Dr. Paul Brand, a missionary surgeon who heads the rehabilitation branch of America's only leprosarium. "If I had one gift which I could give to people with leprosy, it would be the gift of pain," Dr. Brand says.

The gift of pain. An alien, paradoxical concept. One that might never have occurred to us but, as we shall see, one that flows naturally from the experience of a surgeon who treats leprosy victims.

Seen from this viewpoint, pain, like man and nature, is an essentially good creation which has been bent in the Fall. It fits neatly into the cosmic Christian scheme.

Consider earth, which brightly mirrors the handiwork of God: brilliant hues and delicate shadings of a sunset or a rainbow; the roiling foam and spray of a dependable ocean tide; the magnificent abstract designs on butterflies—ten thousand wild variations, all compressed into tiny swatches of flying fabric. Yet the sun which lavishes the sky with color can bake African soil into dry, cracked glaze which may doom millions of people. The pounding, steady rhythm of a surf can, when fomented by a storm, roll in as a twenty-foot wall of death, obliterating towns, villages, even countries. And the harmless swatches of color which spend their lifetimes fluttering among flowers are snatched and destroyed in the daily, bloody ferocity of nature's life cycles. The world, though God's showplace, is also a rebel fortress. It is a good thing, bent.

Consider man: the country which produced Bach, Beethoven, Luther, Goethe, and Brahms also gave us Hitler, Eichmann, Goering. The country which fathered the Constitution of the United States brought us Watergate. In all of us, streaks of brilliance, creativity, talent, and compassion jostle with deceit, selfishness, and cruelty.

And so it is with pain. The nervous system which carries it makes possible man's noblest works. Have you ever watched a concert violinist? Each time his finger lowers on a string he has controlled the synchronized movement of a dozen muscles, supported by the balanced tension of scores of others. His fingers fly through the twelve positions, now falling with power and surety, now searching delicately for a harmonic on the E string, now plucking a loud pizzicato. The nervous system, with its intricate variations of pressure sensations, makes possible his performance.

Of course, you might say, the nervous system has good built within it. But what about when the circuits are shorted out, when a piercing shot of pain races to the brain, drowning the meek sounds of all other sensations? Can that be a gift?

Pain itself, the hurt of pain, is a gift. After years of working with leprosy patients Dr. Paul Brand learned to exult in the sensation of cutting a finger, turning an ankle, stepping into a too-hot bath. "Thank God for pain!" he says.

Doctors once believed the disease of leprosy caused the ulcers on hands and feet and face which eventually led to rotting flesh and the gradual loss of limbs. Mainly through Dr. Brand's research, it has been established that in 99 percent of the cases, leprosy only *numbs* the extremities. The decay of flesh occurs solely because the warning system of pain is absent.

How does the decay happen? Visitors to rural villages in Africa and Asia have sometimes observed a horrible sight: the person with leprosy standing by the heavy iron cooking pot watching the potatoes. As they are done, without flinching he thrusts his arm deep into the scalding water and recovers the cooked potatoes. Dr. Brand found that abusive acts such as this were the chief cause of body deterioration. The potato-watching leprosy victim had felt no pain, but his skin blistered, his cells were destroyed and laid open to infection. Leprosy had not destroyed the tissue; it had merely removed the warning sensors which alerted him to danger.

On one occasion, as Dr. Brand was still formulating this radical theory, he tried to open the door of a little storeroom, but a rusty padlock would not yield to his pressure on the key. A leprosy patient, an undersized, malnourished ten-year-old, approached him, smiling.

"Let me try, sahib doctor," he offered and reached for the key. He closed his thumb and forefinger on the key and with a quick jerk of the hand turned it in the lock.

Brand was dumbfounded. How could this weak youngster out-exert him? His eyes caught a telltale clue. Was that a drop of blood on the floor?

Upon examining the boy's fingers, Brand discovered the act of turning the key had slashed the finger open to the bone; skin and fat and joint were all exposed. Yet the boy was completely unaware of it! To him, the sensation of cutting a finger to the bone was no different from picking up a stone or turning a coin in his pocket.

The daily routines of life ground away at these patients' hands and feet; but without a warning system to alert them, they succumbed. If an ankle turned, tearing tendon and muscle, they would adjust and walk crookedly. If a rat chewed off a finger in the night, they would not discover it until the next morning. (In fact, Brand required his departing patients to take a cat home with them to prevent this common occurrence.)

His discovery revolutionized medicine's approach to leprosy. And it starkly illustrates why Paul Brand can say with utter sincerity, "Thank God for pain!" By definition, pain is unpleasant, so unpleasant as to *force* us to withdraw our finger from boiling water, lightning-fast. Yet it is that very quality which saves us from destruction. Unless the warning signal demands response, we might not heed it.

Brand's discovery in the physical realm closely parallels the moral argument for pain offered by C. S. Lewis in *The Problem of Pain*. Just as physical pain is an early warning signal to the brain, it is a warning signal to the soul. Pain is a megaphone of God which, sometimes murmuring, sometimes shouting, reminds us that something is wrong. It is a "rumor of transcendence" that convinces us the entire human condition is out of whack. We on earth are a rebel fortress, and every sting and every ache reminds us.

We could (some people do) believe that the purpose of life here is to be comfortable. Enjoy yourself, build a nice home, engorge good food, have sex, live the good life. That's all there is. But the presence of suffering complicates that philosophy. It's much harder to believe that the world is here for my hedonistic fulfillment when a third of its people go to bed starving each night. It's much harder to believe that the purpose of life is to feel good when I see people smashed on the freeway. If I try to escape the idea and merely enjoy life, suffering is there, haunting me, reminding me of how hollow life would be if this world were all I'd ever know.

Something is wrong with a life of wars and violence and insults. We need help. He who wants to be satisfied with this world, who wants to think the only reason for living is to enjoy a good life, must do so with cotton in his ears; the megaphone of pain is a loud one.

Pain, God's megaphone, can drive me away from him. I can hate God for allowing such misery. Or, on the other hand, it can drive me to him. I can believe him when he says that this world is not all there is and take the chance that he is making a perfect place for those who follow him on pain-wracked Earth.

If you once doubt the megaphone value of suffering, visit the intensive-care ward of a hospital. It's unlike any other place in the world. All sorts of people will pace the lobby floors: rich and poor, beautiful and plain, black and white, smart and dull, spiritual and atheistic, white-collar and blue-collar. But the intensive-care ward is the one place in the world where none of those divisions makes a speck of difference, for all those people are united by a single awful thread—their love for a dying relative or friend. You don't see sparks of racial tension there. Economic differences, even religious differences, fade away. Often they'll be consoling one another or crying quietly. All of them are facing the rock-bottom emotions of life, and many of them call for a pastor or priest or rabbi for the first time ever. Only the megaphone of pain is strong enough to bring these people to their knees and make them reconsider life.

The concept of pain as a gift directly contradicts the common evangelical attitude of avoiding pain at all costs. We seem to reserve our shiniest merit badges for those who have been healed, with the frequent side-effect of causing unhealed ones to feel as though God has passed them by. The church needs to confront pain realistically and to affirm that a sick person is not unspiritual. A tornado bearing down on my house will not magically swerve and hop to the houses of pagans.

Nothing in Scripture hints that we Christians should expect life to be easier, more antiseptic, or safer. We need a mature awareness of the contributions of pain, and we need the courage to cling to God, Job-like, despite the world of pain and sometimes because of it. Christianity calls us to complete identification with the world—the *suffering* world—not an insulated scarfree pilgrimage through the world.

There are those for whom pain seems to be in revolt. Bodies wracked with cancer so that nerve cells scream in unison a message to the brain which cannot be heeded. Muscular athletes who suffer a freak accident which bruises the spinal cord and condemns them to a life of paralysis and excruciating misery. To these people, all philosophical explanations and all phrases like "the gift of pain" must sound hollow and sadistic. It is as if they are connected to the pain machine in *1984*; pain has left its natural cycle and becomes a Frankenstein.

There are two contributions to the problem of pain that hold true in any circumstance, whether healing or death ensues. The first is the simple fact of Jesus' coming. When God entered humanity, he saw and felt for himself what this world is like. Jesus took on the same kind of body you and I have. His nerve fibers were not bionic—they screamed with pain when they were misused. And, above all, Jesus was surely misused. This fact of history can have a large effect on the fear and helpless despair of sufferers.

The scene of Christ's death, with the sharp spikes and the wrenching thud as the cross was dropped in the ground, has been told so often that we, who shrink from a news story on the death of a race horse or of baby seals, do not flinch at its retelling. It was a bloody death, an execution quite unlike the quick, sterile ones we know today: gas chambers, electric chairs, hangings, injections. This one stretched on for hours in front of a jeering crowd.

Jesus' death is the cornerstone of the Christian faith, the most important fact of his coming. You can't follow Jesus without confronting his death; the gospels bulge with its details. He laid out a trail of hints and bald predictions about it throughout his ministry, predictions that were only understood after the thing had been done, when to the disciples the dream looked shattered. His life seemed prematurely wasted. His triumphant words from the night before surely must have cruelly haunted his followers as they watched him groan and twitch on the cross.

What possible contribution to the problem of pain could come from a religion based on an event like the Crucifixion? Simply this: we are not abandoned. The Alaskan boy with an amputated foot, grieving Salvadoran Christians, survivors of catastrophes—none has to suffer alone. Because God came and took a place beside us, he fully understands. Dorothy Sayers says:

> For whatever reason God chose to make man as he is—limited and suffering and subject to sorrows and death—He had the honesty and courage to take His own medicine. Whatever game He is playing with His creation, He has kept His own rules and played fair. He can exact nothing from man that He has not exacted from Himself. He has Himself gone through the whole of human experience, from the trivial irritations of family life and the cramping restrictions of hard work and lack of money to the worst horrors of pain and humiliation, defeat, despair, and death. When He was a man, He played the man. He was born in poverty and died in disgrace and thought it well worthwhile.

By taking it on himself, Jesus in a sense dignified pain. Of all the kinds of lives he could have lived, he chose a suffering one. Because of Jesus, I can never say about a person, "He must be suffering because of some sin he committed." Jesus, who did not sin, also felt pain. And I cannot say, "Suffering and death must mean God has forsaken us; he's left us alone to self-destruct." Because even though Jesus died, his death became the great victory of history, pulling man and God together. God made a supreme good out of that day. T. S. Eliot wrote in *Four Quartets* (*Collected Poems 1909-1962*, p. 187):

> The wounded surgeon plies the steel
> That questions the distempered part;
> Beneath the bleeding hands we feel
> The sharp compassion of the healer's art
> Resolving the enigma of the fever chart.

That uniquely Christian contribution is a memory. But there is another one—a hope. To the person with unrequited suffering, it is the most important contribution of all. Christ did not stay on the cross. After three days in a dark tomb, he was seen alive again. Alive! Could it be? His disciples couldn't believe it at first. But he came to them, letting them feel his new body. Christ brought us the possibility of an afterlife without pain and suffering. All our hurts are temporary.

How can we imagine eternity? It's so much larger than our short life here that it's difficult even to visualize. You can go to a ten-foot blackboard and draw a line from one side to another. Then, make a one-inch dot in that line. To a microscopic germ cell, sitting in the midst of that one-inch dot, it would look enormous. The cell could spend its lifetime exploring its length and breadth. But you're a human, and by stepping back to view the whole blackboard you're suddenly struck with the largesse of the ten-foot line compared to the tiny dot that germ calls home.

Eternity compared to this life is that way. In seventy years we can develop a host of ideas about God and how indifferent he appears to be about suffering. But is it reasonable to judge God and his plan for the universe by the swatch of time we spend on earth? No more reasonable than for that germ cell to judge a whole blackboard by the tiny smudge of chalk where he spends his life. Have we missed the perspective of the timelessness of the universe?

Who would complain if God allowed one hour of suffering in an entire lifetime of comfort? Yet we bitterly complain about a lifetime that includes suffering when that lifetime is a mere hour of eternity.

In the Christian scheme of things, this world and the time spent here are not all there is. Earth is a proving ground, a dot in eternity—but a very important dot, for Jesus said our destiny depends on our obedience here. Next time you want to cry out to God in anguished despair, blaming him for a miserable world, remember: less than one-millionth of the evidence has been presented.

Let me use another analogy to illustrate the effect of this truth. Ironically, the one event that probably causes more emotional suffering that any other—death—is in reality a translation, a time for great joy when Christ's victory will be appropriated to each of us. Describing the effect of his own death, Jesus used the simile of a woman in travail, full of pain and agony until all is replaced by ecstasy.

Allow yourself to go back in time to an unremembered state—the sterile security of your mother's womb:

Your world is dark, safe, secure. You are bathed in warm liquid, cushioned from shock. You do nothing for yourself; you are fed automatically, and a murmuring heartbeat assures you that someone larger than you fills all your needs. Your life consists of simple waiting. You're not sure what to wait for, but any change seems far away and scary. You meet no sharp objects, no pain, no threatening adventures. A fine existence.

One day you feel a tug. The walls are falling in on you. Those soft cushions are now pulsing and beating against you, crushing you downwards. Your body is bent double, your limbs twisted and wrenched. You're falling, upside down. For the first time in your life you feel pain. You're in a sea of rolling matter. There is more pressure, almost too intense to bear. Your head is squeezed flat, and you are pushed harder, harder into a dark tunnel. Oh, the pain. Noise. More pressure.

You're hurting all over. You hear a groaning sound and an awful sudden fear rushes in on you. It is happening—your world is collapsing. You're sure it's the end. You see a piercing, blinding light. Cold, rough hands pull at you. A painful slap. A loud cry.

You have just experienced birth.

Death is like that. On this end of the birth canal, it seems fiercesome, portentous, and full of pain. Death is a scary tunnel and we are being sucked toward it by a powerful force. We're afraid. It's full of pressure, pain, darkness—the unknown. But beyond the darkness and the pain there's a whole new world outside. When we wake up after death in that bright new world, our tears and hurts will be mere memories. And the new world is so much better than this one that we have no categories to understand what it will be like. The best the Bible writers can tell us is that then, instead of the silence of God, we will have the presence of God and see him face to face. At that time we will be given a stone, and upon it will be written a new name, which no one else knows. Our birth into new creatures will be complete (Rev. 2:17).

Do you sometimes think God does not hear? God is not deaf. He is as grieved by the world's trauma as you are. His only son died here. But he has promised to set things right.

Let history finish. Let the orchestra scratch out its last mournful warm-up note of discord before it bursts into the symphony. As Paul said, "In my opinion whatever we may have to go through now is less than nothing compared with the magnificent future God has planned for us. The whole creation is on tiptoe to see the wonderful sight of the sons of God coming into their own....

"It is plain to anyone with eyes to see that at the present time all created life groans in sort of a universal travail. And it is plain, too, that we who have a foretaste of the Spirit are in a state of painful tension, while we wait for that redemption of our bodies which will mean that at last we have realized our full sonship in Him" (Rom. 8:18, 19, 22, 23).

As we look back on the speck of eternity that was the history of this planet, we will be impressed not by its importance, but by its smallness. From the viewpoint of the Andromeda galaxy, the holocaustic destruction of our entire solar system would be barely visible, a match flaring faintly in the distance, then imploding in permanent darkness. Yet for this burnt-out match, God sacrificed himself. Pain can be seen, as Berkouwer puts it, as the great "not yet" of eternity. It reminds us of where we are, and creates in us a thirst for where we will someday be.

Dr. Paul Brand is known in medical circles for two major accomplishments. As I mentioned in the last chapter, he pioneered the startling idea that the loss of fingers and toes in leprosy was due entirely to injury and infection and was thus preventable. The theory, radically new when Brand first proposed it as a missionary surgeon in India, has gained worldwide acceptance.

Second, he is hailed as a skilled and inventive hand surgeon, and most major textbooks on hand surgery contain chapters by him. Brand was the first to apply tendon transfer techniques to the specific problems of leprosy patients, whose hands often harden into rigid "claw-hands." (An interview with Brand can be interrupted by long distance phone calls from surgeons who are stumped in the very process of surgery. He shouts complicated directions to them over the phone, and they resume their procedures.) For these accomplishments, Brand has been given the USPHS Gold Medallion Award and the prestigious Albert Lasker Medical Award and has been made a Commander of the Order of the British Empire.

I have spent many days with Dr. Brand in his home at the leprosarium in Carville, Louisiana, and in other cities as well. Our conversations have ranged over many aspects of Christianity—the doctrine of the atonement, the Trinity, evolution, verbal inspiration, social concern—as well as his own avocations of genetics, carpentry, and ecology. He ranks among the handful of brightest minds in evangelicalism and yet, until recently, few evangelicals had ever heard of him. I liked that about him. He had not written a book or started a radio program or named an organization after himself. A promising British surgeon, he had worked humbly among the lowest class of people in the entire world: the leprosy-afflicted "untouchables" of India.

I have spent much of the past five years working on books which have grown out of my relationship with Dr. Brand: Where Is God When It Hurts?, Fearfully and Wonderfully Made, *and its sequel*, In His Image. *The following interview pulls together snatches of our many conversations.*

12

Creation and Restoration: Dr. Paul Brand

Question: You once headed up a research project in which you tried to develop an alternative pain system for people who are insensitive to pain, such as leprosy patients. In a sense, you and your team of scientists and bioengineers were playing creator with the human body. What did this teach you about the creation process God went through?

Answer: Our most overwhelming response, of course, was a profound sense of awe. Our team worked specifically with the pain system of the human hand. What engineering perfection we find there! I could fill a room with volumes of surgical textbooks that describe operations people have devised for the injured hand: different ways to rearrange the tendons, muscles, and joints, ways to replace sections of bones and mechanical joints—thousands of operations. But I don't know of a single operation anyone has devised that has succeeded in improving a normal hand. It's beautiful. All the techniques are to correct the deviants, the one hand in a hundred that is not functioning as God designed. There is no way to improve on the hand he gave us.

I concur with Isaac Newton, who said, "In the absence of any other proof, the thumb alone would convince me of God's existence." I think of the complex mechanical hands you see in nuclear labs for handling radioactive materials. Millions of dollars went into the circuitry and mechanical engineering to develop those hands. Yet, they are so bulky and slow and limited compared to ours.

Question: Nearly everyone would acknowledge the marvelous structure of the human body. But what of the one in a hundred abnormal hands? Why did God's creation include the potential for these exceptions that fill our hospitals?

Answer: A partial answer to that lies, I believe, in the inherent limitations of any medium that obeys physical laws. In his creation of the world, God chose to work with atomic particles that he made to operate according to physical and chemical laws, thus imposing certain limits. Those were the building blocks of creation. At the upper end of the whole process, for his highest creative achievement, God chose to make a human brain that would be independent and have freedom of choice.

C. S. Lewis' example of wood illustrates the limitations of law-abiding material. To support leaves and fruit on a tree, God had to create a substance with properties of hardness and impliability. We use wood for furniture and to build homes because of these qualities. Yet, in a free world, that characteristic invites abuse. Wood can be used as a club to bash someone's head. The nature of the substance allows the possibility of a use other than that for which it was intended.

I am glad that the world is governed by laws: that fire is hot and ice is cold, that wood is hard and cotton is soft. As a doctor and scientist, I must rely on those properties for my techniques of experimentation and surgery. If I could not rely on plaster to be firm, it would be useless as a splint for a broken bone.

At Carville, we eventually had to abandon our own attempts at an alternative pain system partly because of these laws. The substances we tried to use—metal and electronic components—would break down after a few hundred uses, whereas the body requires millions of uses from each of its pain cells. We were unable to come close to duplicating the complexity and flexibility built into the simplest nerve cell.

Question: As you studied the human body, especially in its sensitivity to pain, and as you tried to think like God, did you see anything at all that you would have designed differently?

Answer: I would not be so bold as to express it like that, but I have contemplated the choices God must have considered in creating the body. One of the beauties of the pain system in the body is the way in which each pain ending in a tissue fires off its message at a level of stress appropriate to the preservation of that particular tissue. Your foot, for example, reacts dully to pain, since it must be tough enough to face a daily rigor of pounding and stomping. Yet your eye is incredibly sensitive. I visualize the Creator pondering the pain reflex in the cornea. Here is a tissue highly specialized for transparency and thus it must do without a regular blood supply (which would make it opaque). A wound there is a special disaster, and even a small wound could cause blindness. The pain endings are so sensitive that they call for a blink reflex when a thin eyelash touches the surface—no other part of your body would react to the weight of an eyelash.

In setting the levels of sensitivity, the Designer must have recognized that if the eye were made even more sensitive it would be impossible to keep it open in a slightly dusty atmosphere, or in smoke, or perhaps when the wind is blowing. Yet as a doctor concerned primarily with disease and injury, I might have wished for that greater sensitivity.

The same is true with the lining of the trachea and larynx. We get impatient when we are forced to cough, but patients dying of lung cancer must sometimes wish that the Creator had made the mucosa of the trachea less tolerant of tobacco smoke so that their own physiology would prohibit smoking. Even omnipotence cannot please everybody.

Question: Let's talk for a moment about your concept of omnipotence. As I understand it, you view omnipotence in terms of the potential power, not the process it describes. For example, a Russian weightlifter can be called the most powerful man in the world. But his task of lifting the weights he attempts is no easier for him than my lifting to the level of weights that challenges me; he still has to grunt and sweat and exert. Is there an analogy there to the way you interpret God's omnipotence?

Answer: There may be. I don't even like the word *omnipotence*. The word conveys a simplistic view of the Creator and Sustainer of the Universe, as if he merely had to wave a magic wand and it all came into being. Man's creative effort in producing the Sistine Chapel or the lunar landing craft required tremendous planning and forethought, and I can envision God going through a similar process of planning and experimentation in his act of creation.

The more I delve into the natural laws—the atom, the universe, the solid elements, molecules, the sun, and, even more, the interplay of all the mechanisms required to sustain life—I am astounded. The whole creation could collapse like a deck of cards if just one of those factors were removed. To build a thing like our universe had to require planning and thought and that, I believe, is the strongest argument for the presence of God in creation.

From the chance collision of molecules you may sometimes derive a sudden, exciting pattern, but it quickly disperses. Some people really think that all the design and precision in nature came by chance, that if millions of molecules bombard each other for long enough, a nerve cell and sensory ending at exactly the right threshold will be bound to result. To those people I merely suggest that they try to make one, as I did, and see what chance is up against.

I see God as a careful, patient designer, and I don't think that the fact that I call him God makes it easy. There are billions of possible ways in which atoms could combine, and he had to discard all but a very few as being inadequate. I don't think I can fully appreciate God unless I use the word *difficult* to describe the creative process.

I like to think of God developing his skills, as it were, by creating amoebae and then ants and cockroaches, developing complexity until he comes to humankind, the zenith of creation. Again, he was confronted with options at every decision. A person who breaks his leg skiing could wish for stronger bones. Perhaps bone could have been made stronger (though scientists have not been able to find a stronger, suitable substance for implanting), but he then would have made the bones thicker and heavier. If they were heavier you probably wouldn't be able to ski, because you would be too bulky and inert.

Take a model of the human skeleton and look at the size of the tiny bones in the fingers and toes. Those bones in the toes support all your weight. If they were larger and thicker, many athletic events would be impossible. If fingers were thicker, so many human activities—such as playing stringed instruments—would be impossible. The Creator had to make those difficult choices between strength and mobility and weight and volume.

Question: And animals were given different qualities based on their needs. Some are stronger and faster than man and can see and hear better.

Answer: Right, you can only call creation perfect in relation to other options available. Even human types differ. Is an American better than a Vietnamese? The American is bigger, but it takes more food to sustain him. If food becomes short, the Vietnamese will survive because they can get by on a bowl of rice and the Americans will die out. So physical qualities are not good or bad, but good in certain circumstances. I have tremendous admiration for how the world has come out, with evidence of thought behind it. But every stage of development—moving from the inanimate to the animate, single-cell to multi-cell, developing the nervous system—required thought and choice. That's why I define omnipotence the way I do.

Question: When you speak of pain, and even death, you seem to include these within God's overall design for this planet. These are generally seen as evidence of the twisted, or fallen, state of the world. How do you reconcile these elements with your belief in a wise, loving Creator?

Answer: I cannot easily imagine life on this planet without pain and death. Pain is a helpful, essential mechanism for survival. I could walk with you through the corridors of this leprosarium and show you what life is like for people who feel little pain. I see patients who have lost all their toes simply because they wore tight, ill-fitting shoes that caused pressure and cut off circulation. You or I would have stopped wearing those shoes or adjusted our way of walking. But these patients didn't have the luxury of pain to warn them when they were abusing their flesh.

You're familiar with the stereotyped image of leprosy, with its loss of fingers. That abuse comes because the leprosy bacillus destroys pain cells, and the victims are no longer warned when they harm their bodies through normal activity. In this world, given our material environment, I would not for a moment wish for a pain-free life. It would be miserable. I mentioned earlier that ninety-nine of a hundred hands are perfectly normal. The statistics are nearly reversed for those people insensitive to pain: Nineteen of each twenty of them have some sort of malformity or dysfunction, simply because their pain system is not working properly.

As for death, when I look at the world of nature its most impressive feature as a closed system is the lavish expenditure of life at every level. Every time a whale takes a mouthful it swallows a million plankton. Every garden pond is a scene of constant sacrifice of life for the building up of other life. Death is not some evil intruder that has upset beautiful creation; it is woven into the very fabric and essence of the beautiful creation itself. Most of the higher animals are designed so that they depend for their survival on the death of lower levels of life. Having created this food pyramid and placed man at its apex, the Creator instructed him to enjoy and to use it responsibly. In modern, Western culture, we tend to see a certain ruthlessness and lack of love in nature, but I believe that viewpoint comes from a civilization whose main contact with animal life is through domestic pets and children's anthropomorphic animal stories.

Question: Just a minute, now. It is true that pain and death fit into the present system of life on earth, but weren't these factors introduced as a result of man's rebellion and fall? Are you saying that the Garden of Eden contained pain and death?

Answer: Well, anything I say about the Garden of Eden must be conjecture, because we've been given very little data about it. I feel reasonably sure that Adam felt pain, if his body was like mine. If there were sharp rocks on which he could have hurt himself, I hope he had a pain system to warn him. The pain network is so inextricably woven into bodily functions—it tells you when to go to the bathroom and how close you may stand to the fire, and it carries feelings of pleasure as well as pain—that I could not imagine a worthwhile body in this world without it. Note also that in the curse God told Eve he would *multiply* her pain in childbirth.

And, I believe physical death was present before the Fall also. The very nature of the chain of life requires it. You cannot have soil without the death of bacteria; you cannot have thrushes without the death of worms. The shape of a tiger's teeth is wholly inappropriate for eating plant matter (and even vegetarians thrive off the death of plants, part of the created order). A vulture would not survive unless something died. I don't see death as being a bad thing.

Question: But the explicit warning given Adam was, "In that day you shall surely die."

Answer: I think the precise phrasing is important: "in that day." The whole story strongly indicates to me that God was speaking of spiritual life—the breath of God, the image of himself that he reserved exclusively for human beings. I believe Adam was biologically alive before God breathed into him the breath of life; the Hebrew suggests a spiritual life, a direct link of communication and fellowship between God and man. And after Adam's rebellion, immediately, "in that day," the link was broken. God had to search out Adam after his sin. I don't think his curse referred to physical death at all, and I assume Adam would have died biologically if he had not rebelled. As for thorns and thistles and the pain of childbirth, I'm not really adequately prepared to interpret those. We're given so few details of the creation before and after the Fall.

Question: It still sounds strange to hear someone vigorously defending pain. You work in a hospital populated by people insensitive to pain. Having met leprosy patients, I can easily agree to the void created in their lives by the absence of pain. But if you worked in a cancer ward, say, among people who feel constant, unrelieved pain, could you praise pain so confidently there?

Answer: I have worked in places of great suffering: the clinics treating victims of the London bombings during the war, surgical wards in Indian hospitals. The one legitimate complaint you can make against pain is that it cannot be switched off. It can rage out of control, as with a terminal cancer patient, even though its warning has been heard and there is no more that can be done to treat the cause of pain. I'm sure that less than 1 percent of pain is in this category that we might call out of control. Ninety-nine percent of all the pains that people suffer are short-term pains, correctable situations that call for medication, rest, or a change in a person's lifestyle.

In our experiments with alternative pain systems, we learned it was self-defeating to attach a cut-off switch. We had a glove that, when pressed hard, would emit an electric shock. But if the patient was turning a screwdriver too hard and the electric shock went off, he simply overruled the pain signal and switched it off. As a result, he often injured himself. To make a useful system we would have to eliminate the cut-off switch, or place it out of the patient's reach. I can see why God didn't allow a cut-off switch.

Don't forget, absolutely the best pain-relieving drug in the world is the opium seed of the poppy, which people have used throughout recorded history. God did make allowances for pain that rages out of control. There are many ways open to us to relieve the pain of a person with terminal cancer.

Question: Have you given any thought to the resurrected world of the afterlife? The Bible gives little evidence about it; and yet you insist so strongly on the necessity of pain in this world, what about the next? The Bible hints that in the matter of pain heaven will be radically different.

Answer: I really don't know. Jesus could walk through a solid door in his resurrection body, so it seems clear the afterlife will be governed by a different set of physical laws. There will be some continuity. His body and those of the three on the Mount of Transfiguration were recognizable, and it's true that Jesus even bore the scars of his pain from this world. Thomas touched them.

Heaven is a spiritual world, and it's difficult to conjecture what we will be like when our spiritual forms are fully developed. Will children still have resurrection bodies of children? I think of my mother, Granny Brand, who lived to be ninety-five. She struggled as a missionary for seventy years under harsh conditions in India. Gradually the decades of poor sanitation and Indian diseases and poor nutrition caught up with her, and her body was bent and twisted. She thought herself so ugly that she would not allow a mirror in her house. Yet when she rode her donkey into a village, the people who knew her saw her as a beautiful person, a messenger of love. Perhaps we will relate in heaven so much on that basis that physical appearance will become irrelevant. I don't know how pain fits in. If the verse "tears shall be no more" is to be taken literally, then our eyes will be very different, for in this world we quickly go blind without tears.

Question: What about some of the psychological parallels to physical pain? I'm thinking particularly of emotions we generally view as negative, such as guilt and fear. Do you see these as contributing to health in the same way that physical pain does?

Answer: Guilt has spiritual value: it impels you toward cleansing. It is a pain to the conscience that something is wrong that should be dealt with. Two steps are necessary. First, the person must find the cause of the guilt, just as a person must find the cause of his pain. Much of modern counseling deals with this process of rooting out reasons for guilt.

But then a further step must follow: a pathway out of the guilt. Unless it is aimed at cleansing, guilt is a useless encumbrance. Guilt as such doesn't lead you anywhere, just as pain does not: they both simply point out a condition that needs attention. In this sense, guilt is certainly a good thing, if it is directional, pushing you toward something. The *perceived* purpose of it is for you to get rid of the sense of guilt, which you don't like. Underlying that is the more significant purpose of uprooting and dealing with the cause of guilt. It's the same with pain.

In modern society we tend to approach pain as if it were the enemy. We get rid of the pain without asking why the pain came. Pain-killing medicine can quiet the pain, but that can be bad if its cause is not determined. Similarly, I believe modern psychology has concentrated on guilt as an evil and attempted to suppress or excise guilt. Just stop feeling guilty, they say. Live your life as you want. But in the Christian context, guilt is very valuable. It pushes you to right the wrong that is the cause of your guilt and gives you the outlet of forgiveness to purge it.

When used properly, fear, too, is an essential element of human life, a protective instinct without which the human race would never have survived. A mother isn't happy to leave a baby alone until it has grown to have a healthy fear of fire or of heights. Fear also supplies, through adrenalin, increased heart rates, and other mechanisms, to tap abnormal reserves of strength. The trick is to have the right amount of fear and to control it properly.

Question: We know that pain and struggle produce character and that often in the realm of music and art the tensions of childhood result in creative genius. Do you think the tendency in America to try to balance everyone out through self-help books, counseling, advice, and so forth, can be unhealthy? I often wonder how a psychiatrist would have handled Beethoven.

Answer: There are problems in this area. One is a trend to eliminate variety. I think variety is exciting and lovely, yet we set up norms and tend to reject people who do not match. If one does not have the proper standard of height, weight, figure, shape of nose, outgoing personality, and extroversion, the psyche is bruised and he or she loses the will to succeed. Anyone who doesn't conform to our artificial goals does badly. When a child is bookish and is clumsy with sports and doesn't shine in conversation, society tends to discard him or her. But that's the material from which research scientists come. I feel we try too much to push people into molds.

Another danger is the tendency of modern culture to remove risk and adventure from life. Most of our excitement happens to us vicariously, as we watch it on television. We shelter our kids, removing them from risky situations, and as a result stunt their growth. I have always maintained that of our six children, I would much rather have four survivors who truly lived, with adventure and self-determination in the face of risk, than end up with six fearful, timid youngsters. Fortunately, all six have survived, but they could all tell you some hair-raising tales of what they went through in finding their own independence.

This tendency to eliminate risk is compounded upon the old. I visited a very tidy hospital for old people, where the superintendent showed me with great pride how each person had a separate room and a clean bed. They lie there all day. I asked why they were not allowed to get up and walk about. He said, "Well, if they do, we find that they sometimes fall and break their hips. If they go outdoors they catch cold and if they meet with each other they exchange infections. By keeping them in their separate little rooms they don't get infected, they don't break their legs, they don't catch cold." I carried away from there a memory of bodies that were alive, but of spirits that were caged.

Question: Your emphasis on restoring the human spirit brings up an interesting line of questions. In rehabilitation, you work with very few patients, lavishing thousands of dollars and man-hours a year on each one. In fact, at Carville the ratio of staff to patients is almost one-to-one, isn't it? Does it bother you that in India millions of people are going without the most primitive kind of medical treatment while these patients receive so much?

Answer: I don't like the juxtaposition of the two cases—people in India and patients here. I work with quadriplegics and other disabled persons who require lavish expenditures of money, yes. The opportunity to work with a person and to help set his spirit free is one of my most inspiring challenges. No effort is too great and no expense should be spared to restore activity to such a one or to help the spirit rise above its physical limitations.

Even in India I was faced with terrible choices of priorities. After I applied hand surgery techniques to the specific case of leprosy, our staff was able to remake hands. We could turn a rigid, frozen claw-hand into a flexible, usable hand and allow a beggar to find work. But our time and resources were limited, so we had to make choices just as hospitals in the United States recently had to make choices among their kidney dialysis patients. Did we give a hospital bed to one long-term case for a year, or to twelve short-term cases for one month each, or fifty cases for one week each? Did we repair an older patient with gross deformities or a younger one who had a whole life ahead of him? The most pathetic cases—those with missing limbs and exposed bones—were often the last we would treat; we tried to focus on less advanced cases to prevent further abuse. These were wrenching choices. Yet in no way did that background of alternatives devalue the worth of the human spirits we eventually treated.

Question: I have heard it said, by an Indian in fact, that Western medical advances applied to India upset the natural balance. Years ago, the birth rate was high, but only a third of the babies survived infancy. Now the birth rate remains high, but most of them live. He accused the West, and missionaries in particular, of causing India's overpopulation because of their "charitable" aid.

Answer: And in a real sense he's right. Missionaries on the whole have not been the chief offenders. They're too inefficient and localized. But the World Health Organization comes in with massive resources and wipes out killing diseases. I would have to say I would not go to India with a life-saving mission without tying it to education for limiting population. While in India, my specific task was with crippling diseases; I helped remake human spirits; and that, I think, is wholly legitimate. The expense required by one of our operations could have saved a hundred people from cholera, but I still maintain that spirit-saving activity was worth it.

Question: Jesus said, "Love your neighbor as yourself." Modern media have made that command infinitely more complex and burdensome. Because of television, the whole world is our neighbor. On evening news programs we watch the progress of famines, wars, and epidemics. How can we possibly respond to all of these disasters?

Answer: You can't, not in the sense in which Jesus meant it, at least. You must remember the context in which he was speaking. He meant family, nearby villages, Capernaum. Jesus healed people, but in a very localized area. In his lifetime he did not affect the Celts or the Chinese or the Aztecs. And I think an intolerable burden of guilt such as you describe merely numbs us and keeps us from responding. We must have a sense of touch to those we love.

Westerners, with our opulent lifestyles, are very sensitive on this point. But I really don't believe that children born in Bangladesh amid poverty suffer all that much more than a spoiled child in a rich country. Plato's *The Cave* pictures people being born and brought up entirely in darkness, and as a result their range of appreciation of beauty, light, and joy is very different from that of a person outside. When they come up to the light, dazzled, they learn to appreciate a new range of happiness. This, to me, is a deep perception of the human spirit. A child develops a norm, above which is happiness and below which is suffering.

Not long ago I was in Bombay, among the awful refugee villages between the airport and the city. Children live in stinking, ghastly shacks, held up by sticks, reeking with human excrement, fleas, and lice. Yet you'll see a child coming out of the hovel and playing tag and hopscotch with a lighthearted air. Their ability to enjoy the basics of life seems greater than that of a spoiled kid the day after Christmas, whining and smashing his new toys out of boredom.

Question: How do you maintain a sense of Christian compassion in your work? In India you saw thousands of patients regularly with the same afflictions. After examining three thousand abused hands, how can you maintain your compassion?

Answer: I don't know that I do it very well. In India I did learn the importance of a sense of touch. Sometimes when we were treating a serious case and had prescribed some drug, the relatives of the patient would go and purchase the medicine, then come back and ask me to give it to the patient "with my good hands." They believed the medicine was more able to help the patient if it was given by the hand of the physician. Interesting, isn't it, that Jesus always touched his patients?

I probably remember a person's hands better than his or her face. I connect a person's occupation with his hands—sometimes I can read it in the hand. I try to individualize what the loss of sensation or the stiffness in his hands means in his work. When I return to India to teach, I can often remember a patient's hands with startling vividness. I'll recognize someone and say right off, "You've lost some more of your ring finger."

Question: Doesn't your emphasis on the personal aspect of mission run counter to some of the trends in missions today, where we isolate which groups are most responsive to the gospel and go after those groups with a specific approach?

Answer: Yes, it does contradict those trends. I don't believe mission work is necessarily more effective as it becomes more specialized. My father moved into a mountain community in India to preach the gospel. Within a year his tasks were part medical, part agricultural, part education, evangelism, and translation. He responded to the needs of the people around him. I think that's Christian mission at its best.

The Christian way of multiplying is the biological way, not the arithmetical way: One becomes two and two becomes four and four becomes eight. I have seen good Christian medical works in India gradually lose their original mission. They become institutionalized, with a building and staff to support, and soon they have to charge fees for their patients. To make the work more self-supporting, they branch out into specialized surgery techniques. Soon they're doing brain surgery with all sorts of sophisticated equipment, and the people they originally came to reach, the poor, malnourished Indians, cannot afford the hospital. Christian witness shines when a young person goes out to work among villagers, working with their sanitation, treating diarrheal disease, improving nutrition, educating on childbirth. Eventually more good is done through this kind of personal ministry, I believe.

Jesus Christ did not have to touch people as he healed them. He could easily, with that same power, have waved a magic wand. In fact, a wand would have reached more people than a touch. He could have divided the crowd into groups: paralyzed people over there, febrile people here, people with leprosy there, and raised his hands to heal each group *en masse*, but he chose not to. No, his mission was to people, individual people who happened to have a disease. They came to him because they had a disease, but he touched them because they were humans and because he loved them. You can't readily demonstrate love to a crowd. Love is generally person to person.

*Editors of Christian magazines become inured to occasional venom-
ous letters. Still, I was not quite prepared for the hate mail generated
by my* Christianity Today *articles on Mahatma Gandhi. "So it's Gandhi on the cover this month," wrote one reader. "Who will it be next
month, the Ayatollah?"*

*Most of the complaints boiled down to one question: do we Christians
have anything to learn from someone who rejected our faith? It is
true that Gandhi never accepted the claims of Christian theology,
but, ironically, he based his life philosophy on principles learned from
Christianity.*

*Gandhi represents a great threat to the West, because he passionately
believed the West had forfeited its ability to lead the human race. He
looked for a new way, based on people's spiritual, not material,
strength. He broke every rule in the political handbook, yet he helped
found the largest democracy in the history of the world.*

*I do not write about Gandhi because he had the answers for our
planet. To the contrary, I write merely because he asked the questions
most eloquently. We may reject his answers, surely, but can we do so
before first considering his questions?*

13

Gandhi: A Man Who Triumphed over Suffering

Beginning in 1983 the books, long out of print, began to appear again. Many had a photo of Ben Kingsley, rather than Gandhi, on the cover and a slash of color heralding "the book that inspired the epic film," or words to that effect. Mahatma Gandhi, The Great Soul, the wizened old man whose personal force struck down an empire, was back in the news, thanks to Richard Attenborough's film *Gandhi*. The media granted a few more nanoseconds of historical time to the man who changed the landscape of the globe, thirty-five years after his death.

Gandhi lived life in italics. There was no one like him: no one more disciplined, or stubborn, or consistent, or creative, or baffling, or lovable, or infuriating. Many of the political principles we take for granted today, as well as the sounds of protest that echo in the streets of Poland and Chile and South Africa, originated in the mind of this man who led a fifth of humanity into the twentieth century.

Now, thirty-five years later, it is time to begin to assess Gandhi, his life and beliefs, by asking what relevance he has in our speeded-up world of nuclear tension, environmental carnage, and militant nationalism. And because he was called a saint—a Hindu saint, certainly, but one strategically informed by Christian thinkers—we in the church should pause to ponder what message he has for us also. Gandhi died three years after America used the atom bomb, an event which convinced him more than ever that, for the planet to survive, the world must look to the East, not the West, for solutions. The West had always looked to the East, he claimed, citing Jesus, Buddha, Moses, Zoroaster, Mohammed, Rama. The alternative he foresaw was a global cataclysm brought on by decadence, materialism, and armed conflict.

In India today, Gandhi's homeland, he is honored, even revered, but hardly followed. Giant textile mills have supplanted the wooden spinning wheels. The corruption of India's bureaucracy is legendary. And, three bloody wars after Gandhi, his nation flirts with the ring of power that haunted him: nuclear weaponry. Even so, India cannot get the strange little man out of her consciousness. Nor, as Attenborough's film reminds us, can the rest of the world.

If someone staged a beauty contest to select the least likely world leader, Gandhi would win hands down. Barely five feet tall, he weighed a mere 114 pounds, and his skinny arms and legs stuck out from his body like the limbs of a malnourished child. His ears flared straight out from his shaved head; his squat, oversized nose looked fake, like one of the rubber noses attached to glasses that people wear to costume parties. Steel rimmed spectacles kept slipping from that nose, tilting down towards his mouth, itself oddly shaped due to his habit of wearing dentures only while eating. His lips curled over nearly toothless gums. "He's rather like a little bird," said Lord Mountbatten, the last British viceroy of India, "a kind of sweet, sad sparrow perched on my armchair."

As Gandhi walked, he leaned either on a bamboo stave or on the shoulders of his "crutches," as he called his two young grandnieces. He wore the same clothes every day: a loose Indian loincloth and sometimes a cotton shawl, both of coarse homespun material he had spun at his own wheel. He carried all his possessions in a small sack, except for one, an Ingersoll pocket watch which he proudly wore on a string; among his other idiosyncracies was an obsessive punctuality.

Gandhi followed a strict schedule every day; and no one, not the King Emperor of the British Empire, nor the leaders of India, nor his closest friends, could alter it. He would arise daily at 2:00 A.M. to read his beloved *Gita* and say prayers, spend the next quiet hours answering correspondence, then do his ablutions and his toilet, completing them with a ritual salt-and-water enema. At noon every day he insisted on another health regimen—a porous cotton sack packed with oozing mud placed on his abdomen and head.

"Those who are in my company," he warned his followers, "must be ready to sleep upon the bare floor, wear coarse clothes, get up at unearthly hours, subsist on uninviting, simple food, even clean their own toilets." Somehow he mobilized his followers, millions of them, into a moral and spiritual crusade with profound political repercussions. They fought with prayers, jail sentences, and flattened bodies, not machine guns. Finally, four hundred million people were set free without armed revolt against their colonialist rulers.

It is popular today for historians to pick at the scabs of great men, exposing their flaws and inconsistencies. For a time after his death Gandhi was apotheosized, but revisionists have since dug up evidence about his petty demands on associates, his outbursts, his bizarre personal habits, his cranky stubbornness. Certainly that serene demeanor concealed an irascible streak. The man who could galvanize millions failed badly as a leader of his own family: he admittedly mistreated his wife and imposed such strictness on his children that his eldest son rebelled and became an embezzler, gambler, and penniless alcoholic.

Even the major principles that guided Gandhi's life proved highly problematic. He made major advances in village-level health and sanitation by encouraging peasants toward cleanliness and self-administered health treatments. But when his wife lay dying from acute bronchitis and the British flew in a vial of rare penicillin that could save her life, Gandhi refused the doctor permission to give it to her intravenously; the violence of the needle would violate her body, he said. As a result, she died.

Nevertheless, after all the gossip is heard, and the idealism of Gandhi corrodes upon exposure to the polluted atmosphere of world politics, and his own nation continues to forsake so much of what he lived and died for—even after all that—still Gandhi radiates a unique and prescient wisdom that cannot fail to affect all who contact him. Mountbatten, a seasoned military commander, concluded hyperbolically that Gandhi's impact on history would rival that of Jesus and Buddha. Is it time to look East again, to give another thought to the principles that formed this eccentric prophet?

No single essay can begin to acquaint a reader with even a cursory sketch of Gandhi's life. But before drawing out the principles which have special relevance to the church today, I must at least trace a few of the major events. The measure of a man like Gandhi depends on his actions at hinge moments in life. Those few moments reveal Gandhi's true greatness.

Prophets in the tradition of an Elijah or John the Baptist are not easily imagined in a modern setting. What would one look like? What would he wear? What would he say if confronted by shopping centers and nuclear bombs, if followed by an army of reporters? Resembling some of those prophets but in a modern context, Gandhi offers a startling, innovative response. He redefined politics and spirituality, along the way helping to change the globe forever.

Though not a Christian by belief or practice, Gandhi attempted to an impressive degree to live out some of the very same principles that characterized Jesus. His life merits our reflection.

Protests

Gandhi's doctrine of civil disobedience evolved gradually. In two decades in South Africa he had led marches, taken his share of beatings, spent a few hundred days in jail, and had experienced the mixed results of protest under oppressive regimes. Upon return to India he confronted a very different situation. There, his concern was not for a minority of tightly knit Indians in a strange land, but a majority, 400 million citizens strong, composed of diverse subcultures in a subcontinent ruled by the powerful British. As Britain started tightening the screws against Indian nationalism and protest, notably in the Rowlatt Act, Gandhi meditated long hours about the appropriate response. It came to him early one morning, in the dawning moments between sleep and consciousness. He decided to call for a day of mourning. No activity at all. India would respond with utter quietness. Shops would close, traffic would cease, the country would simply shut down for one day. Nothing like it had been attempted before in history. We who live in its wake, after dozens of adaptations around the world, can easily miss the extraordinary genius of that response.

Gandhi devised a suitable reply to the classically colonialist economic system. Britain was growing raw cotton in India, transporting it to England for milling and manufacture, and shipping the finished product back to India for sale at high prices. To break the chain, Gandhi urged every Indian, villager or city dweller, to spend at least an hour a day spinning cotton. He set the example himself, digging up an old wooden spinning wheel that he used the rest of his life.

In response to Britain's tax on salt, a staple that every person, no matter how poor, required, Gandhi countered with his famous Salt March, a 250-mile, painstakingly slow march to Bombay. Millions of cheering peasants hailed his entourage along the way while nervous officials back in London anxiously followed every step of his snaillike progress. When he arrived in Bombay, he waded out into the sea and scooped up a fistful of salt. He held it in the air like a sceptre as a symbol of defiance to the Empire. Let India gather her own salt and boycott everything British. (Contrast that approach with the American colonists' response to Britain's stamp tax.)

Gandhi proved to be a thorn in the side of the British because orthodox means could not put down his unorthodox protests. When they hauled him into court and threatened a jail sentence, he calmly asked for the maximum sentence. Far from being a discipline, the jail environment offered more luxury than he allowed himself when free and gave the additional benefit of extended periods of time for reflection and writing. In all, Gandhi spent 2,338 days in British jails. He said, "Freedom is often to be found inside a prison's walls, even on a gallows; never in council chambers, courts, and classrooms."

When the British tried more traditional methods of oppression—opening fire on the demonstrators—they created martyrs and only served to unite the nation further. In one notorious incident at Amritsar, British-led troops trained machine guns on a peaceful but illegal gathering, shooting 1,650 rounds and causing 1,516 casualties.

Later in his life, Gandhi's inner voice led him to the most devastating tactic of protest, a tactic that sealed the fate of the Empire and eventually saved the new nation from anarchy. He simply fasted, depriving himself of food. Gandhi planned his fasts as carefully as a general plans military strategy. Sometimes he set them for specified lengths of time, such as twenty-one days, and sometimes he announced a fast unto death unless certain demands were met. The ironies defy comprehension: an ultimate weapon of intentional starvation within a nation of starving masses, a single man's self-sacrifice as the most potent force in defeating the most widespread empire in history.

Against all odds, the tactics worked. Churchill foamed at "the nauseating and humiliating spectacle of this one-time Inner Temple lawyer, now seditious fakir, striding half-naked up the steps of the Viceroy's palace, there to negotiate and parley on equal terms with the representative of the King Emperor." But Gandhi became "Mahatma, The Great Soul." He guaranteed morality with his own life: no one was willing to risk being responsible for letting The Great Soul die. One by one, the generals, viceroys, prime ministers, and finally the king yielded to the demands of "that half-naked fakir."

Untouchables

When Gandhi lived in India one-sixth of the population comprised a group of people who seemed more animal than human. They lived in dark, putrid slums, amid open sewers in which swarmed rats and every other disease-bearing agent. The Hindu doctrine of *karma* gave a theological basis for the elaborate system of 5000 subcastes, and the lowest caste of all, the Untouchables, did not dare protest.

You could tell Untouchables by their dark color and by their posture, for they cringed like beaten animals. The name defined them— if a caste Hindu so much as touched one, or touched a drop of water one had polluted, he would shriek away and begin an elaborate purification process. An Untouchable had to shrink from the path of a caste Hindu to avoid casting a shadow and thus defiling him. Some parts of India allowed Untouchables to leave their shacks only at night; there, they were known as the *Invisibles*. Untouchables gave a valuable service to society; they swept the streets and cleaned the latrines and sewers, acts a caste Hindu would never perform.

With nothing to gain but abuse and rejection from the rest of his peers, Mahatma Gandhi took up the cause of the Untouchables. In a singularly brilliant stroke, he bestowed on them a new name; they were no longer to be called *Untouchables*, but rather *Harijans*, the Children of God. At his first *ashram*, a commune in South Africa, Gandhi stirred up a storm of protest by inviting an Untouchable to move in with him and the others. When the chief financial backer of the commune experiment withdrew his support, Gandhi made plans to move to the Harijans' own quarters. Finally he committed the most defiling act possible for a Hindu to perform: he cleaned the latrines of the Untouchables. Back in India he adopted them as his brothers and stayed in their hovels in Calcutta whenever possible.

Years later, after independence, when all other leaders in India pressed Lord Mountbatten to accept the honorary post of Governor-General, Gandhi proposed his own alternative candidate: an Untouchable sweeper girl "of stout heart, incorruptible and crystallike in her purity." His candidate did not get the nomination, of course, but by such symbolic actions Gandhi helped change the perception of Untouchability all across India. Laws were changed and strictures removed. Today in India, the caste system continues in a milder form. But 100 million people there now call themselves not by a curse—Untouchable—but by a blessing: they are the Children of God.

India's Ointment

As the momentum for independence swept across India and its citizens realized they were going to get their country back at last, centuries-old animosities began to boil to the surface. In sudden spasms of violence, Hindus and Moslems turned on each other with ferocity on a scale without historical precedent. Moslems in the Bengal and Noakhali districts burned the huts of their Hindu neighbors, forced them to eat sacred cows, raped the Hindu women, and butchered their husbands. Hindus fought back with a vengeance, and thousands of Indians died in the months leading up to independence. Increasingly it appeared that the whole country would burst into flames. In New Delhi, Congress Party leaders met anxiously with British and Moslem officials to try to work out some compromise. Mohammed Ali Jinnah, the Moslem leader, stood firm against compromise. To him, the Hindu-controlled Congress Party had already proven itself untrustworthy by excluding Moslems from power. He and 100 million Moslems were demanding a separate country called Pakistan. But Congress leaders, most notably Gandhi, saw partition as a terrible blow to their dream of a unified India. In an emotional appeal, Gandhi cried out that his own body would be broken before he could ever allow Mother India to break in two. The debates went on, and so did the rapine.

Gandhi proposed his own solution. In order to avoid partition, he suggested that the Congress Party should turn over all the government to the Moslems, the Hindus thus voluntarily subjecting themselves to a Moslem minority one-third their size. Not everyone was up to his ideals; the Congress leadership permanently broke with Gandhi and a separate Pakistan became inevitable.

While the officials sat in elegant palace rooms and bartered for power and land, Gandhi went on an "ointment" crusade. Let them argue, he said; he was going back to the people, to the angry hordes that were assailing each other so viciously. At the age of seventy-seven he headed to the Noakhali region where the most violence had occurred and roamed among the charred villages. He simply wanted to be there, he said, to absorb their pain and to hold prayer meetings for the love and brotherhood that he cherished. Though a Hindu, he led his ragtag group into Moslem villages to face their taunts and rocks and bottles. When he approached a village, the most famous Asian alive would beg for shelter and live on the charity of the villagers. If turned away, he would look for a tree to sleep under. If accepted, he would read from the Gita and Koran and New Testament, teach simple principles of health and hygiene, then trudge on to the next village. In all he visited forty-seven villages, walking 116 miles barefoot.

In each village Gandhi tried to persuade one Hindu and one Moslem leader to move into the same house together and serve as guarantors of peace. He asked them to pledge themselves to fast unto death if one from their own religion attacked an enemy. Incredibly, the method worked. While debates continued in the Delhi palaces, Gandhi's personal ointment began to palliate the open wounds across the state and nation For a while the killing stopped.

Soul Force

After independence, however, India needed more than ointment; she needed huge swaths of gauze bandages to staunch the flow of blood that quite literally turned her rivers red and filled her skies with vultures. As Gandhi had predicted in his eloquent appeals against partition, independence ushered in a holocaust of death and destruction such as the world had never seen. When the boundary lines were finally announced, millions of Hindus found themselves caught within the borders of a newly created and hostile Pakistan, and millions of Moslems found themselves in Hindu India. Thus began the greatest mass migration in human history. In all, ten million people left their homes and attempted a frantic march across the searing plains to a new home.

Lord Mountbatten, the British viceroy who oversaw independence, knew that two areas were potential conflagrations. On the west where India bordered West Pakistan, site of the largest migration, hostilities would undoubtedly erupt. But the east, along the gerrymandered border of East Pakistan, threatened even greater danger. Sitting beside that border was Kipling's City of Dreadful Night, Calcutta, the most violent city in Asia. No city in the world matched its squalor, its pullulating masses (more than 400,000 beggars), its religious bigotry, its unrestrained passions. Calcutta brazenly worshiped the Hindu deity Kali, the goddess of destruction. Months before, in a one-day preview of what was to come, violence had erupted in Calcutta. On that day known as the "Great Calcutta Killings," 6000 Hindu and Moslem bodies were tossed in the Hooghly River, stuffed in gutters, or left to lie in streets. Most had been beaten or trampled to death.

Mountbatten responded first to the western frontier as reports of atrocities came flooding in over the telegraph wires. Ultimately, as many as 500,000 people were to die on that frontier. The viceroy had no choice but to deploy there his Boundary Force, 55,000 of the most dependable British and Gurkha army troops. But that left him no reserves for the eastern front. In total desperation, Mountbatten pleaded with Gandhi to go to Calcutta and there, among the Untouchables he had embraced as brothers, somehow to work a miracle.

Gandhi firmly declined, for he had pledged to spend the time around independence spinning, fasting, and praying with the beleagured Hindu minority in Noakhali.

This time, on the eve of his departure to Noakhali, Gandhi was led to change his mind. He was convinced not by Mountbatten but by a Moslem leader who came personally from Calcutta to beg Gandhi to come to his city. The man, Suhrawardy, was one of the most corrupt politicians in Calcutta and was widely believed responsible for inciting his Moslem League followers to much of the violence on the day of the Great Calcutta Killings. Now he feared for the life of every Moslem in Calcutta and for the very survival of the city. Only Gandhi could ward off disaster, he said.

Gandhi listened, reconsidered, and came up with two conditions for his coming to Calcutta. First, Suhrawardy must pledge that the Moslems of Noakhali (where Gandhi had been headed) would not kill a single Hindu. If the pledge was broken, Gandhi would fast to death. In effect, Gandhi was placing his own life in Suhrawardy's hands.

The second condition was appalling to Suhrawardy, known for his decadent, luxurious lifestyle. Gandhi proposed that he and Suhrawardy live together day and night, unarmed, in the heart of one of Calcutta's worst slums. Suhrawardy swallowed hard and reluctantly agreed to the two conditions.

So it was that two days before India's independence Mohandas Gandhi arrived in the City of Dreadful Night. A massive crowd of Indians awaited him as usual, but this one, unlike so many others, greeted him not with cheers but with shrieks of hatred and anger.

They were Hindus out for revenge, and to them Gandhi represented a meek submission to the injustices Moslems had already wreaked. Many of them had seen relatives slaughtered and wives and daughters defiled by Moslem mobs. Gandhi got out of his car amid a shower of rocks and bottles. Raising one hand in a frail gesture of peace, the seventy-seven-year-old man walked alone into the crowd. "You wish to do me ill," he called, "and so I am coming to you." The crowd fell silent. "I have come here to serve Hindus and Moslems alike. I am going to place myself under your protection. You are welcome to turn against me if you wish. I have nearly reached the end of life's journey. I have not much further to go. But if you again go mad, I will not be a living witness to it."

Peace reigned in Calcutta that day, and then Independence Day, and the next, and the next, for sixteen days in all. Huge throngs gathered each evening, not as mobs bent on violence but as a congregation at Gandhi's prayer meetings. At first a thousand came, then ten thousand, and finally a million people jammed the streets of Gandhi's slum to hear him lecture on peace and love and brotherhood. Once again Gandhi was confronting a political crisis with what he called "soul force," the innate power of human spirituality.

While whole states in India were going up in flames, with millions of people fleeing their homes and thousands dying in the process, not one act of violence occurred in that most violent city. "The miracle of Calcutta" it was called worldwide. Lord Mountbatten wrote in grateful tribute, "In the Punjab we have 55,000 soldiers and large-scale rioting on our hands. In Bengal, our force consists of one man and there is no rioting." "My One-Man Boundary Force," he called Gandhi.

Nevertheless, the miracle did not endure. On the seventeenth day two Moslems were murdered, then a rumor spread about a Hindu victim, and before long a few hundred yards from Gandhi's house a grenade was lobbed into a bus full of Moslems. The people had broken their pledge; Gandhi was to keep his. He began a fast unto death, this one not against the British but against his own countrymen. He would not eat food again unless he received repentance from all those who had committed violence, and solemn vows that no more would occur.

At first no one cared. What was the life of one shriveled old man in the face of an assault on one's religion and family and honor? Revenge seemed far more appropriate than forgiveness. Gunfire echoed through the streets of Calcutta all during the first day of Gandhi's fast. But within a day his already weak heart started missing one beat in four, and his blood pressure dropped precariously. The next day, as his vital signs plummeted toward death, rioters paused and began listening to reports of the old man's blood pressure and heart rate and the analysis of his urine. Gandhi was having an effect. Soon the attention of every citizen of Calcutta was riveted on the straw pallet where he lay, too weak to speak. The violence stopped. No one was willing to take an action that might allow the Great Soul to die.

One day more and the gang responsible for the brutal murders came to confess to Gandhi, to plead forgiveness, and to lay their arms at his feet. A truck arrived at his house filled with guns, grenades, and other weapons that people had turned in voluntarily. The leaders of every religious group in the city agreed on a declaration guaranteeing that no more killing would take place.

Convinced of their sincerity, Gandhi took his first few sips of orange juice and said his prayers. This time the miracle held. Calcutta was safe. As for Gandhi, as soon as he regained strength he made plans to head west, into the heart of the violence that had killed half a million people.

14

East Challenges West

Gandhi's own account of his life presents events in a strange proportion. Maybe one paragraph will mention the Great Salt March, a turning point in Gandhi's career and India's history, but four consecutive chapters will explore Gandhi's internal agony on whether or not goat's milk should be included in his vegetarian dictum against dairy products. Gandhi portrays his life as a straight-line progression, a gradual honing of the soul. *The Story of My Experiments with Truth* he subtitled it, presenting the events of his life as merely the stage on which the internal drama of his own character development was being played out. What mattered most was the spiritual warfare going on inside.

The Christian church, birthed in the East but formulated and structured in the West, shares many of the crises of Western civilization as a whole. For a new perspective on the challenges we face, perhaps we would benefit by listening to this enigmatic figure who, although not a Christian, adapted many biblical principles to a modern context. Christian saints before him addressed these same issues, but we have grown so accustomed to our Christian saints that we no longer hear their message clearly. When a sound is too loud, sometimes we can discern it better in its echo.

From Gandhi's autobiography and books about him, I have extracted these principles which seem to me to have acute relevance to the Western church. Now, for the first time, more nonwhites than whites call themselves Christians. The center of the church is moving to Africa and Asia. Whether we can comprehend, appreciate, and to some extent embrace these principles may determine how successfully we can meet the challenge thrown to us by the East. It may, in fact, determine our planetary survival.

Simplicity

Gandhi came to symbolize this virtue more effectively than any other man in history. He had tried Western ways once, as a law student in London when he outfitted himself in an evening suit, silk top hat, patent leather boots, white gloves, and a silver-tipped walking stick. He held on to Western dress and was something of a dandy when he returned to India. Between England and India, he spent his twenties and thirties working as a lawyer in South Africa, and there the guiding principles of his life began to coalesce.

First Gandhi began to iron his own shirts, much to the ridicule of his law colleagues. Then he practiced cutting his own hair, leaving patches of unevenness that drew even more laughter. Although drawing a fat salary of five thousand pounds a year, he experimented by halving household expenses, then halving them again. (At the end of every day he made a meticulous accounting of every penny spent.) He found that the process of spending less money and acquiring fewer possessions vastly simplified his life and gave him an inner peace. In addition, it allowed him to identify more completely with the poor people he often represented.

Gandhi had fought vigorously for the right to travel first class on South Africa's railways, ever since one critical incident when he was thrown off a train because of skin color, despite possessing a first-class ticket. Yet voluntarily Gandhi began to travel third class. In India, where third-class travel combines crowdedness, noise, filth, and smells in an experience unimaginable to most Westerners, Gandhi continued the practice. He got little rest sitting bolt upright, squeezed onto the wooden slat railway benches, but he rejected overtures to upgrade.

Gandhi's autobiography devotes whole chapters to his lifelong process of refining eating habits. He broadened his vegetarianism to exclude eggs and milk. Gradually he began eliminating salt, spices, tea, and most exotic vegetables and fruits. Finally he took a vow to partake of only two meals a day, never after sunset, and to consume a maximum of five different items a day, including medicines. A typical meal consisted of two segments of grapefruit, some goat's curds, and lemon soup.

After Gandhi renounced material possessions he carried all his belongings in a single sack. To answer correspondence he used pads made from the cut-up envelopes of the letters he was answering. He ate with a spoon that had been broken off and repaired with a piece of bamboo lashed to it with string.

Ironically, the impetus for all this emphasis on simplicity came not from a Hindu holy man, but from books by Westerners, *The Kingdom of God Is Within You* by Tolstoy and *Unto This Last* by John Ruskin, as well as some of Thoreau's essays. Those authors convinced him that riches were a trammel, and that only the life of labor was worth living.

Gandhi maintained his simple, uninterrupted routine even after he had become one of the most famous people in the world. If anything, he grew even more strict, keeping to his daily schedule and diet whether in the viceroy's palace or Calcutta's Sweepers' Colony. He also observed every Monday as a day of silence, both to rest his vocal cords and to promote harmony in his inner being. He held to that silence even when summoned to Lord Mountbatten's office in the heat of intensive negotiations on India's future.

Today the American church, set in the midst of the most technologically complex society in history, is hearing calls for a return to simplicity. Voices of people like Richard Foster, Ron Sider, and the editors of *Sojourners* and *The Other Side* uphold the virtues of a simple lifestyle and raise questions about the morality of American standards in the light of world inequities (though, in fairness, the level of simplicity they recommend more closely resembles what Gandhi started with than what he later attained). I will leave the subjective issue of lifestyle to others more confident than I. Rather, Gandhi's unique contribution is the reason for simplicity, not its level. For Gandhi, simplicity was motivated not so much by guilt or a comparison with others but rather by the salubrious effect it can have on the leader himself.

Gandhi had dined with great leaders. He had seen the seduction of power, the reliance on servants to carry out every whim, the endless spiral staircase of luxury, the absorbing anxiety over investments, the deluge of letters and speaking invitations and endorsements and phone calls. Knowing well the burden of fame, he also knew the only way to combat it was to seek simplicity with all his heart. If he did not, his soul force, the inner strength from which he got all his stamina and courage for spiritual confrontations, would leak away.

From the inside, I have watched a disturbing pattern in what we do to our Christian leaders. We reward them with applause, fame, enticing new contracts, and a flurry of requests for speaking engagements and media appearances and publicity tours. We insist that the spiritual leaders of our organizations become experts in management while carrying a crushing load of personal appearances. We push our pastors to function as psychotherapists, orators, priests, and chief executive officers. When a leader shows special acumen, we offer temptation with radio shows, a TV series, and of course a massive direct-mail machine to keep the organization's superstructure intact. In short, we in the church slavishly copy the secular model of media hype and corporate growth.

I wonder how much more effective our spiritual leaders would be if we granted all of them Monday as a day of silence for reflection, meditation, and personal study. I cannot imagine a leader's business manager—or, for that matter, constituency—permitting such a frivolous plan. Of course, daily demands are pressing, but were not those of Gandhi, leader of the second most populous country on earth?

Human Dignity

I have already mentioned the personal impact Gandhi had on a five-thousand-year-old tradition of caste consciousness. In a momentous stroke, he renamed Untouchables the *Harijans*, or Children of God, and then risked his entire career by inviting them to live with him on his commune. Gandhi devoted his life to recognizing the inherent dignity in every human being. He strove to devote the same care in making a mudpack for a leprosy victim as in conducting an interview with the Viceroy of India. Along the way, he helped elevate the status of women in the country by surrounding himself with highly competent women followers.

Gandhi summarized his beliefs in three points, which he credited to John Ruskin's book *Unto This Last*:

1. That the good of the individual is contained in the good of all.
2. That a lawyer's work has the same value as a barber's inasmuch as all have the same right of earning their livelihood from their work.
3. That a life of labor, i.e., the life of the tiller of the soil and the handicraftsman, is the life worth living.

Those principles transformed Gandhi's life, and he sought out ways to inculcate them. In cities like Bombay and Calcutta, he preferred the hovel of the Sweepers' Colony to a hotel. He used a pencil until it was reduced to an ungrippable stub, out of respect for the human being who made the pencil.

In a sense the Christian church has led the way in this principle of human dignity. Missions movements have responded to the downtrodden, such as those with leprosy and the underclass, more quickly and often more effectively than governments. But we in the West are still learning the difference between charity, which we're good at, and changing a person's self-perception, which we're not. Evangelicals (with notable exceptions among Catholics and Pentecostals) have been notoriously deficient in communicating a sense of dignity to the blue-collar worker and the unemployed.

Too often our motives smack of paternalism (so do the words: *down*trodden, *under*class). I, the educated, healthy, wealthy American, reach out in compassion to help you improve yourself. We see ourselves as on the side of Christ, giving in love to the needy. But Matthew 25 makes it quite clear that Jesus is on the side of the poor, and we serve best by elevating the downtrodden to the place of Jesus. Charity is not condescending, but rather ascending—we have an opportunity to serve someone far better. Somehow Gandhi communicated that spirit to those whose lives he touched; he made even the Untouchables feel like favored children of God.

Self-Discipline

In his personal habits Gandhi moved far beyond self-discipline into renunciation. He held up the Hindu/Buddhist ideal of passionlessness that has generally been rejected by Christian orthodoxy, save for a few ascetic movements. He allowed no room for sensuous pleasures, and in his autobiography you read nothing of a pleasant experience with music or with nature or sensory pleasures of taste or smell.

You do read, however, of his lifelong struggle to stamp out the residue of human passion. At the age of thirty-seven, after a twenty-four-year struggle against lust for his wife (yes, he was married at thirteen), he took a solemn vow of celibacy. He spent much energy investigating what foods might have the slightest aphrodisiacal quality, concluding that milk of any kind, salt, and certain fruits contributed to sexual urges. For thirty years he managed to avoid having an erection, with the exception of one night when he awoke from a dream. He called that night "my darkest hour" and immediately undertook a six-week vow of silence to atone for it.

Applying the same rigid standards of restraint in his speech and emotions, Gandhi sought to suppress any sign of anger, violence, and hatred. This tendency, of course, totally contradicts the stream of development recommended by modern psychology. Commenting on similar trends in Christian saints, Jürgen Moltmann has observed that "what are virtues for the mystic are torment and sickness for the modern man or woman: estrangement, loneliness, silence, solitude, inner emptiness, deprivation, poverty, not-knowing, and so forth....What the monks sought for in order to find God, modern men and women fly from as if it were the devil."

By citing these instances of ascesis, I do not mean to hold them up for us to emulate. Yet one fact intrigues me. Gandhi's variety of discipline did not influence his own son, but it seeped into the consciousness of his nation and is still revered in India today. America has a parallel in legalistic fundamentalism with its strictures against premarital touching, makeup, smoking, drinking, modern music, and sometimes even bowling and roller skating, counterbalanced by its emphasis on personal devotion and discipline. Yet in recent years that fundamentalism has tended to spawn a generation with a great distaste for discipline. Richard Quebedeaux coined the term "worldly evangelicals" to describe those who seem religiously to push the limits of grace by trying all the habits that were anathema to their parents. What makes Gandhi's ascesis mystically attractive to some of these same young people when the self-discipline of fundamentalism repels them?

Could it be that the difference in appeal lies not so much with the specifics of the discipline—what is given up—as with the motive for it? In fundamentalism, restraint, care for health, sexual control, temperance of vices—wise principles all—usually come interlarded with guilt and motivated by a desire for moral superiority. Gandhi's regimen, though far more strict—I haven't met a Bob Jones graduate yet with a Gandhian diet or lifestyle—derived from his personal search for peace. Discipline opened doors of freedom; it did not close them, he said. The right action brings peace, and he sought to eliminate any possible diversion from that peace "not as this world giveth."

It is for *my* sake, explained Gandhi, that I insist on such spartan practices. I am the one who will suffer if I give in to my carnal nature, and I am the one who will profit from whatever artificial controls I can erect around it. Fear of internal destruction and a desire for wholeness just may be more effective motivators than fear of punishment.

Sadly, the concepts of grace and forgiveness from God do not appear in Gandhi's works; Hinduism stumbles at grace. "If one is to find salvation," said Gandhi, "he must have as much patience as a man who sits by the seaside and with a straw picks up a single drop of water, transfers it, and thus empties the ocean." He contributed a legalism without judgment, yes, but a legalism nonetheless.

The East has a rich legacy of holy men, culminating in the Buddha who came to personify control over human passions. An ascetic in the East is not pitied or laughed at or made to feel a marytr, as often happens in the West, but rather admired for having achieved a deeper plane of existence. Discipline has lost its appeal for us. Is it possible to recover some of that implicit value in self-discipline without also pulling in the concomitant reliance on works rather than grace? One cannot deny that the "soul force" of Gandhi's leadership radiated power because of his unimpeachable personal example. Could anyone other than a holy man have saved Calcutta?

Humility

To anyone who has been to India, I need cite only one instance of Gandhi's self-imposed humility: his willingness to travel third-class on trains all his life. (Why? he was once asked. And he replied, "Because there is no fourth class.") In a few rare persons, "humility" describes a natural outflowing of a deferring, submissive personality. To others it is a learned trait imposed against every impulse to act arrogantly and assertively. Gandhi would, I think, put himself in the latter category. He had no innate desire to be stepped on and had shown his assertive qualities splendidly in his battles for personal rights in South Africa. But gradually, as he immersed himself in the scriptures of Hinduism, Islam, Buddhism, and Christianity, he became convinced that the humility of a servant was the one posture required by God. Only then did he dispossess himself of material things, strip off his European clothes, and seek out companionship with the poor and suffering.

Later in life, Gandhi's humility was so integral that he allowed no important personage, not even royalty, to interfere with it. When Lord Mountbatten offered to fly him to an important meeting on his private plane, Gandhi chose instead his third-class railway compartment. He caused something of a scandal on a famous visit to England to meet with the leaders of Parliament and with King George. He arrived amid great fanfare and press coverage, and the nation gasped as he tottered down the steamship gangplank wearing only a cotton loincloth and leading a goat (his source of milk) by a rope.

Declining offers from the best hotels, he chose instead to stay in an East End slum. He would not even change his uniform or diet for meetings in the palace. Some reporters were scandalized that he would dare meet with a king in a "half-naked" state. Gandhi quietly pondered their objections and replied with a smile, "The king was wearing enough clothes for both of us."

In India, as the issues of independence and partition began reaching the critical mass just before explosion, Gandhi took off on his celebrated barefoot pilgrimage through the riot-torn Noakhali district. Some Congress leaders questioned his decision to waste time in jerkwater villages while the party was negotiating the future of the subcontinent. "A leader," said Gandhi, "is only a reflection of the people he leads." If the small villages do not live in peace, how will the entire nation?

Gandhi never insisted that political leaders follow his path of rigid discipline; his was a moral and religious crusade and not just a political one. But he did ask that each government minister live in a simple home with no servants and no car, practice one hour of manual labor daily, and clean his or her own toilet box. For more than a decade after his death, Congress leaders wore the homespun cotton uniform he espoused and often conducted party meetings while spinning cotton threads. Despite this cosmetic gesture, Congress soon slipped into wealth, corruption, and venality; nothing pained Gandhi more during the last few years of his life.

Gandhi's adopted style of humility permeates his autobiography. In it, he treats rivals who caused him intense pain and strife with respect and courtesy. Look at your own errors with a convex lens, said Gandhi, and at others' with the reverse.

A convex lens applied to American culture would not reveal a surfeit of humility. Cultural observers have often noted our national characteristic of narcissism. Tom Wolfe described the 70s as the "me decade" and historian Christopher Lasch diagnosed our "culture of narcissism." Two recent comprehensive studies—Yankelovich's *New Rules* and Amitai Etzioni's *An Immodest Agenda*—have confirmed that the pervasive spirit of self-fulfillment and narcissism challenges the structure of our society.

Unfortunately, the gospel message that gets widest exposure in America today follows the cultural mainstream. It offers the appeal "God has something good in store for you" and a pilgrimage toward self-discovery. Jesus' frequent statements about finding oneself by losing one's self and carrying a cross are left unexegeted. In America a success-based theology as often as not works out plausibly well, if only because the resources of this nation are so large. But such a theology has little to say to Christians in Poland or Albania or Nepal or Iran; there, faith in Christ guarantees compounded suffering.

In his own study of the New Testament, Gandhi found an appeal to seek truth with the whole heart, expecting nothing, regardless of results. He used to sing an Indian poem as he walked among the rice paddies of Noakhali as his own people were persecuting him, "If they answer not your call, walk alone, walk alone." In America that message, frankly, does not sell. The fact that Western Christianity exclusively stresses the success side of faith may, however, explain why Asia of all continents has proven least receptive to the gospel.

Nonviolence

History will remember Gandhi for the principles of nonviolence and civil disobedience which he extended for the first time to national scale. He would likely have rejected both these negative terms—why define a movement by something it is not, *non*violent and *dis*obedient?—and chosen a positive term such as "Truth Force." The principles evolved in his thinking, expanding outward from his personal response to beatings and discrimination and culminating in a universal principle with no exceptions.

South Africa had given Gandhi ample opportunity to prove his personal courage. He was tossed off trains, ejected from hotels and restaurants, charged by mounted police, and jailed for almost a year. He learned to face danger with no force but courage. In those early days, he did not apply nonviolence nationally. He supported Britain in the Boer War and in World War I, organizing an Indian ambulance corps in each conflict to help the British cause. Indians were not yet ready for nonviolence, he claimed.

In India he turned to nonviolent means as much out of pragmatism as out of religious conviction. "Great Britain," he warned, "wants us to put the struggle on the plane of machine guns where they have the weapons and we do not. Our only assurance of beating them is by putting the struggle on a plane where we have the weapons and they have not." If his supporters ever turned violent during one of his campaigns, Gandhi would call it off. No cause, no matter how just, was worth bloodshed.

Gradually, a deeply felt religious doctrine formed in his mind which gave sacred sanction to the principles he already lived by. Violence against another human being contradicted everything he believed about universal human dignity, even if the particular human might be a British officer firing into an unarmed crowd. You cannot change a man's conviction through violence, he believed. Violence only brutalizes and separates, it does not reconcile. Gandhi records that he reached a turning point in his life when he came across Jesus' admonition that his followers should turn the other cheek to their persecutors. That statement provided the moral plinth for a doctrine he had already accepted personally.

In later years, Gandhi became absolutely inflexible on this issue. During World War II he counseled first the Ethiopians invaded by Nazi armies, then the Jews, then Great Britain, to invite their enemies in and stand before the slaughter with serenity and a clear conscience. He told his followers if an atom bomb were dropped on India they should stand, "looking up, watching without fear, praying for the pilot."

"I would die for the cause," he concluded, "but there is no cause I'm prepared to kill for." Since Gandhi, other political leaders have adopted his tactics. Martin Luther King, who considered himself a spiritual successor, brought those concepts to America and fought violence with nonviolence. Historically, the results have been mixed. Relatively free societies have proved open to change based on moral force. With media attention, nonviolent protest can arouse the conscience of a nation. In closed societies such as Nazi Germany, Poland, Czechoslovakia, and Russia, as well as in Chile, South Korea, and the Philippines, nonviolent dissent and civil disobedience have done little but strengthen the grip of the oppressors.

Of all Gandhi's guiding principles, this one has lodged most firmly in Western consciousness, and today the doctrine of nonviolence is being hotly debated by American Christians. Groups as diverse as Catholic bishops and a gathering of evangelicals at Fuller Seminary have reconsidered war in light of the preponderance of nuclear arms. Articles on nonviolence and pacifism appear in major Christian periodicals, many with a strident tone that does little justice to the complexity of the issues involved. (Ironically, some Hindu leaders, Gandhi's own religious heirs, are suggesting that this principle grew out of his Christian influences and has no place in Hinduism.)

Civil disobedience also has gained respectability as a force for change in democracies. Francis Schaeffer in *A Christian Manifesto* gave his blessing to selected calls for civil disobedience. Still, Martin Luther King's example stands as the most direct application of Gandhian principles in modern Western society. Legally, at least, he broke the back of discrimination in the United States by mimicking Gandhi's tactics. The climax came on the bridge to Selma, Alabama, when King's unarmed followers met policemen armed with fire hoses, clubs, and snarling German shepherds. Nonviolent force met violent force. When King instructed his followers to kneel down and the television cameras ground away, in a few minutes the civil rights struggle was all over.

Christians will continue to disagree on the question of when armed force is justified. But Gandhi's example does show that a very large change—freedom for the second most populous nation on earth—did come about through nonviolent means.

Village Self-Sufficiency

Gandhi held this principle dear above all others, and yet his teaching on the subject has been rejected by India as well as by the West, which had already gone too far to listen. Gandhi truly believed the only hope for the East lay in forming economically self-sufficient village units. He had seen the colonialist methods of taking raw materials overseas, manufacturing them, and shipping the finished product back to India at high profit. He had also seen the West's own labyrinthine system: corn grown in Iowa is shipped to Colorado for feeding cattle, which are in turn shipped to Kansas City for processing and packaging, then back to Iowa via Chicago for sale in supermarkets. To him, industrialization was a dubious blessing; he desired that each of India's half-million village units learn to feed, clothe, treat medically, and educate its members.

Gandhi advocated closing down textile mills and replacing them with wooden spinning wheels. When time came for India to choose a new flag, he strongly lobbied for the spinning wheel as the national symbol to place on the flag. Presaging a new shift to come, Congress leaders adopted a more conventionally nationalistic symbol: ancient emperor Ashok's pole with a three-headed lion. Gandhi's beliefs stemmed not from a quixotic back-to-the-land idealism but rather came as a practical response to what he had observed in India's cities. Urbanization was sucking people out of the villages, destroying centuries-old family patterns, breeding crime and violence, and choking the skies of India with pollution. Only in a small village context could his goals of human dignity and simplicity find truly fertile ground.

Gandhi also had doubts about modern technology. He believed people who had cars, radios, and well-stocked refrigerators and clothes closets would become psychologically insecure and morally corrupt. He knew enough about soil conservation to realize that India's land, farmed without interruption for five thousand years, could not tolerate even a few decades of the kind of soil abuse brought about by high-technology farming. He had questions about how long energy sources would hold up. And besides, Gandhi said, he would continue to recommend cows until a tractor was invented that could produce milk, yoghurt, and dung.

On this issue, Gandhi's words reverberate prophetically. Too late we in the West are realizing the cost of pell-mell industrialization. Dependence on energy has changed the entire world economic order. We may find ways to reclaim lakes killed by acid rain and may be able to restock forests and wildlife, but certain things will never be regained. In 150 years, Iowa has lost more of its topsoil than India has lost in 5000 years.

Perhaps the most insidious result of our consumer society has been its effect on the plausibility of alternative lifestyles. A society whose economic fabric depends on constant growth requires that its citizens have ever-expanding needs and wants. If ten million Christians, with the highest of motives, decided to cut out all extravagance and live more simply by trading in their cars, wearing unfashionable clothes, raising their own food, and eliminating appliances, economic chaos would result. By their actions those Christians would immediately put tens of thousands of people out of work. That dilemma is exactly what Gandhi wanted to avoid in India.

In the West, it will take one with soulforce equal to Gandhi's to change the prevailing dogma. Some prophets, such as Jacques Ellul, cry out. We may be forced to change our profligate ways some day, when the soil is depleted, the aquifers drained, and all the oil wells pumped dry. But those crises will wait another fifty years at least; those yet unborn will worry about them.

Vicarious Suffering

Very early in his career, while Gandhi was organizing a commune, or *ashram*, in South Africa, two of the young people under his tutelage lapsed into an act he would only call "a moral fall." Grieving deeply, Gandhi agonized for days over an appropriate response. Most members of the *ashram* were calling for strict punishment of the offenders. But it seemed to Gandhi a guardian or teacher was at least partly responsible for the failures of his ward or pupil. He doubted whether the other students would realize the depth of his distress and the seriousness of sin unless he did some penance. And so, in response to the students' transgression, he went on a total fast for seven days and took only one meal a day for four-and-a-half months. "My penance pained everybody," he concluded, "but it cleared the atmosphere. Everyone came to realize what a terrible thing it was to be sinful, and the bond that bound me to the boys and girls became stronger and truer."

Over the next decades, Gandhi expanded his reach to embrace the suffering of all India. In a supreme irony, his most powerful weapon turned out to be the most primitive of all denials, the refusal to take food, in a nation famous for its starvation and malnutrition. He fasted to oppose repressive taxes and to oppose the violence done to demonstrators. He fasted when his fellow politicians were acting divisively. Gandhi sought out and absorbed the sufferings of his people, and in the process a bond of love joined them to him as to no other leader.

I have already recounted the stunning effects of Gandhi's penultimate fast in Calcutta. Out of fear that indirectly they might be responsible for the death of The Great Soul, millions of Hindus and Moslems steadfastly resisted the violence that was erupting in other parts of India. After Calcutta, Gandhi announced one last fast. This one occurred in New Delhi, the capital of the brand new country, a capital that in early 1948 lay under a pall of smoke.

Five million refugees had staggered across the Punjab from Pakistan toward the capital, and many of them were now living in the squalor of Delhi's refugee camps. They had been preyed upon, raped, and brutalized by hordes of Moslems, and these Hindus wanted revenge. They looted Moslem homes, mosques and shops, and punished their owners. As a government, India was refusing to pay 55 million pounds it owed Pakistan, fearing that the money might be used for arms against its own nation. Delhi was in no mood for mercy or compromise.

When Gandhi arrived and sensed the hatred for himself, he announced a fast unto death. His doctors pleaded against it; he had not yet recovered from the near-fatal fast in Calcutta. Outside, the crowds had a different reaction. They had had their fill of the shriveled old man and his hallucinations of peace and brotherhood. Gangs of Hindus marched past Gandhi's house with a new chant on their lips, one he had never before heard: "Let Gandhi die! Let Gandhi die!"

For a few days it seemed that the city of Delhi and the nation of India had gone incurably mad. Somehow, one more time, The Great Soul—contained within a body weighing barely one hundred pounds and slipping in and out of comas—cast his spell on the country. That crumpled figure on a straw pallet became a kind of plexus in which all the nerve fibers of India met. The horrible sufferings of the last few months that had afflicted Moslems, Hindus, and Sikhs came to rest in this one man who refused to eat. His kidneys stopped functioning. His heart missed beats. He breathed with great difficulty. All India Radio began broadcasting hourly bulletins on his condition.

On the fourth day, in desperation, the most powerful leaders in India—Nazis, Communists, and all movements in between—filed past Gandhi's bed and took a solemn vow to protect Moslems and renounce violence. Truckloads of arms were collected and destroyed. Civic leaders brought him petitions guaranteeing the return of thousands of homes, shops, and mosques to their rightful Moslem owners. The Indian parliament voted to pay the archenemy Pakistan 55 million pounds. At last, after every one of Gandhi's strict conditions had been met and the country again was at peace, Gandhi agreed to break his fast. It had lasted 121 hours.

Two weeks later, his wasted body again lay on that straw pallet, killed not by a fast but by three bullets from a Hindu fanatic who resented what he saw as Gandhi's betrayal of his nation. In that last act of death, Gandhi accomplished more than the thousands of policemen and soldiers who were vainly patrolling villages in the Punjab. Because of Gandhi's death all India paused; communal killing stopped; the young nation was shocked to its senses. A holy man in Bombay walked through the city crying, "The Mahatma is dead. When comes another such as he?"

Many of Gandhi's accomplishments died with him. His beloved nation took a different path than the one he had advocated. Since his death, the world has grown more violent, more belligerent, more repressive, and less receptive to his core beliefs. But this strange, baffling man had somehow called forth a heroic goodness inherent in all people. He had raised men and women above the level of their usual selves. His only claim to leadership was the force of his own soul. He held no office, and any who obeyed him did so voluntarily. Yet had any man in history commanded such allegiance from so many of his contemporaries?

Gandhi and Christianity

Finally let's look at Gandhi's perception of Christianity and the reasons he was never seriously tempted to become a Christian.

Gandhi credited Christianity with two of his most significant guiding principles: nonviolence and simple living. But he had often seen the disparity between Christ and Christians. He said, "Stoning prophets and erecting churches to their memory afterwards has been the way of the world through the ages. Today we worship Christ, but the Christ in the flesh we crucified."

Growing up in India, Gandhi had little contact with Christians as a youngster. Rumors spread in his town that if a Hindu converted to Christianity he would be forced to eat meat, drink hard liquor, and wear European clothes. Gandhi recalls one very distasteful memory of a Christian missionary on the street corner of his town pouring abuse on the Hindu gods.

As a law student in England, Gandhi had a more prolonged exposure to Christianity. Out of obligation to a friend, he read through the entire Bible. He admits that the Old Testament was uninspiring and put him to sleep, especially the book of Numbers. But the New Testament produced a profound impression. Throughout his life, Gandhi found himself going back to the teachings of Jesus.

Gandhi lived in South Africa during the most formative period of his life, and a few nasty incidents there did little to disabuse him of his notions of Christianity. He encountered blatant discrimination in that ostensibly Christian society, being thrown off trains, excluded from hotels and restaurants, and made to feel unwelcome even in some Christian gatherings.

One white woman who used to invite Gandhi for Sunday meals made it clear that he was unwelcome when she saw the influence Gandhi's strict vegetarianism was having on her five-year-old son. Before that incident, he had attended the Wesleyan church with her family every Sunday. "The church did not make a favorable impression on me," he concluded laconically, citing uninspiring sermons and a congregation who "appeared rather to be worldly-minded, people going to church for recreation and in conformity to custom."

Besides Tolstoy's *The Kingdom of God Is Within You* and Ruskin's *Unto This Last* (both mentioned earlier) he was profoundly influenced by the Bible. He also read Pearson's *Many Infallible Proofs* (which "had no effect on me") and Butler's *The Analogy of Religion* among a host of other Christian books and commentaries.

In his autobiography, Gandhi recounts several episodes of Christians attempting to convert him. One kindly man even went so far as to take him to the Wellington Convention, a revival-type service similar to Keswick conventions. The Rev. Andrew Murray spoke, and Gandhi was quite impressed by stories he told about George Muller's faith. This is how Gandhi recalls the convention and summarizes his difficulties with Christianity: "Mr. Baker was hard put to it in having a 'coloured man' like me for his companion. He had to suffer inconveniences on many occasions entirely on account of me. We had to break the journey on the way, as one of the days happened to be a Sunday, and Mr. Baker and his party would not travel on the sabbath....

"This convention was an assemblage of devout Christians. I was delighted at their faith. I met Mr. Murray. I saw that many were praying for me. I liked some of their hymns, they were very sweet.

"The Convention lasted for three days. I could understand and appreciate the devoutness of those who attended it. But I saw no reason for changing my belief—my religion. It was impossible for me to believe that I could go to heaven or attain salvation only by becoming a Christian. When I frankly said so to some of the good Christian friends, they were shocked. But there was no help for it.

"My difficulties lay deeper. It was more than I could believe that Jesus was the only incarnate son of God, and that only he who believed in him would have everlasting life. If God could have sons, all of us were His sons. If Jesus was like God, or God Himself, then all men were like God and could be God Himself. My reason was not ready to believe literally that Jesus by his death and by his blood redeemed the sins of the world. Metaphorically there might be some truth in it. Again, according to Christianity only human beings had souls, and not other living beings, for whom death meant complete extinction; while I held a contrary belief. I could accept Jesus as a martyr, an embodiment of sacrifice, and a divine teacher, but not as the most perfect man ever born. His death on the Cross was a great example to the world, but that there was anything like a mysterious or miraculous virtue in it my heart could not accept. The pious lives of Christians did not give me anything that the lives of men of other faiths had failed to give. I had seen in other lives just the same reformation that I had heard of among Christians. Philosophically there was nothing extraordinary in Christian principles. From the point of view of sacrifice, it seemed to me that the Hindus greatly surpassed the Christians. It was impossible for me to regard Christianity as a perfect religion or the greatest of all religions.

"I shared this mental churning with my Christian friends whenever there was an opportunity, but their answers could not satisfy me."

Gandhi graciously omits from his autobiography one more painful experience that occurred in South Africa. The Indian community especially admired a Christian named C. F. Andrews whom they themselves nicknamed "Christ's Faithful Apostle." Having heard so much about Andrews, Gandhi sought to hear him. But when C. F. Andrews was invited to speak in a church in South Africa, Gandhi was barred from the meeting—his skin color was not white.

Commenting on Gandhi's experiences in South Africa, E. Stanley Jones concludes, "Racialism has many sins to bear, but perhaps its worst sin was the obscuring of Christ in an hour when one of the greatest souls born of a woman was making his decision."

Christianity in India Today

I had occasion to spend a month in the land of Gandhi in 1982. Toward the end of the trip, I found myself in a Christian community in New Delhi, a kind of *ashram* composed of young Indians who are trying to work out corporately Jesus' radical call to discipleship. For some time we discussed parallels between Gandhi and Jesus Christ. In many external ways, the two lives followed similar tracks, and Gandhi freely admitted his most important principles derived directly from Jesus' teaching. Yet while Gandhi nearly reshaped the whole country, Christianity has barely made a dent in India—less than 3 percent of the population call themselves Christian. Together, we explored whether perhaps the body of Christ had presented Christianity to India, but not the true Christ.

We talked about the perception of Christianity by the average educated Indian. Those who have been to America come back very impressed with the churches. They tell stories about the television evangelists and how much money they take in each day. They tell of Christian leaders meeting with the President and Presidents themselves claiming to be Christian. Christian leaders tend to be slick, middle-class, well-groomed, not the austere holy men they are accustomed to in India. No one is called "The Great Soul" in the West. Reflecting on Christianity, these Indians tend to revert to hackneyed words like "power," "money," "success." When they describe American Christianity, in fact, what they are describing is American culture. They rarely talk about Jesus' life or the principles he laid down.

Wanting to encourage my fellow Christians in New Delhi, I reminded them of Gandhi's statement that the answer to the world's problems must come from the East and not the West. I urged them to take the best of what their continent has produced, some of the same principles I have reviewed above, and trace their Christian roots. They could challenge our nation in a way that we Americans could not, as shown by the fact that young Americans will sometimes listen to a Gandhi before they will listen to Jesus. The world may be ready for this message again, I said.

One thoughtful young Indian who had sat quietly throughout the discussion spoke up at this. "I don't understand," he said. "You seem to say that the West in general is receptive to a saint, someone like Gandhi who stands apart from culture. But is the *church* receptive? You have said that American Christianity has never produced a saint who follows along the lines of a Gandhi. All the Christian leaders are so different from Gandhi. You seem to imply that if a Gandhi rose up in the American church today, he would not be taken seriously, would perhaps be laughed at and rejected. And yet those same Christians say they worship Jesus Christ. Why don't they reject him? He lived a simple life, preached love and nonviolence, refused to compromise with the powers of this world. He called on his followers to "take up a cross" and bear the sufferings of the world. Why don't American Christians reject him?"

It was a good question. One I still cannot answer.